Spade & Archer's

SECRETS OF PARIS

A Guidebook for the Discerning Traveler

*Edited by
Ginette Billard*

THOMASSON-GRANT
Charlottesville, Virginia

Secrets of Paris
Published in 1994 by Thomasson-Grant, Inc.

Copyright © 1994 by Spade & Archer, Inc.:
J. C. Suarès, Dominique Bluhdorn, and
Stephen D. Kaplan. All rights reserved.

Editor: Ginette Billard
Associate Editor: Pierre Billard
Managing Editor: Catherine Schurdak
Copy Editors: John Anderson and
    Louise Marinis
Map Editor: Laura Victoria Levin
Production: Thomasson-Grant, Inc.
Front Cover Illustration: Nina Duran

No portion of this book may be reproduced or transmitted in any form or manner by any means including but not limited to graphic, electronic, or mechanical methods, photocopying, recording, taping, or any information storage and retrieval system without explicit written permission from the publisher. The publisher and the author assume no legal responsibility for the appreciation or depreciation in value of any premises, commercial or otherwise, by reasons of their inclusion in or exclusion from this book. The information contained in this guide is subject to change but was correct to the best knowledge of the publisher at the time of publication. Many of the maps are diagrammatic and may be selective of street inclusion.

Printed and bound in the United States.

00 99 98 97 96 95 94   5 4 3 2 1

Any inquiries should be directed to
Thomasson-Grant, Inc., One Morton Drive,
Suite 500, Charlottesville, VA 22903-6806
Telephone (804) 977-1780

Library of Congress Cataloging-in-Publication Data:

Spade & Archer's secrets of Paris : a guidebook for the discerning traveler.
        p. cm.
    Includes index.
    ISBN 1-56566-041-2 (softcover)
    1. Paris (France)—Guidebooks. 2. Celebrities—France—Paris—Social life and customs. I. Spade & Archer. II. Title: Secrets of Paris.
DC708.S575 1994
914.4'36104839—dc20   93-24072
                                                                                    CIP

Contents

	Introduction	1
1	Provincial Dining with Paul Bocuse	7
2	More Provincial Dining—with Alain Dutournier	10
3	Patrice de Nussac's Best Chefs of Paris	15
4	The Most Beautiful Restaurants	18
5	Garden Restaurants Around Town	22
6	Garden Restaurants Out of Town	25
7	Wine Bars, Bistros, and Brasseries	28
8	Jean-Louis Scherrer's Pick of the Restaurants, Bistros, and Brasseries	32
9	Exotic Cuisine	36
10	Tea Time in Paris	42
11	Irresistible Ice Creams	44
12	Gourmet Shopping and More with Jeanne Moreau	46
13	Régine's Parisian Chocolate Assortments	50
14	Isabelle Adjani's Organic Food and Health Spots	55
15	Grand Hotels	57
16	Jean-Paul Rappeneau's Favorite Left Bank Hotels	61
17	Paris at Night	64
18	Givenchy's Paris	69
19	Hervé Aaron's Personal Choices in Le Louvre	72
20	André Courrèges' Favorite Museums	76
21	Unusual Museums	78
22	More Museums	82
23	Michèle Morgan's Selection of Contemporary Art Galleries	88
24	Claude Lelouch Out with the Kids	90
25	Day Trips Around Paris	93
26	Mstislav Rostropovich's Survey of the Concert Halls	101
27	Michel Legrand's Favorite Jazz Spots	105

28	Costa-Gavras' Cinephilia	107
29	Gérard Oury's Walking Tour of Montmartre	112
30	Touring L'Ile de la Cité with Charlotte Rampling	117
31	L'Ile Saint-Louis with Charlotte Rampling	120
32	A Walk Through the Marais with Sophie Marceau	122
33	19th-Century Monuments with Andrzej Zulawski	124
34	A Tour of the Shops of Saint-Germain-des-Prés	129
35	Along the Route of Famous American Authors: A Walking Tour	133
36	François Reichenbach Explores the 19th-Century Hidden Malls and Arcades	136
37	Sir Dirk Bogarde's Park Meanders	138
38	Catherine Deneuve's Secret Gardens	143
39	Browsing the Flea Markets with Pierre Hebey	145
40	Outdoor Markets	150
41	Famous Graves in Père-Lachaise Cemetery	153
42	Designer Haute Couture and Prêt-à-Porter	155
43	Haute Couture at Discount	158
44	Louis Malle and Candice Bergen's Pick of the Kids' Shops	164
45	Danièle Thompson's Tools of the Trade for the Sophisticated Hostess	167
46	Diane Von Furstenberg's Most Precious Paper Shops	172
47	Emmanuelle Khanh's Flower Basket	175
48	Inès de la Fressange: Paris on a Leash	178
49	Japan in Paris: Fashion, Food, Books, Art	180
50	The Métro: Subway and Culture	184
	Acknowledgments	187
	Index	188

INTRODUCTION

SECRETS OF PARIS offers an artfully detailed, handheld tour of a very select Paris. As a visitor, you will get to know the City of Light from the point of view of its most notable citizens. Here are their personal *coups de coeur*, the aspects of Paris that tug at their heartstrings. These worldly celebrities and passionate locals share their private favorites with a sense of joy and hospitality that the sophisticated tourist will relish. This is a luxury look at Paris with an appreciation of value. Many of the restaurants are pricey, while the discount couture represents a true bargain. All of the shopping, dining, and touring is guided by those who really know superlative Paris—the insiders.

Paris is a city of neighborhoods or districts known as *arrondissements*. There are 20 such districts (designated in French as 1er, 2e, 3e, 4e, and so on), laid out in the shape of a snail. The 1er arrondissement is in the center of the city, then the 2e, 3e, 4e, and 5e form a circle around it. The remaining arrondissements continue in a widening spiral as they extend to the outskirts of Paris. Most of the chapters in this book are organized by arrondissement, except when the author's preference or the subject (such as a walking tour) dictate another order.

The postal code for Paris addresses always begins with 75, which represents Paris; the arrondissement number is found in the last two numerals. A starting number other than 75 denotes an address outside the city limits, in the suburbs or beyond.

Gentrification has become the social norm for almost all major European cities. Paris is no exception. Slowly, the affluent have taken over and renovated and restored the homes of the working class, displacing them to the eastern and northern *banlieue*, or suburbs. The Bastille district, once on the skids, is becoming fashionable, a phenomenon New Yorkers know as *Soho-ization*.

The socioeconomic configuration of Paris is in a constant state of flux. Traditionally, "west" is affluent, "east" less so. The old Paris comprises the 1er, 2e, 3e, and 4e arrondissements. The Left Bank, which encompasses the three "intellectual" arrondissements (5e, 6e,

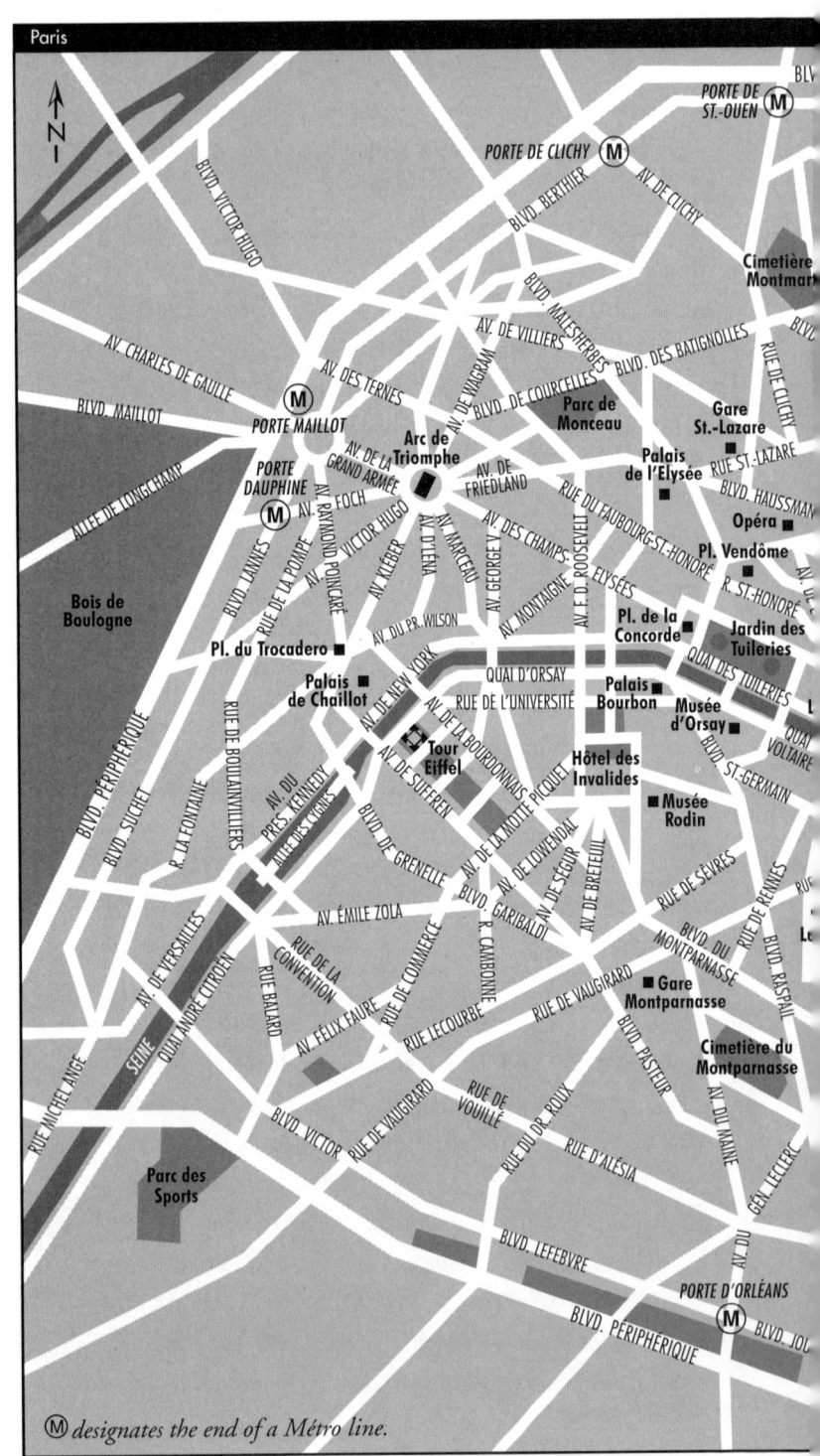

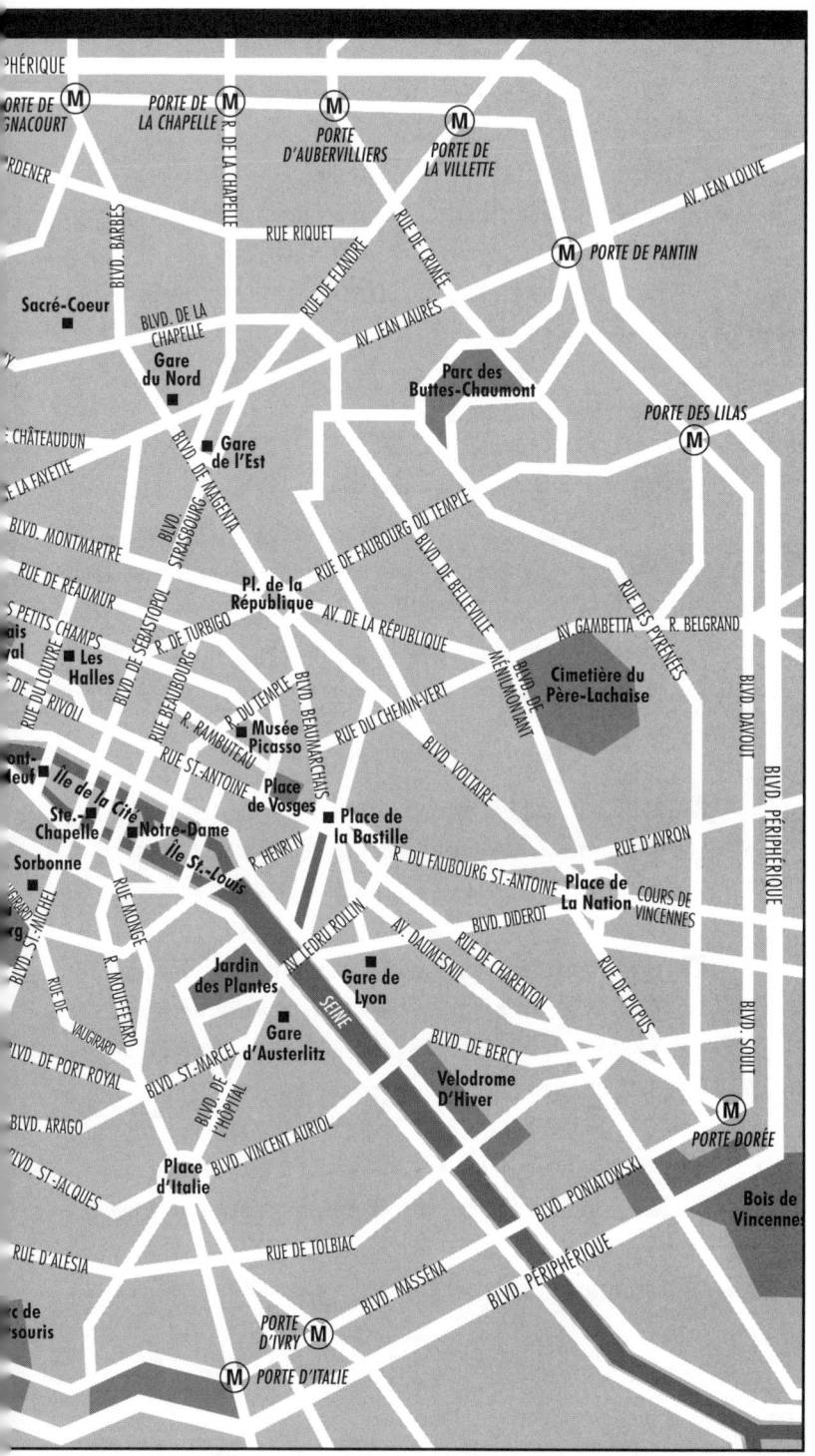

and 7e) as well as the 13e, 14e, and 15e, is characterized by publishing companies, universities, and an intellectual atmosphere. The 8e is the chic Champs-Elysées and avenue Montaigne. The *grande bourgeoisie* is in the 16e and 17e arrondissements. However, Paris loves to break its own rules, so it is not uncommon for a starving student to share a maid's room on the Champs-Elysées, or for a banker to inhabit a huge loft in the shabby 19e arrondissement.

Here are capsule summaries of the character and attractions of the city's arrondissements.

1 The 1er, 2e, 3e, and 4e arrondissements (La Cité, Notre-Dame, Ile Saint-Louis, Le Louvre, La Bourse, Beaubourg, Place des Vosges) *The heart of the Old City, and a great attraction for tourists. The Louvre, the Forum des Halles, the Centre Beaubourg, and the renovated Marais are all here, along with mansions and town houses of the aristocracy dating back to the 17th century. Many are now open to public view.*

2 The 5e, 6e, and 14e arrondissements (Sorbonne, Luxembourg, Montparnasse, Montsouris) *The Latin Quarter, the Left Bank, the universities—intellectual Paris with its publishers and art galleries.*

3 The 7e arrondissement (Invalides, Champ de Mars, Tour Eiffel) *Traditionally, a seat of power, where all the ministries are located. Also convents and houses of the aristocracy of the old Faubourg Saint-Germain, which reigned over Paris in days of yore.*

4 The 8e arrondissement (Champs-Elysées, Parc Monceau, Madeleine) *Built around its royal axis, the Champs-Elysées, from Place de la Concorde to the Arc de Triomphe. It attracts haute couture models, show-biz stars, and tourists from around the world.*

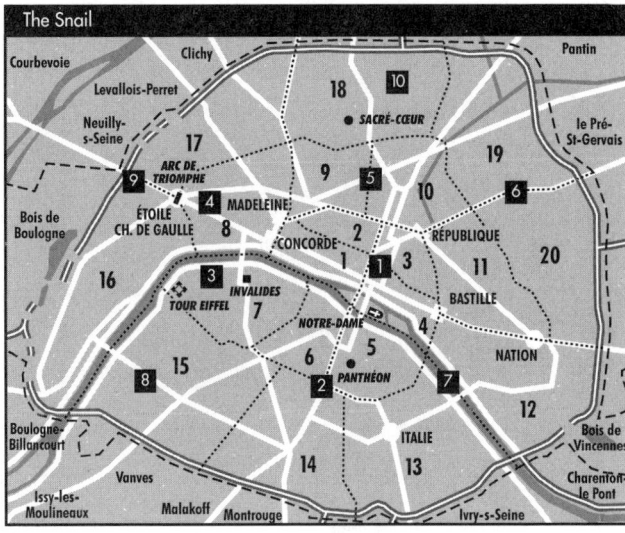

5️⃣ The 9e and 10e arrondissements (from the Opéra to the Gare du Nord and Gare de l'Est and the Grands Boulevards) *Big department stores, a slightly passé neighborhood. The centers of interest have moved elsewhere; opera performances have been moved to Opéra-Bastille, and there is now only ballet at the grand old Opéra Garnier.*

6️⃣ The 11e, 19e, and 20e arrondissements (Place de la République, Buttes-Chaumont, Père-Lachaise) *These three northeast arrondissements are the poorest. But La Villette is coming to life with its Cité de la Musique et des Sciences, and Ménilmontant is being renovated. Perhaps the future is here.*

7️⃣ The 12e and 13e arrondissements (Palais de Bercy, Gobelins) *They were going downhill but are now in full renovation. The 12e includes the Bercy district, and the 13e has become Chinatown.*

8️⃣ The 15e arrondissement (from Champ de Mars to Parc des Expositions) *A traditional neighborhood of petite bourgeoisie, completely renovated a few years ago under the "Front de Seine" building program that introduced skyscrapers along the Seine.*

9 The 16e and 17e arrondissements (Auteuil, Passy, avenue Foch, Trocadéro, Les Ternes, Wagram) *The 16e is the quartier chic between the banks of the Seine and the Bois de Boulogne. An annex of the 16e, the 17e is a peaceful refuge for the higher bourgeoisie.*

10 The 18e arrondissement (Pigalle, Barbès, Montmartre) *Neon, glitter, bisexual prostitutes in Pigalle, folklore artists on the Butte Montmartre, North African ghettos at La Goutte d'Or—an effervescent neighborhood full of contrasts, with some impoverished pockets.*

GINETTE BILLARD
Editor

A few practical details:

Museums and restaurants often keep hours you may find unusual, or close one or two days a week. Be sure to check hours of operation by phoning in advance.

In French buildings, the ground floor (the *rez-de-chausée*) is not numbered. A first-floor shop or restaurant, therefore, is actually on the second level.

Some establishments (restaurants, hotels) mentioned in this guide are exceptionally expensive. Here again, phone in advance.

And finally, a few vocabulary hints:

Place is the French word for *square:* it is neither a street, nor an avenue, nor a boulevard.

Hôtel can mean a *hotel*—a place that rents rooms to tourists. Or it can mean *hôtel particulier.* These 17th- to 19th-century mansions were occupied by the aristocracy and the affluent. Many have been transformed into museums.

The word *table* is used in French for *cuisine.* A restaurant with a good *table* is a restaurant with fine food.

1 PROVINCIAL DINING WITH PAUL BOCUSE

"If French cuisine is so highly and so justly famous, it is due to the quality of the products it uses, its traditions, and also its diversity. Each province of France offers a special dish, a special flavor. Here are some restaurants in Paris that create extraordinary provincial cuisine. Do not be surprised by the preponderance of cooking from Lyons: it is the cuisine I prefer. I call this province the *garde-manger* (pantry) of France."

PAUL BOCUSE, *the "Pope" of French cuisine. His restaurant,* Paul Bocuse *at Collonges au Mont d'Or, nine kilometers from Lyons, is world-famous for the quality and inventiveness of his cuisine and the number of awards he has received.*

Auvergne

1 L'Ambassade d'Auvergne
22 rue du Grenier Saint-Lazare
75003
42 72 31 22
Chef Patrick Hun: *chou farci, boudin aux châtaignes.*

2 Le Vivarois
192 avenue Victor Hugo 75016
45 04 04 31
Chef Claude Peyrot:
aspic de foie gras avec truffes, poularde aux morilles.

3 Lamaison
42 rue des Acacias 75017
43 80 28 54
Chef Bernard Fournier, cuisine from Aubrac: *rognonnade de veau de lait.*

Lyons

4 Chez Pauline
5 rue Villedo 75001
42 96 20 70
Chef André Génin: *terrine de lapereau, salade de tête de veau.*

5 L'Ambroisie
9 place des Vosges 75004
42 78 51 45
Chef Bernard Pacaud:
blanc de turbot à l'huile, tarte sablée au chocolat.

6 Chez Moissonnier
28 rue des Fossés Saint-Bernard
75005
43 29 87 65
Chef Louis Moissonnier:
saladiers lyonnais et gras double aux oignons.

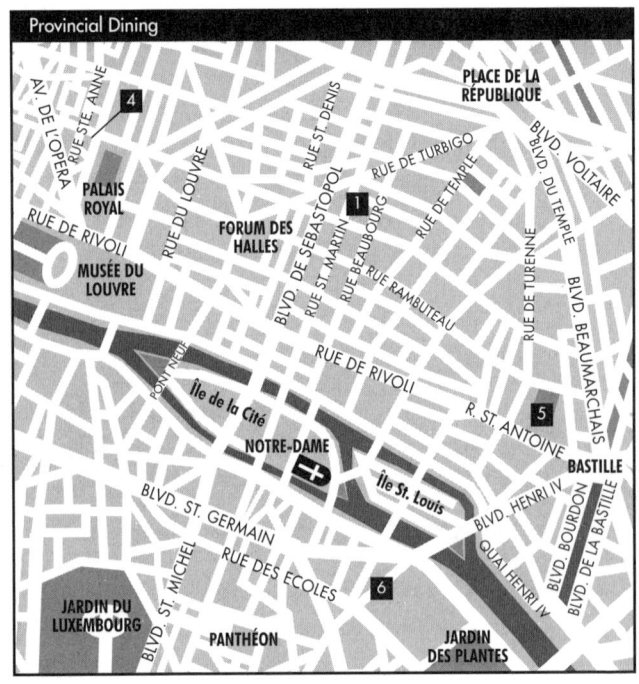

Normandy

7 L'Amphiclès
78 avenue des Ternes 75017
40 68 01 01
Chef Philippe Groult: *galantine de lapin aux aubergines, canette rôtie à l'orange.*

Dauphiné and Savoie

8 Guy Savoy
18 rue Troyon 75017
43 80 36 22
Cuisine from Dauphiné: *volaille de Bresse au jus de truffe, tarte tiède à la rhubarbe.*

9 Michel Rostang
20 rue Rennequin 75017
47 63 40 77
Cuisine from Savoie: *poêlée d'écrevisses, pintades à la chapelure.*

Les Landes

10 La Petite Bretonnière
2 rue de Cadix 75015
48 28 34 39
Chef Alain Lemaison: *terrine de confit d'oie, foie gras chaud.*

PROVINCIAL DINING WITH PAUL BOCUSE

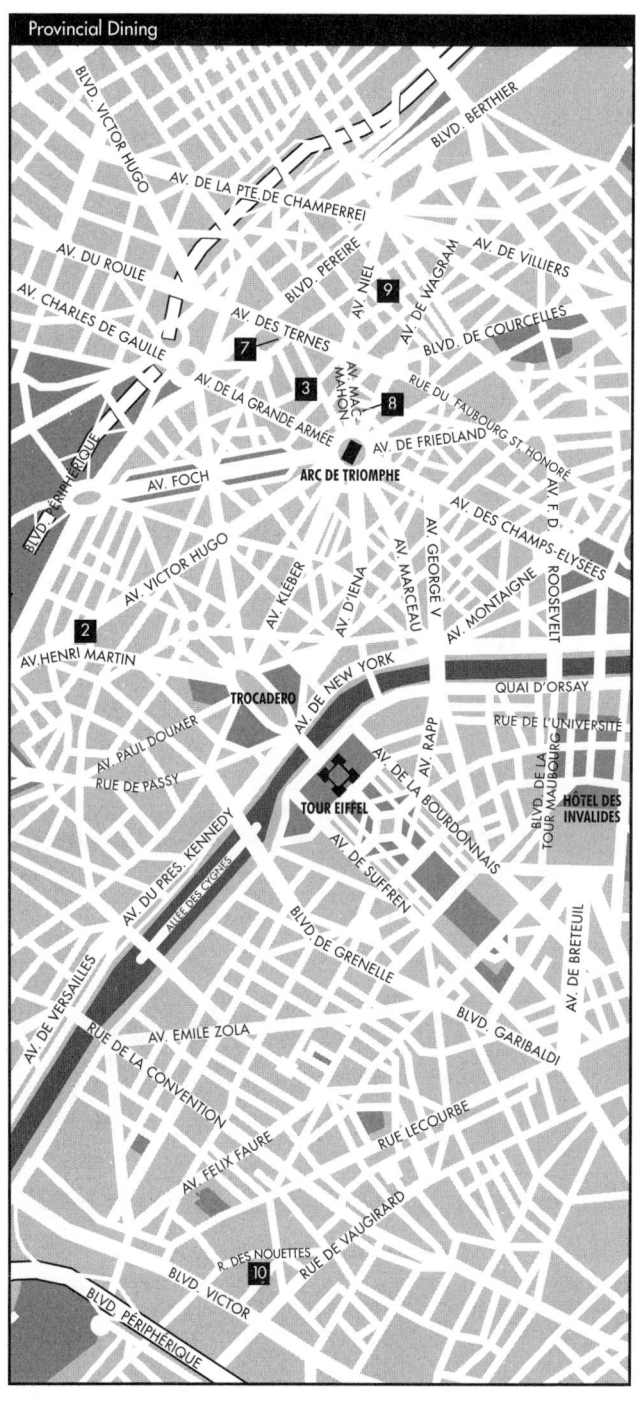

2 MORE PROVINCIAL DINING— WITH ALAIN DUTOURNIER

From his native Landes, the great food-producing region in the southwest of France, Alain Dutournier has transplanted Gascogne cuisine to the heart of Paris. His restaurant, Le Carré des Feuillants at 14 rue de Castiglione 75001 (42 86 82 82), lovingly prepares Gascogne specialties such as *foie gras, chapon aux cèpes, agneau de lait,* and *boeuf de la Chalosse.*

Dutournier also savors gustatorial creations from other provinces. Here is his list of favored provincial *tables* in Paris.

Alsace

1 Baumann
15 rue Marbeuf 75008
47 20 11 11
Famous for fish *choucroute* and succulent meats. Marble décor with chandeliers and mirrors signed by Slavik.

2 Brasserie Flo
7 cour des Petites-Ecuries 75010
47 70 13 59
A charming old stagecoach station, always full. Known for its Riesling *foie gras*, oyster dishes, and extraordinary pheasant *choucroute*.

Jura/Franche-Comté

3 Le Saint-Moritz
33 avenue de Friedland 75008
45 61 02 74
Escargots en meurette, feuilletés aux morilles, poularde au vin jaune, all served in a handsome redwood-paneled room.

Lyonnais

4 La Foux
2 rue Clément 75006
43 25 77 66
Near Saint-Germain-des-Prés, Alex Guini serves his *saucisson chaud, tripes, pot-au-feu* with *poularde de Bresse,* but also *daubes* and macaroni from Nice.

5 Le Bellecour
22 rue Surcouf 75007
45 51 46 93
Fine bourgeoise cuisine: *saladiers lyonnais, quenelles de brochet, andouillette au Mâcon, navarin d'agneau.*

6 Le Récamier
4 rue Récamier 75007
45 48 86 58
Publishers and politicians come here for the *jambon persillé, oeufs en meurette, boeuf bourguignon,* and Martin Cantegrit's Bourgogne wines.

7 Le Bistrot d'à Côté
10 rue Gustave Flaubert 75017
42 67 05 81
Next door to his grand restaurant, Michel Rostang's bistro offers Lyonnaise and Dauphinoise cuisine: *salade de langue et pied de veau, gâteau de foies de volaille, ravioles de Romans.*

Midi—Pyrénées

8 Auberge Pyrénées-Cévennes, chez Philippe
106 rue de la Folie Méricourt 75011
43 57 33 78
Philippe Serbource has been serving typical *auberge* cuisine for the last 25 years: copious *cassoulets*, paellas, *boeuf bourguignon*, with the best Madeira and Beaujolais wines.

Nice—Provence

9 Aux Senteurs de Provence
295 rue Lecourbe 75015
45 57 11 98
Aromas of *bouillabaisse, aioli, bourride,* and *loup au fenouil* combine to create an inviting welcome.

10 La Niçoise
4 rue Pierre Demours 75017
45 74 42 41
Television personality Denise Fabre concocts her *petits farcis:* tomatoes, eggplants, *courgettes,* sweet peppers, *daubes,* ravioli, *lapin au romarin,* and the polenta of her childhood home in Nice.

11 Le Clodenis
57 rue Caulaincourt 75018
46 06 20 26
Actress Nicole Courcel recently bought this restaurant on the Butte Montmartre. Fresh pasta with basil, *filets de rougets grillés, daube de boeuf à la provençale.*

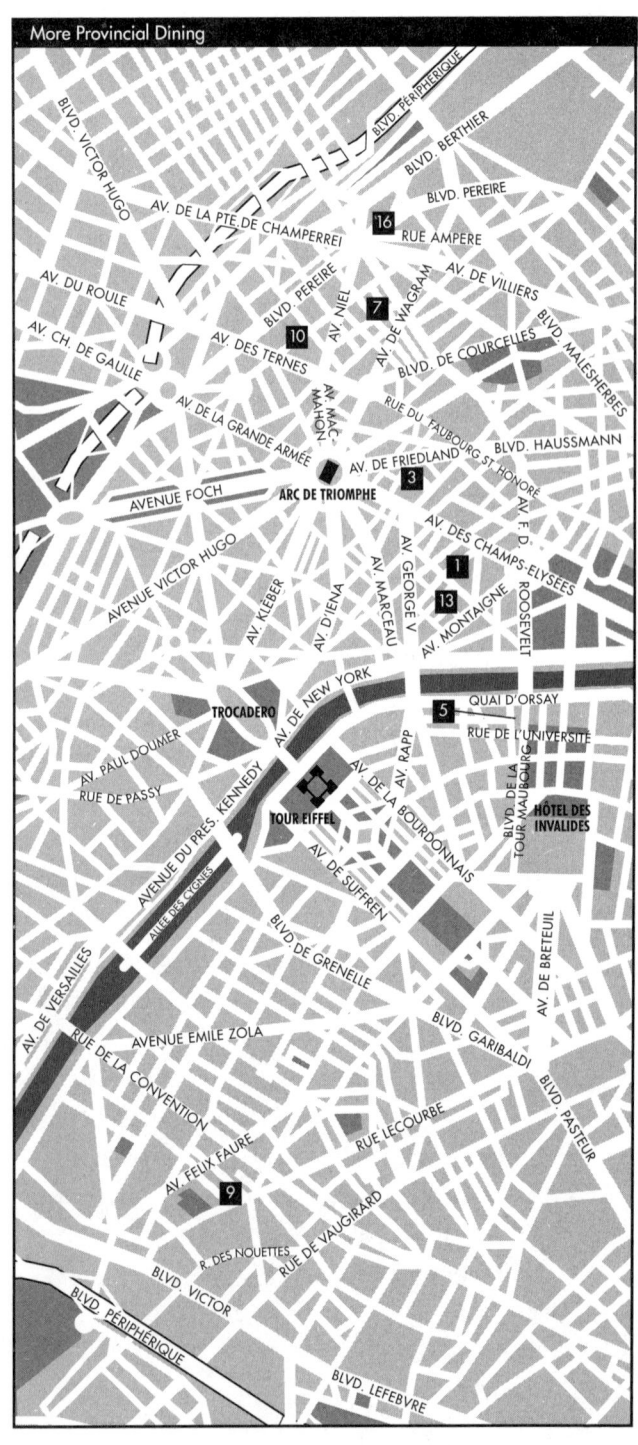

MORE PROVINCIAL DINING — WITH ALAIN DUTOURNIER

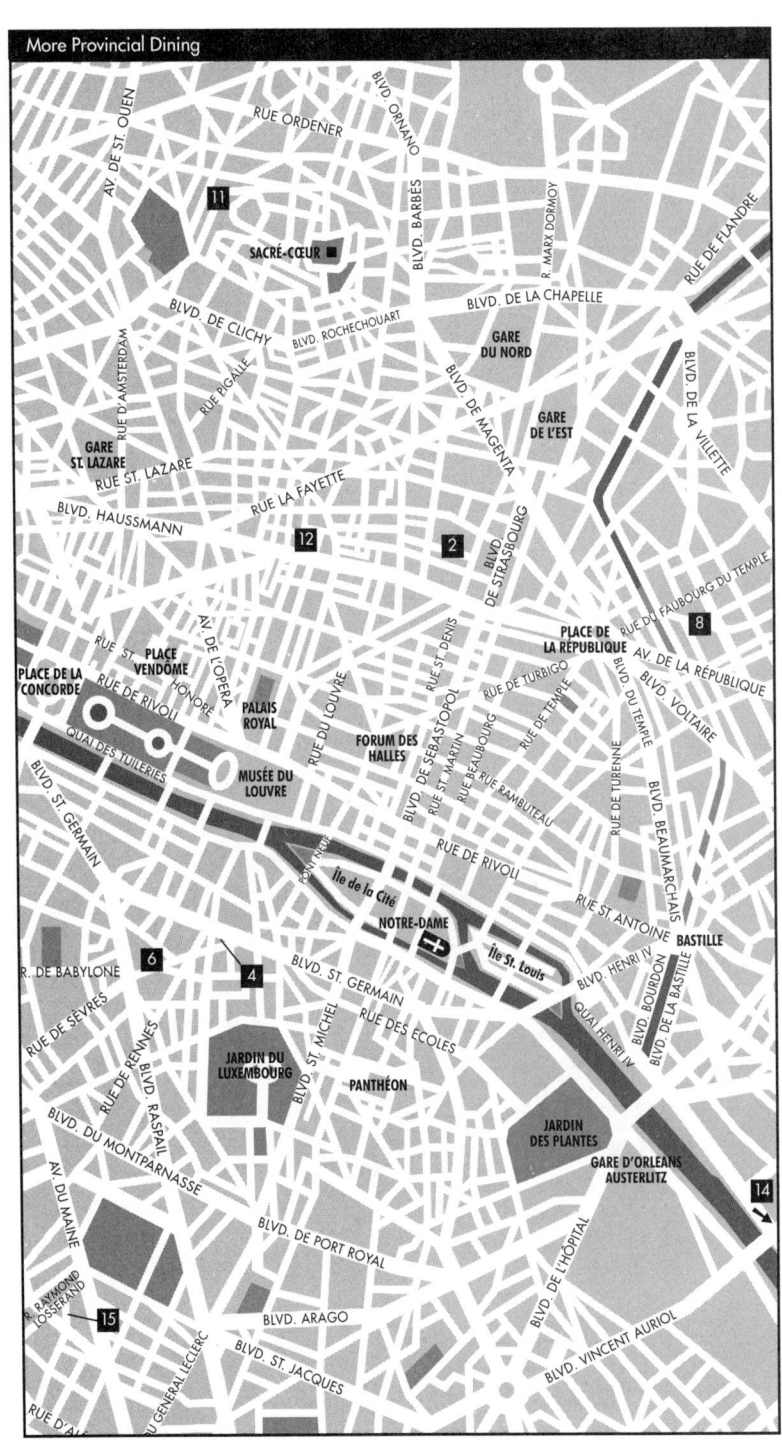

Pays de Loire

12 Au Petit Riche
25 rue Le Peletier 75009
47 70 68 68
Cuisine from Touraine: *rillons, andouillettes au Vouvray, poissons au beurre blanc,* and wines from the Loire region. Wonderful wood-paneled décor with copper lamps.

Southwest

13 Jean Charles et ses Amis
10 rue de la Trémoille 75008
47 23 53 53
A warm welcome: customers are treated as friends, and feast on inspired cuisine from the Landes and the Pays Basque.

14 Le Trou Gascon
40 rue Taine 75012
43 44 34 26
The Gascogne of Nicole Tournier. The best *jambon de Bayonne* in Paris, *pâté chaud aux cèpes, cassoulet de canard, cochons aux haricots tarbais.*

15 L'Assiette
181 rue du Château 75014
43 22 64 86
Yes, some Parisians do wear the famed béret: Lulu la Basquaise feeds "tout Paris" *foie gras de canard* and *magrets* larded with truffles.

16 La Table de Pierre
116 boulevard Pereire 75017
43 80 88 68
Escargot casserole à la tomate, pepper omelette in pastry shell, merlin in green sauce, stuffed duck leg. Outside on Place Pereire, musicians play songs from the Pays Basque.

3   PATRICE DE NUSSAC'S BEST CHEFS OF PARIS

"My choices for the best *grands chefs* of Paris include not only some of the most prestigious names but also brilliant 'outsiders,' the Bocuses and Robuchons of tomorrow. While remaining true to the classic tradition, they are also capable of exciting innovations, bringing ever new progress to French cuisine."

PATRICE DE NUSSAC, *editor in chief of* Gault Millau *magazine that sets the fashions and builds new reputations in French gastronomy.*

The list gives the name of the chef first, then his restaurant.

1 *Alain Dutournier*
Le Carré des Feuillants
14 rue de Castiglione 75001
42 86 82 82
Dutournier preserves the flavors of his native Gascogne. His is one of the great Parisian *tables,* both wise and convivial.

2 *Philippe Bardau*
Le Bourdonnais
113 avenue de La Bourdonnais
75007
47 05 47 96
Exquisite modern cuisine in Micheline Coat's lovely restaurant, fertile ground for training culinary talents.

3 *Alain Passard*
Arpège
84 rue de Varenne 75007
45 51 47 33
A virtuosic young Mozart whose fine and delicate compositions place him among the great names of French cuisine.

4 *Daniel Bouché*
Au Petit Montmorency
5 rue Rabelais 75008
42 25 11 19
Bouché demonstrates exceptional talent for refined and delicate cuisine. Just off the Champs-Elysées, this is a must for the gourmet.

5 *Ghislaine Arabian*
Le Doyen
Carré des Champs-Elysées
75008
47 42 23 23
Although she is married to an Armenian, this blonde Belgian continues to carry high the flag of Flemish-inspired cuisine. *Turbot à la bière* and *soupe crèmeuse aux moules* are among the most famous specialties of her *table.* She is the only woman chef to have slipped to the top rank of great chefs.

6 *Alain Senderens*
Lucas-Carton
9 place de la Madeleine 75008
42 65 22 90
Modern cuisine in a Belle Epoque setting—a happy marriage and a delight for the senses.

7 *Henri Faugeron*
Faugeron
52 rue de Longchamp 75016
47 04 24 53
The cuisine of a perfectionist chef in a quiet atmosphere. The *sommelier* is simply the best in the world.

8 *Joël Robuchon*
Jamin-Joël Robuchon
59 avenue Raymond Poincarré
75016
42 27 12 27
In his beautiful new restaurant with its Art Nouveau setting, Robuchon has elevated cuisine to a near-perfect art. The Japanese are building a château for him in the heart of Tokyo.

9 *Francis Vandenhende (owner) with Gilles Mery (co-chef)*
Le Manoir de Paris
6 rue Pierre Demours 75017
45 72 25 25
Although he was born in Normandy, Vandenhende has adopted the cuisine of his wife, Denise Fabre, a television personality from Nice. All the flavors of the Mediterranean in a refined cuisine.

10 *Jean-Pierre Vigato*
Apicius
122 avenue de Villiers 75017
43 80 19 66
Charming cuisine in a charming restaurant. Bright and shining, Vigato promises to become one of the best.

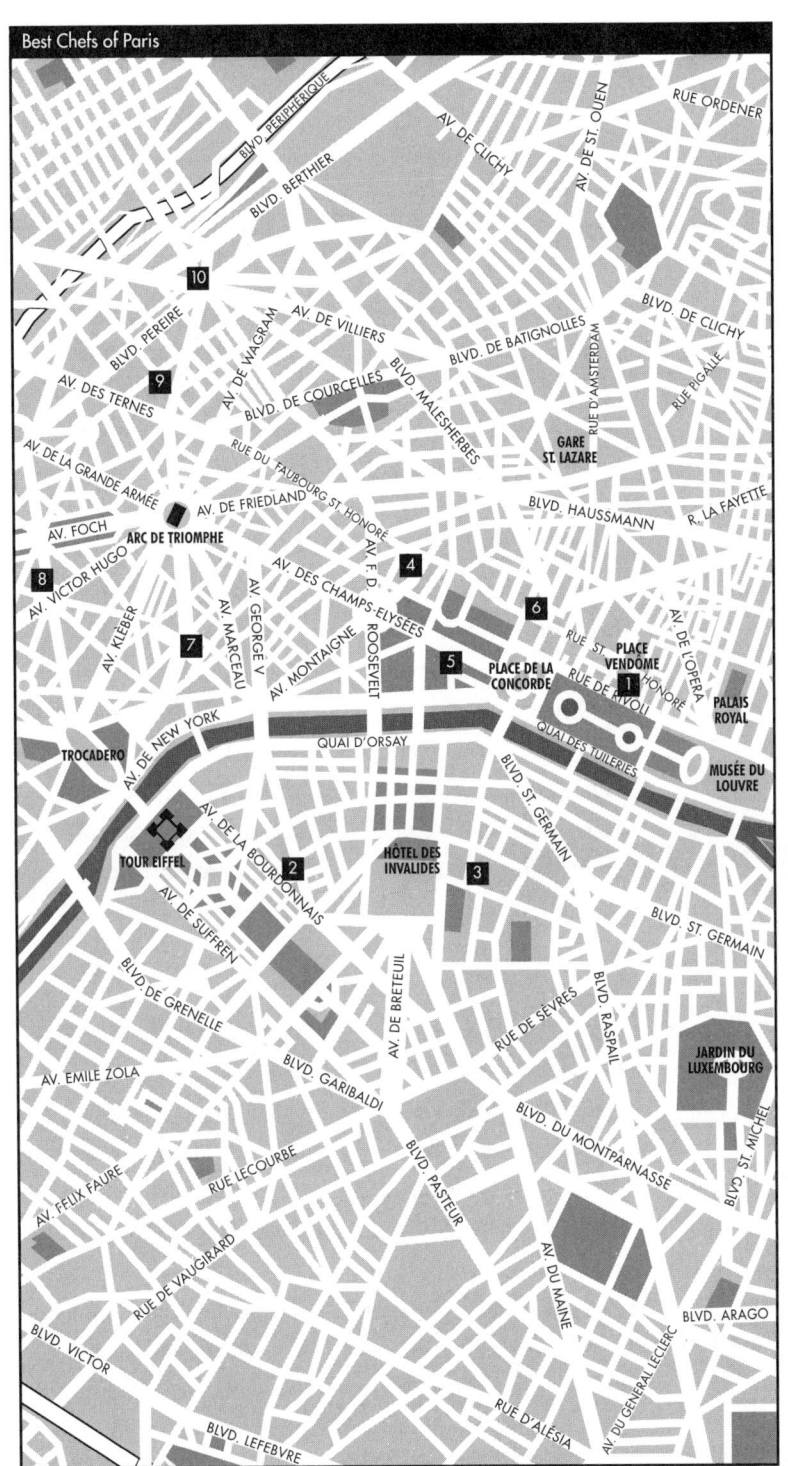

Paris is known throughout the world for superb cuisine, but surprisingly, the atmosphere of some of the most celebrated restaurants does not always measure up to the food. Here are some outstanding restaurants where the ambience offers as much pleasure as the cuisine.

1 Le Grand Véfour
17 rue de Beaujolais 75001
42 96 56 27
Set in the arcaded gardens of the Palais-Royal, where Louis XIV played as a child, Le Grand Véfour is one of the grandest restaurant settings in Paris. The interiors are a monument to Directoire, Napoléon I, and Napoléon III styles, with painted panels, bronze chandeliers, and Directoire chairs. It was Jean Cocteau's favorite eating spot. Solid bourgeoise cuisine.

2 Drouant
Place Gaillon 75002
42 65 15 16
Over a century old, Drouant was renovated in 1923 with engraved mirrors, decorated ceilings, a circular staircase, marble and wrought iron, painted portraits, and murals. It has one of the best wine cellars in Paris, and good cuisine for business lunches and after-theater meals. The Prix Goncourt, France's most important literary honor, is awarded here every year.

3 Allard
41 rue Saint-André-des-Arts 75006
43 26 48 23
An antiquated but hospitable 19th-century *salle de restaurant* with a 1720 façade, sawdust on the floor, and waiters in traditional long white aprons. Cuisine from Berry and Bourgogne.

4 Lapérouse
51 quai des Grands-Augustins 75006
43 26 68 04
An extraordinarily beautiful restaurant to match the fabled cuisine, with an 18th-century façade, gilded windows, paintings à la Boucher and Watteau, decorated ceilings, trompe l'œil frescoes, precious carpets, and more.

THE MOST BEAUTIFUL RESTAURANTS

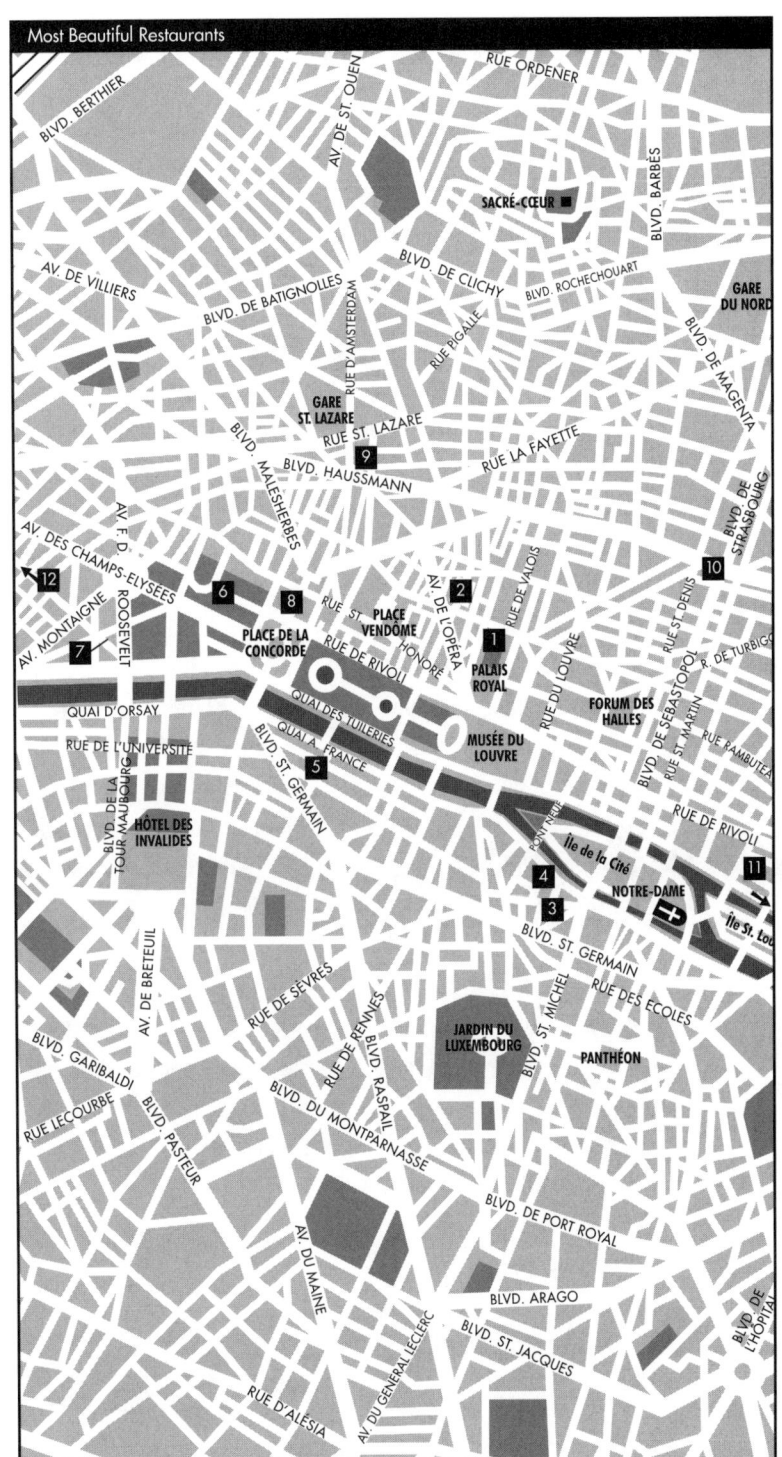

5 Restaurant du Musée d'Orsay
1 rue de Bellechasse 75007
45 49 42 33
The Palais d'Orsay, created for the 1900 World Exhibition, houses the museum of Impressionists and other 19th-century art in a former railway station. The restaurant on the second floor retains the original ceiling, extravagant crystal chandeliers, gilded moldings, marble fireplaces, and light oak floors, and has a superb view of the Seine. Entrance reserved for visitors to the museum. Lunch, plus dinner Thursday evenings. Phone in advance.

6 Elysée Lenôtre
Carré Marigny
10 avenue des Champs-Elysées 75008
42 65 85 10
Gaston Lenôtre, one of the best caterers in Paris, works his miracles in a romantic Belle Epoque pavilion surrounded by metal-and-glass verandas in the gardens of the Champs-Elysées. It was built for the 1900 World Exhibition.

7 Lasserre
17 avenue Franklin Roosevelt 75008
43 59 53 43
Expensive and chic cuisine accompanied by the finest Limoges, silver, and crystal. The dining room has a sliding ceiling that opens to the stars. Decorated by Touchagues with dancing nymphs, it was André Malraux's favorite restaurant.

8 Maxim's
3 rue Royale 75008
42 65 27 94
The most beautiful and most celebrated restaurant in the world: 1900 saw the rise of Maxim's. Pierre Cardin bought it in 1979 and kept the Belle Epoque décor; the *cocottes* are gone, but the charm persists in sumptuous red banquettes, mahogany, silver, and crystal, and in the erotic mural frescoes of nude women—all under the famous glass roof.

9 Mollard
113 rue Saint-Lazare 75008
43 87 50 22
A remarkable 1895 construction with polychrome marble columns, Pompeian ceiling frescoes, wrought iron, Baccarat crystal, and ceramic wall panels depicting the countryside as seen by travelers on the trains leaving the Saint-Lazare station.

10 Le Louis XIV
8 boulevard Saint-Denis 75010
42 08 56 56
Salvador Dali and Andy Warhol were devoted to this place with its 1950s décor, so rare in Paris. Wrought iron, bronze, mahogany, and gilded wood provide the backdrop for rôtisserie, game, and *fruits-de-mer*.

11 Le Train Bleu—Gare de Lyon
20 boulevard Diderot 75012
43 43 09 06
A monument to the opulence of the Third Republic, Le Train Bleu on the second floor of the Gare de Lyon is considered by many to be the most beautiful restaurant in Paris. Enormous bay windows, bronze chandeliers, and tall caryatid sculptures contribute to the grandeur. Painted murals depict the landscape of the south of France and Italy.

12 La Grande Cascade
Bois de Boulogne
Allée de Longchamp 75016
45 27 33 51
This exquisite Belle Epoque metal pavilion in the Bois de Boulogne was built for the 1900 World Exhibition in the style of Hector Guimard's Métro entrances. Mirrored ceilings, crystal chandeliers, and Florentine tiled floors add to the enchantment.

5   GARDEN RESTAURANTS AROUND TOWN

Summers in Paris are often cooler than in the U.S., and dining alfresco is popular with natives and visitors alike. The city offers a rich variety of garden restaurants in beautiful settings. Some are *tables* for gourmets; others offer simpler fare. All provide a refreshing interlude.

1 La Gaudriole
30 rue Montpensier 75001
42 97 55 49
A delightful, shaded restaurant in the unexpected and refreshing gardens of the Palais-Royal, birthplace of the French Revolution, just across the street from Le Louvre.

2 Muscade
36 rue Montpensier
(67 galerie Montpensier) 75001
42 97 51 36
Next door to La Gaudriole in the Palais-Royal gardens, but more modest and casual.

3 La Maison de l'Amérique Latine
217 boulevard Saint-Germain
75007
45 49 33 23
A beautiful 18th-century *hôtel particulier* in a park with old chestnut trees. Tables are set out in the garden in summer.

4 Copenhague—Flora Danica
142 avenue des Champs-Elysées
75008
43 59 20 41
A charming patio brings the countryside onto the Champs-Elysées. Scandinavian cuisine.

5 L'Espace Cardin
1 avenue Gabriel 75008
42 66 11 70
Far from the roar of traffic, Pierre Cardin has set up a charming nook in the shade, just off the Place de la Concorde, overlooking the Jardins des Champs-Elysées. A dozen or so tables for a quick lunch (buffet à la Club Med).

6 Jardin du Carré d'Or
46 avenue Georges V 75008
40 70 05 05
One of the newest garden restaurants in the heart of Paris. The walls are painted in trompe l'œil. Good classic cuisine.

GARDEN RESTAURANTS AROUND TOWN

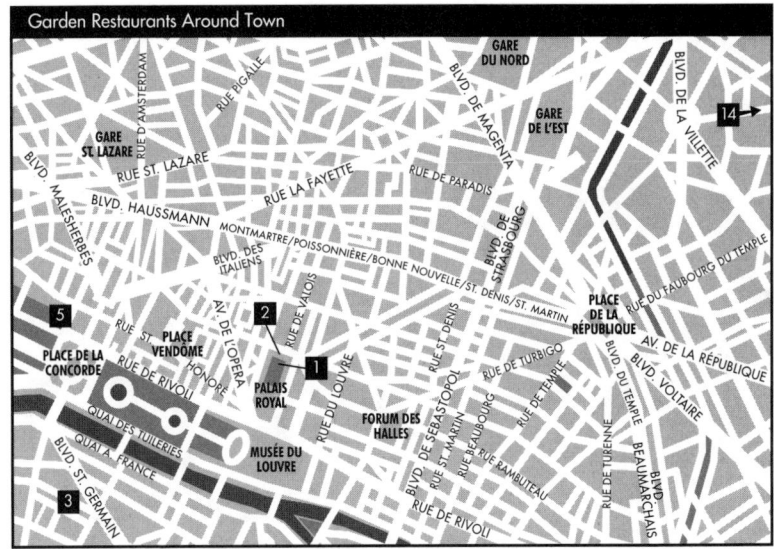

7 Restaurant in Hotel Lancaster
7 rue de Berri 75008
43 59 90 43
In one of the most refined hotels in Paris just off the Champs-Elysées, a quiet courtyard restaurant with flowers and statues. A favorite place for film people from all over the world. Very cool and quiet.

8 Pavillon Montsouris
20 rue Gazan 75014
45 88 38 52
In Parc Montsouris, one of the most beautiful gardens of Paris, across the street from the Cité Universitaire, a pavilion re-creates the atmosphere of 1930s health spas. Good food.

9 L'Auberge du Bonheur
Bois de Boulogne
Allée de Longchamp 75016
42 24 10 17
What once was the eating place for the chauffeurs of diners at La Grande Cascade is now, under the same chestnut trees, a very pleasant bistro for a quick lunch on a sunny day.

10 Le Chalet des Iles
Bois de Boulogne
Lac Inférieur 75016
42 88 04 69
A romantic place for a *diner à deux* on an island in a lake, complete with rowboats.

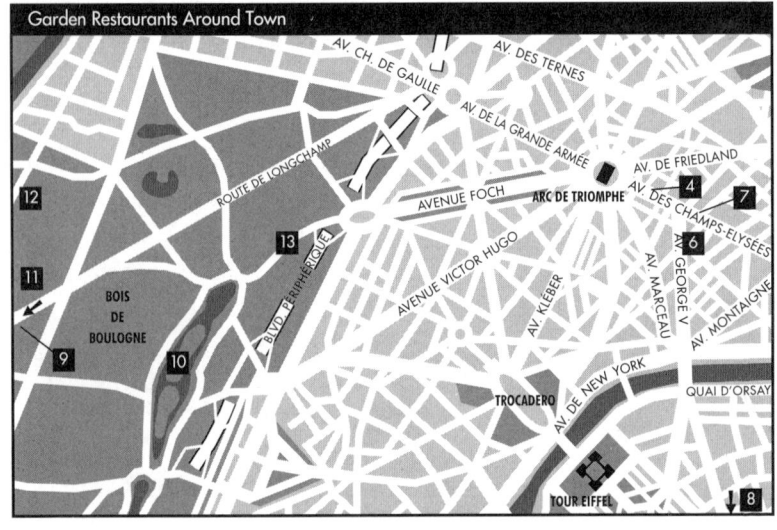

11 La Grande Cascade
Bois de Boulogne
Allée de Longchamp 75016
42 27 33 51
An elegant terrace restaurant of glass and steel surrounded by chestnut trees. Superb cuisine.

12 Les Jardins de Bagatelle
Bois de Boulogne
Route de Sèvres à Neuilly
Parc de Bagatelle 75016
40 67 98 29
A charming garden restaurant in an 800,000-square-foot park with grottoes, waterfalls, ponds, and a rose garden.

13 Le Pré Catelan
Bois de Boulogne
Route de Suresnes
La Croix Catelan 75016
45 24 55 58
Famous caterer and *pâtissier* Gaston Lenôtre offers wonderful cuisine on a shaded terrace overlooking the Bois. Don't miss the desserts.

14 Pavillon Puebla
Parc des Buttes Chaumont 75019
42 08 92 62
A pleasant country house in Napoléon III style overlooking the Parc des Buttes Chaumont and Paris. Fine Mediterranean cuisine.

GARDEN RESTAURANTS OUT OF TOWN

If you have time, drive out into the countryside. Not far from Paris you can find delightful outdoor restaurants in the shade of centuries-old chestnut trees, where you'll be greeted with a pleasant welcome and a cool breeze when the temperature in the city has risen too high.

1 L'Auberge du Relais Breton
27 avenue de Paris
78560 Port Marly
39 58 64 33
Close to Alexandre Dumas' Château de Monte Cristo, with a ravishing garden, a lawn, and birds singing amid groves and thickets. Moderate prices.

2 Le Bas-Bréau
22 rue Grande
77630 Barbizon
60 66 40 05
Spend a summer evening in the paradise of the Impressionists—65,000 square feet of flowers, plants, lawn, vegetables, and fruits, just off the forest of Fontainebleau.

3 Cazaudehore
1 avenue du Président Kennedy
78100 Saint-Germain-en-Laye
34 51 93 80
An immense terrace opening onto a garden filled with acacias, just off the Château de Saint-Germain-en-Laye. Classical cuisine of the southwest, and a magnificent wine list.

4 Le Coq Hardi
16 quai Rennequin Sualem
78380 Bougival
39 69 01 43
Filled with hydrangeas and many other flowers, in a great park that was favored by Monet. Traditional cuisine.

5 L'Ecu de France
31 rue de Champigny
94430 Chennevières-sur-Marne
45 76 00 03
The river flows at your feet at this former stagecoach station on the Marne. A charming *guinguette* (open-air bistro) has been transformed into a good restaurant.

6 Le Moulin d'Orgemont
Rue du Clos des Moines
95100 Argenteuil
34 10 21 47
A park, a river, and a bridge: you dine on top of a tree-lined hill overlooking the Seine. Very good seafood, and a beautiful 19th-century merry-go-round.

7 Le Moulin d'Orgeval
Rue de l'Abbaye
78630 Orgeval
39 75 85 74
The restaurant is in an old mill, with a terrace overlooking the river and the park.

8 Le Pavillon Henri IV
21 rue Thiers
78100 Saint-Germain-en-Laye
39 10 15 15
In the park of the Château de Saint-Germain-en-Laye, this restaurant offers a terrace with a view of the park, the Seine, and Paris. Dine in a building of stones and bricks where Louis XIV was born and where Dumas wrote *The Three Musketeers* and *The Count of Monte Cristo.*

9 Le Restaurant de la Fondation Cartier
3 rue de la Manufacture
78350 Jouy-en-Josas
39 56 46 46
This beautiful restaurant in a 19th-century garden features exhibitions of modern art and excellent Cahors wines. After lunch, go for a stroll in the sprawling park.

10 Le Tastevin
9 avenue Eglé
78600 Maisons-Laffitte
39 62 11 67
In the park near the famous racetrack, enjoy a romantic dinner under a weeping willow or catalpa tree. Excellent seafood and a magnificent wine list.

11 La Terrasse de l'Etang
Route Forestière des Etangs
Etangs de Villebon
92190 Meudon
46 26 09 57
Deep in the forest of Meudon, 20 minutes from Paris, this terrace restaurant on the Pond of Villebon is a soothing retreat. Mostly seafood.

GARDEN RESTAURANTS OUT OF TOWN

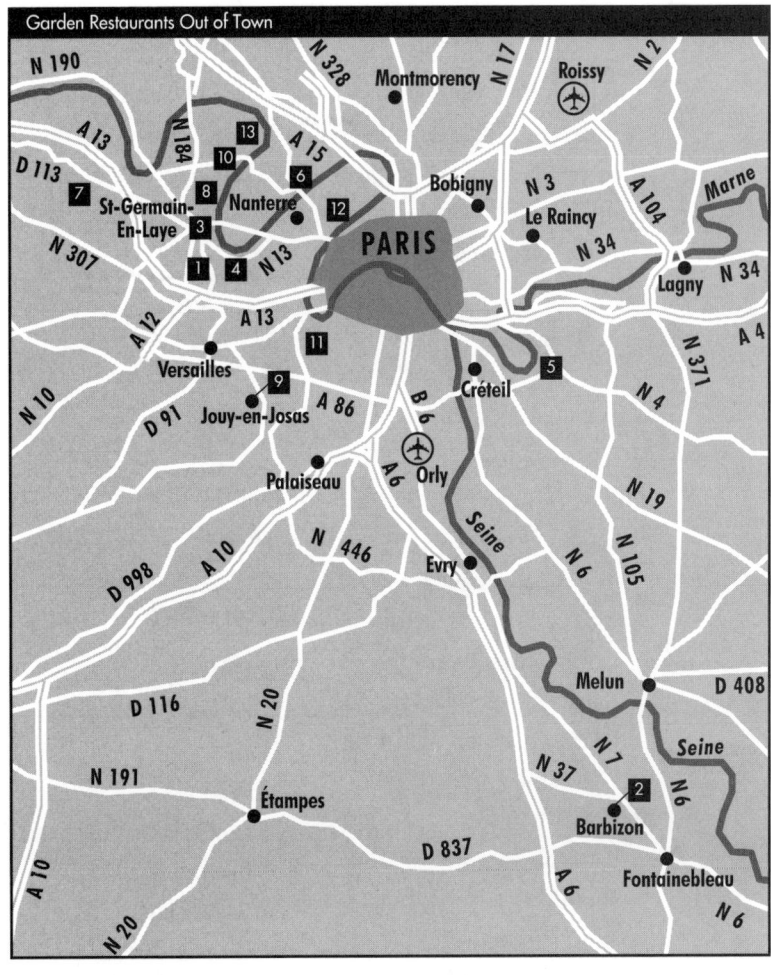

12 Le Van Gogh
2 quai Aulagnier
92600 Asnières
47 91 05 10
The works of Vincent van Gogh and other painters come immediately to mind on this terrace overlooking the Seine, surrounded by boats. Remarkable seafood.

13 La Vieille Fontaine
8 avenue Gretry
78600 Maisons-Laffitte
39 62 01 78
On a terrace overlooking the Parc de Maisons-Lafitte, with its pond and its majestic old trees, the Old Fountain restaurant boasts a Napoléon III façade and superb cuisine.

7 WINE BARS, BISTROS, AND BRASSERIES

Bistros are a Parisian trademark. It is said the word comes from the Russian *bistro*, which means "quick!" When the Cossacks occupied Paris in 1815 after the Napoleonic debacle at Waterloo, it seems they wanted a drink, and quickly. Originally, bistros were places to drink—usually wine. Most of them now serve meals of typical home-cooked cuisine. Their larger versions are called *brasseries*.

Wine Bars
Where you can sip a glass of good wine in a convivial atmosphere.

1 Le Relais Chablis
4 rue Bertin Poirée 75001
45 08 53 73
This typical Burgundy inn with a low, wood-beamed ceiling specializes in North Burgundy wines (Chablis and others). Sandwiches and meals.

2 Willie's Wine Bar
13 rue des Petits Champs
75001
42 61 05 09
Wines from the Rhône Valley, Alsace, and the southwest. Meals.

3 Au Sauvignon
80 rue des Saints-Pères 75007
45 48 49 02
Specializing in Beaujolais wines, this is *the* wine bar of the Left Bank, just off Saint-Germain-des-Prés, with a glass-covered terrace. Sandwiches.

4 Ma Bourgogne
133 boulevard Haussmann
75008
45 63 50 61
Beaujolais wines in a Rabelaisian atmosphere.

Bistros—Restaurants

5 L'Epi d'Or
25 rue Jean-Jacques Rousseau
75001
42 36 38 12
In the old Halles district, this 1950s-style bistro with comfortable décor serves rabbit, *jambonneau, petit salé aux lentilles, rognons de veau.*

6 Lescure
7 rue de Mondovi 75001
42 60 18 91
Just off the Concorde, amid strings of garlic and country sausages, enjoy *poule au pot, poule au riz, porc aux choux.*

WINE BARS, BISTROS, AND BRASSERIES

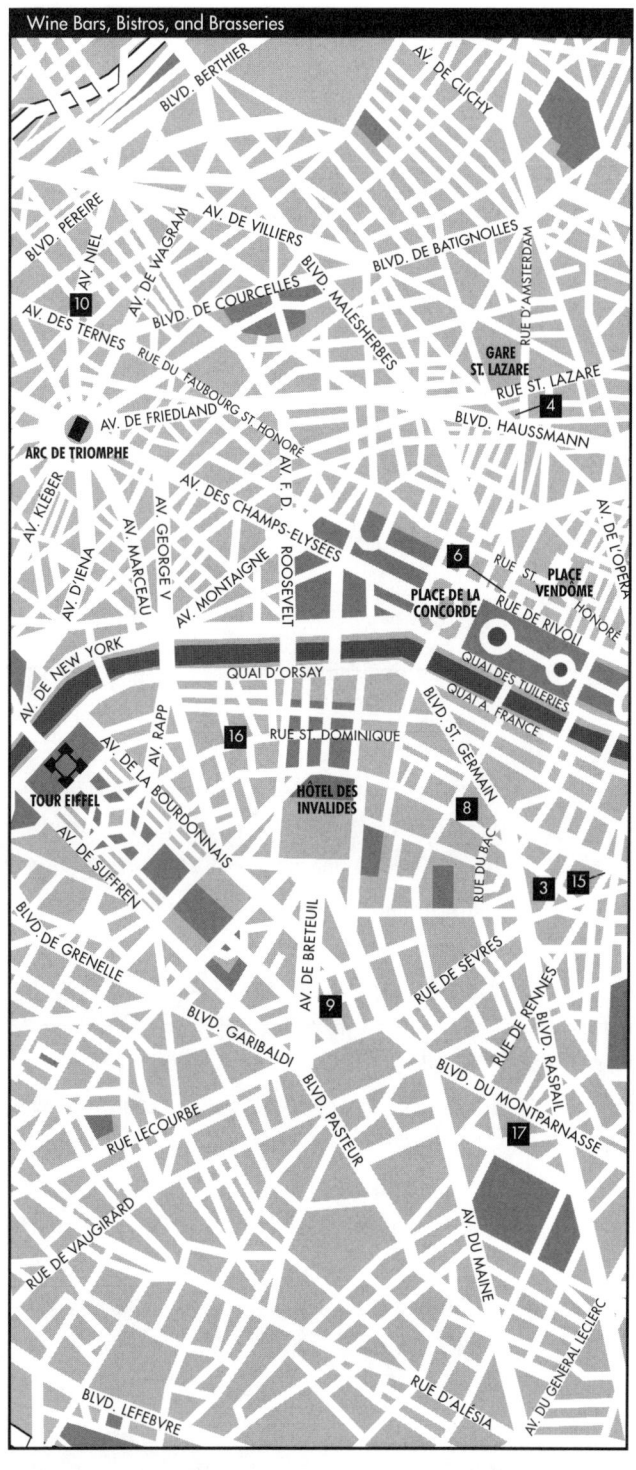

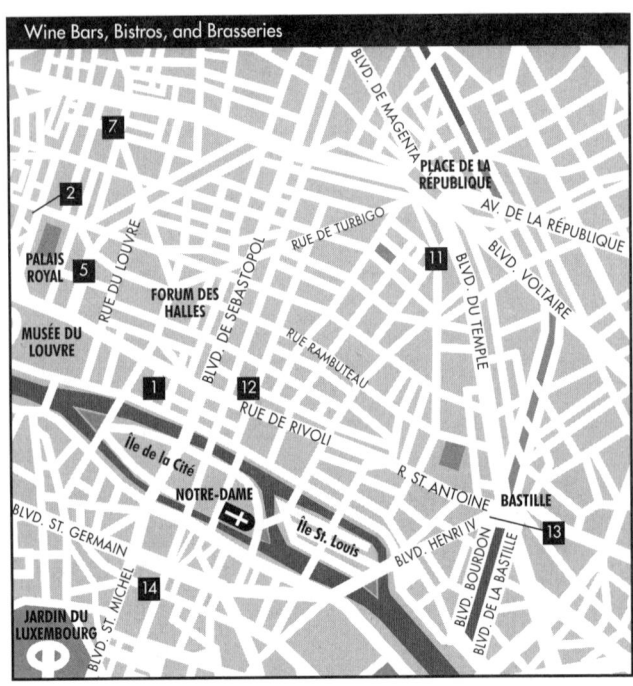

7 Aux Lyonnais
32 rue Saint-Marc 75002
42 96 65 04
Typical bistro cuisine in the Bourse neighborhood: *salade aux lardons, boeuf gros sel, poule au pot*, and excellent desserts.

8 L'Oeillade
10 rue Saint-Simon 75007
42 22 01 60
Famous for its *pot au feu, cassoulet*, and other standard fare.

9 Le Bistrot de Breteuil
3 place de Breteuil 75007
45 67 07 27
A pleasant terrace on a tree-shaded *place* with a view of Les Invalides and La Tour Eiffel. *Escargot à l'ail*, steak tartare, duck, lentils.

10 Le Bistrot de l'Etoile
75 avenue Niel 75017
42 27 88 44
Renowned chef Guy Savoy has opened a bistro with a quiet terrace a few blocks from his expensive restaurant on rue Troyon. Escargot, raviolis, rabbit, and very good desserts.

Brasseries

Bistros on a larger scale, usually characterized by fast service and a certain busy conviviality.

11 Chez Jenny
39 boulevard du Temple 75003
42 74 75 75
Masterful *choucroute*, sausage and pork dishes, and Riesling wines reign here. Décor entirely Alsatian including waitresses in traditional dress.

12 Chez Benoit
20 rue Saint-Martin 75004
42 72 25 76
The king of *cuisine de ménage* (home cooking) offers *compote de lapin, escalope de foie gras aux lentilles, langue de boeuf au porto*, a glorious *fondue au chocolat*. Good Macon, Sancerre, Beaujolais wines.

13 Bofinger
5 rue de la Bastille 75004
42 72 87 82
Just across the *place* from the new Opera-Bastille. Perfect for late-night meals after a show. Oysters, *choucroute*, steak tartare. Chic clientele.

14 Le Balzar
49 rue des Ecoles 75005
43 54 13 67
The *Lipp* of the Latin Quarter. *Céleri remoulade, gigot, poule au riz, raie au beurre noir*, and, naturally, *choucroute*.

15 Lipp
151 boulevard Saint-Germain 75006
45 48 53 91
The meeting place of show-biz stars, literati, and politicians. *Hareng de la Baltique, pot au feu, choucroute*.

16 Thoumieux
79 rue Saint-Dominique 75007
47 05 49 75
The other Left Bank brasserie: *cassoulet, boudin, pot au feu*, steak tartare, *choucroute*.

17 La Coupole
102 boulevard du Montparnasse 75014
43 20 14 20
While the Art Déco setting is still here, old-timers will say that the old Montparnasse spirit is gone. But the *choucroute* is formidable, the oysters and *andouillettes* excellent.

8 — JEAN-LOUIS SCHERRER'S PICK OF THE RESTAURANTS, BISTROS, AND BRASSERIES

"Here is my list of *restaurants sympas*—personal favorites selected for the quality of their cuisine, of course, which is primordial in Paris, but also for their unique and delightful ambience: charming décor, dramatic setting, and colorful clientele. A foreigner will be happy to discover 'another Paris' in the offbeat bistros and brasseries included here. For the lady from abroad, the list offers beguiling places she might fall in love with, grand establishments to dress up for, and out-of-the-way spots filled with artists and intellectuals."

JEAN-LOUIS SCHERRER, *couturier*

Restaurants

1 Le Grand Véfour
17 rue de Beaujolais 75001
42 96 56 27
One of the most elegant restaurants in Paris. When phoning for a reservation, ask for a seat near the windows for a superb view of the Jardins du Palais-Royal.

2 L'Orangerie
28 rue Saint-Louis-en-l'Ile
75004
46 33 93 98
In the Ile Saint-Louis, a magical place where women still dress for dinner. To invite friends here is like entertaining them at home.

3 Le Jules Verne
Tour Eiffel, 2nd floor 75007
45 55 61 44
A thrilling setting high in the Eiffel Tower, with all of Paris 400 feet below you. In the evening, the effect is magical.

4 Caviar Kaspia
17 place de la Madeleine
75008
42 65 33 32
For late nights after the show: caviar, salmon, borscht, blinis. Attractive antique décor.

5 Laurent
41 avenue Gabriel 75008
42 25 00 39
A favorite. On the terrace in summer you may undergo a total *dépaysement* and think you are in New Orleans.

6 15 Montaigne
15 avenue Montaigne 75008
47 23 55 99
For the superb view at night, overlooking the Seine, the Eiffel Tower, and all of Paris, and known for its sophisticated gray-black interior.

7 Maxim's
3 rue Royale 75008
42 65 27 94
A "must" for its beautiful Belle Epoque décor, and as a souvenir of all the celebrities and crowned heads who haunt it. Complete with a string ensemble, Maxim's is a legend.

8 Relais Plaza
21 avenue Montaigne 75008
47 23 46 36
A very pleasant place in 1920s décor for supper after the theater.

9 La Stresa
7 rue de Chambiges 75008
47 23 51 62
Very good Italian cuisine in a relaxed atmosphere. The décor is from the 1950s.

10 Le Duc
243 boulevard Raspail 75014
43 20 96 30
The best fish restaurant in Paris. Meeting place of the show-business and business worlds, in an interior of polished wood.

11 Les Jardins de Bagatelle
Bois de Boulogne
Parc de Bagatelle 75016
40 67 98 29
A summer lunch in the famous rose gardens is an enchanting experience.

Bistros and Brasseries

12 L'Ami Louis
32 rue du Vertbois 75003
48 87 77 48
In the Halles district, just searching for rue du Vertbois will give you an opportunity to visit the beautiful Marais. L'Ami Louis preserves the authenticity of the true Parisian bistro.

13 Anahï
49 rue Volta 75003
48 87 88 24
Argentine cuisine and atmosphere in a former butcher shop which has kept its ceramic façade. Very few tourists. The patrons are on the intellectual side.

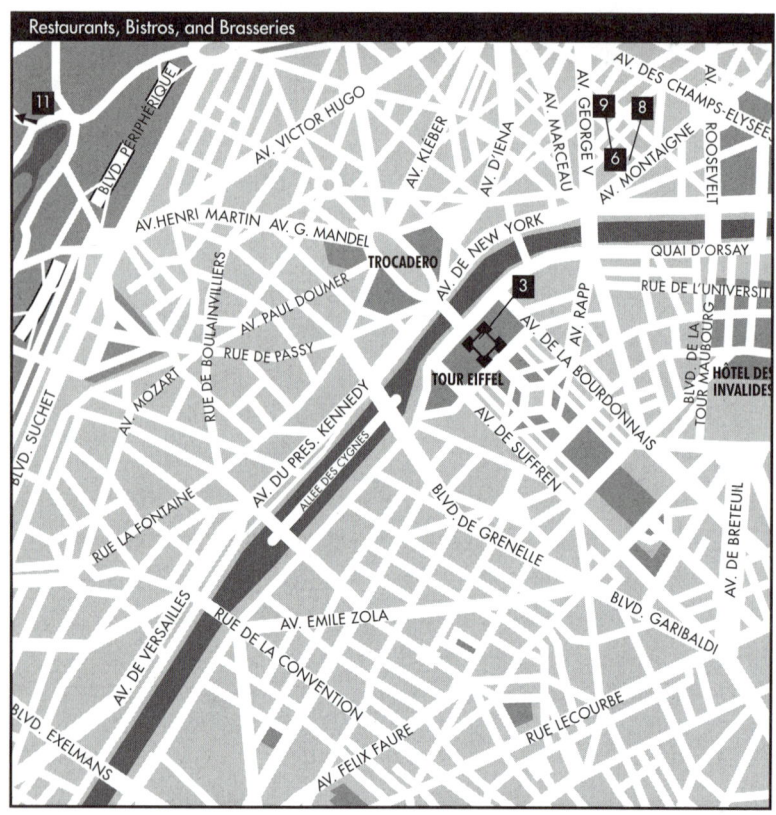

14 Chez Jenny
39 boulevard du Temple 75003
42 74 75 75
For its champagne *choucroute* and its décor of inlay work in a patriotic theme.

15 Benoît
20 rue Saint-Martin 75004
42 72 25 76
Founded in 1912 by an ex-coachman, this is the most Parisian of all bistros.

16 Lipp
151 boulevard Saint-Germain 75006
45 84 53 91
A truly authentic bistro, with waiters in long white aprons, an intellectual crowd, and typical Parisian ambience which has persisted through several decades.

JEAN-LOUIS SCHERRER'S PICK OF THE RESTAURANTS, BISTROS, AND BRASSERIES

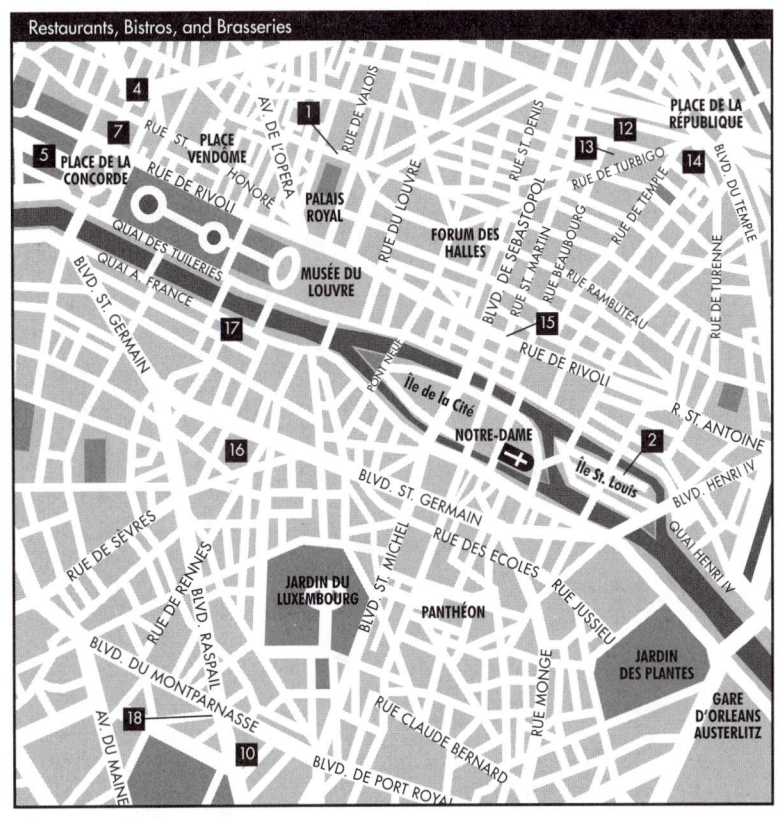

17 Le Voltaire
27 quai Voltaire 75007
42 61 17 49
A meeting place for artists on the quays along the Seine.

18 La Coupole
102 boulevard du Montparnasse 75014
43 20 14 20
Founded in 1927, La Coupole retains its striking environment, Art Déco glass roof, and animated ambience. Filled with all the remembrances of Montparnasse, it is *the* Parisian brasserie.

9 EXOTIC CUISINE

French food is the best in the world. There is no possible discussion about this—at least with a Frenchman. However, if you desire a change of pace, here are some exotic Parisian restaurants where you will find cuisine from around the world.

Asian Cuisine (Chinese, Indian, Thai, Vietnamese)

1 Au Coin des Gourmets
5 rue Dante 75005
43 26 12 92
Amok as cooked in Cambodia, brochettes, seafood, *nhom* made with *mussels à la citronella,* duck stuffed with red dates.

2 Chieng-Mai
12 rue Frédéric Sauton 75005
43 25 45 45
Authentic Thai cuisine: peppered shrimp soup, cuttlefish, mussels.

3 Restaurant A
5 rue de Poissy 75005
46 33 85 54
Chinese imperial classics dating to the 18th century, not found elsewhere in Paris. Salads of shrimp and jellyfish, rabbit stewed in Chinese alcohol, crabmeat cooked in beer.

4 Yugaraj
14 rue Dauphine 75006
43 26 44 91
One of the rare, authentic Indian restaurants in Paris. Specialties from Delhi, Goa, Luchnow: *tandoori, samosa, ghost rada khom* (spiced mutton), *machli massada* (fish *à la mode* de Calcutta).

5 Aux Délices de Szechuen
40 avenue Duquesne 75007
43 06 22 55
Chinese delicacies in an elegant setting in a refined neighborhood. Meals are served on the terrace in summer. Spiced cold noodles, lacquered duck, dim sum, spiced duck, ginger dumplings, sesame chicken, orange beef.

6 Tan Dinh
60 rue de Verneuil 75007
45 44 04 84
Vietnamese. Duck rolls, steamed crabmeat, mangoes. A very good wine cellar.

EXOTIC CUISINE

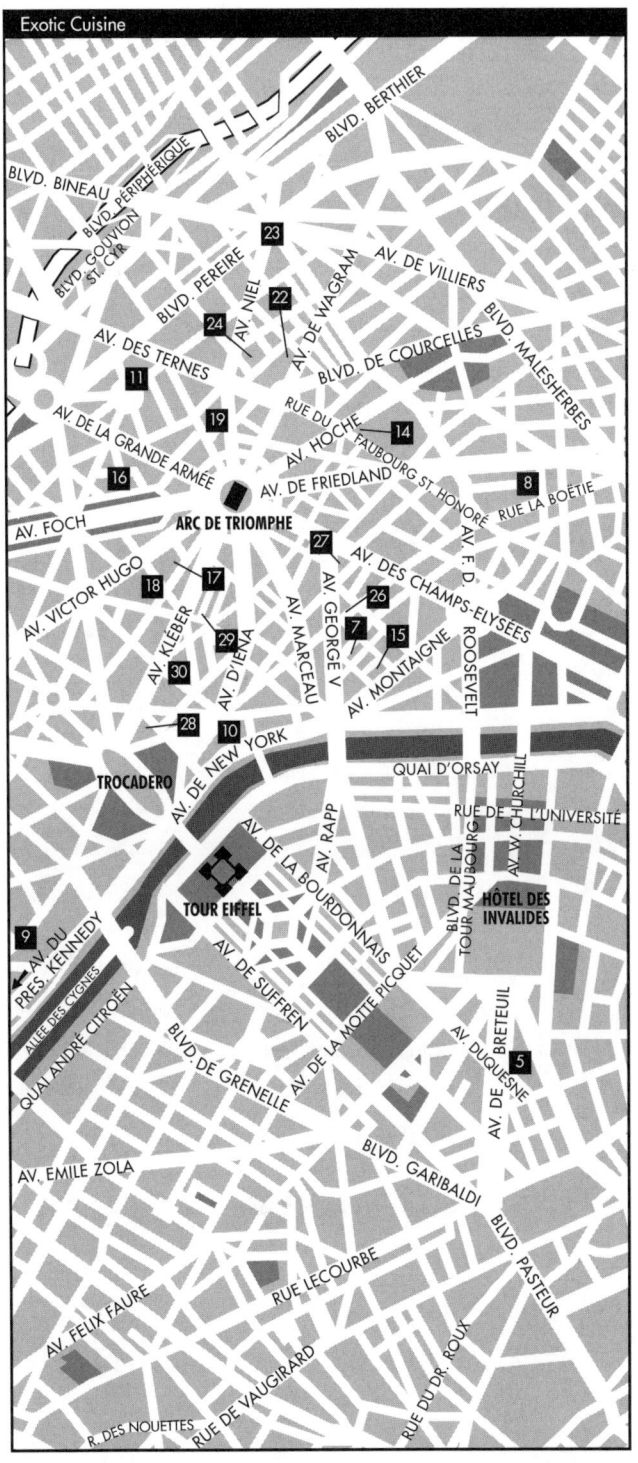

7 Le Chateau de Chine
9 rue La Trémoille 75008
47 23 80 90
Dim sum, lacquered duck, chicken with five flavors.

8 Dynastie Thai
101 rue La Boétie 75008
42 89 09 05
Very spicy, mostly vegetarian fare. Curry gambas, shrimp soup with lemon grass, sautéed pork with pepper and garlic.

9 La Baie d'Ha Long
164 avenue de Versailles 75016
45 24 60 62
Vietnamese. Spiced shrimp soup, duck grilled in ginger, chicken cooked in banana tree leaves.

10 Le Grand Chinois
6 avenue de New York 75016
47 23 98 21
Remarkable lacquered duck and pineapple chicken, but also less classic dishes such as hot oysters with ginger and jellyfish salad. Authentic Chinese cuisine, a splendid wine list, and courteous service.

Greek Cuisine

11 Alexandros
18 rue Saint-Ferdinand 75017
45 74 75 11
Good *pikalias* (hors d'œuvres), pork brochettes, interesting Greek wines. Inexpensive.

12 Les Délices d'Aphrodite-Mavrommatis
4 rue de Candolle 75005
43 31 40 39
Just off Mouffetard, the best of Greek cuisine on a little square. Moussaka, souvlaki, jellyfish.

Italian Cuisine

13 La Bauta
129 boulevard du Montparnasse 75006
43 22 52 35
Venetian cuisine, including octopus with fennel, pasta with anchovies, veal liver with onions, and, of course, *sabayon*. Good chianti wines.

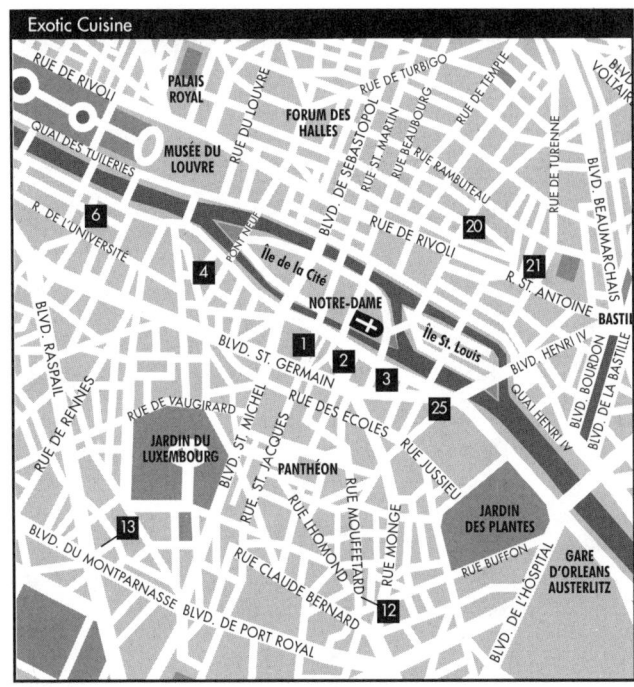

14 Le Carpaccio
Hotel Royal Monceau
37 avenue Hoche 75008
42 99 98 90
Naturally one of the best *carpaccios* in Paris. Tuscan soup, veal with eggplant gratin, Sicilian *paupiettes,* and, to finish, tiramisu and *zuppa inglese.*

15 Le Stresa
7 rue de Chambiges 75008
47 23 51 62
Very chic: antipasto with olive oil from Tuscany, pasta, osso bucco, tiramisu.

16 Bellini
28 rue Le Sueur 75016
45 00 54 20
Very refined: *risotto à la bottarga* (mullet eggs), tiramisu, great wines from Frioul, Tuscany, Venetia.

17 Conti
72 rue Lauriston 75016
47 27 74 67
One of the most delicate Italian *tables* in Paris: pancakes with sweetbreads and oregano, lobster lasagne, Parmesan bacon with *carpaccio,* rigatoni, cream tagliatelle, osso bucco.

18 Villa Vinci
23 rue Paul Valéry 75016
45 01 68 18
Venetian veal liver, *scampi fritti*, tiramisu.

19 Sormani
4 rue du Général Lanrezac 75017
43 80 13 91
The must for chic Italian dining in Paris. *Brandade* of cod in tiny gnocchi, calamari cooked in garlic with red peppers and bacon, kidneys and sweetbreads with Trevisan salad. Voluptuous tiramisu, exquisite Italian wines.

Jewish Cuisine

20 Jo Goldenberg
7 rue des Rosiers 75004
48 87 20 16
In what is left of the Parisian *shtetl*, the grandest and oldest of Ashkenazi restaurants: pickle *fleisch*, kosher *foie gras*, chopped liver, cream borscht, and, of course, strudel.

21 Pitchi Poï
7 rue Caron
Place du Marché Sainte-Catherine 75004
42 77 46 15
The best and most chic Yiddish *table* in Paris, with cumin and poppy seeds, *tchoulent* (Jewish cassoulet with barley and potatoes), stuffed cabbage. Dine on the terrace in summer.

22 Al Rosenberg
69 avenue de Wagram 75017
42 27 34 79
Sauerkraut with pickles and veal sausages, *tchoulent*, fat herrings, stuffed carp. Not far from Place Charles de Gaulle.

And two kosher restaurants:

23 Les Jardins du Belvèdère
111 avenue de Villiers 75017
42 27 16 91

24 Nini
24 rue Saussier Leroy 75017
46 22 28 93

North African and Lebanese Cuisine

25 Institut du Monde Arabe
1 rue des Fossés Saint-Bernard 75005
46 33 47 70
A delightful terrace overlooking the Seine and Notre-Dame. Couscous, *tagines*, *mezze* (cold and hot hors d'œuvres), all the classics of North Africa.

26 Ajani
1 rue Lincoln 75008
42 25 38 44
Lebanese. *Kebbeh amis* (lamb with shallots), *tabouli chawarma* (marinated beef), and gorgeous Middle Eastern pastries.

27 Fakhr El Dine
3 rue Quentin Bauchart 75008
47 23 74 24
Lebanese. *Mezze* with mashed eggplant, sausages, marinades, wines from the Lebanese mountains.

28 Al Mouna
16 rue de Magdebourg 75016
47 27 57 28
In a Moorish décor, the food is served on copper plates. One of the best Moroccan restaurants in Paris. *Tagines*, *harira* soup, couscous.

29 Amazigh
2 rue La Pérouse 75016
47 20 90 38
Moroccan. Very refined *tagines* and stews, lamb with eggplant, *briouats* (ravioli with seafood), stuffed sardines, a royal couscous.

30 Fakhr El Dine
30 rue de Longchamp 75016
47 27 90 00
Rich Lebanese exiles gather here for the unusual variety of *mezze*, *nougadara* (mashed lentils), *thalate* (stuffed lamb spleen), and *makanek* (spiced sausages cooked in wine). Oversweet Lebanese desserts and Lebanese wines (Musar, Ksara).

TEA TIME IN PARIS

When a day of shopping, sightseeing, or walking the museums begins to take its toll, it's time for a tea break. Here is a selection of *salons de thé* where you can rest awhile, sip delicious tea (with a cake, perhaps), or drink a chocolate. Enjoy a late breakfast or a light lunch and a chat with a friend.

1 Angelina
226 rue de Rivoli 75001
42 60 82 00
Successor to the famous Rumpelmayer across the Tuileries Gardens, Angelina serves excellent tea and coffee, even better chocolate, and light meals.

2 Mariage Frères
30 rue du Bourg Tibourg
75004
42 72 28 11
Walls lined with hundreds of tins and boxes make for an incredible décor. In the Marais.

3 La Mosquée de Paris
39 rue Geoffroy Saint-Hilaire
75005
43 31 18 14
Savor mint tea, remarkable Turkish coffee, and *corne de gazelle* pastries in the exotic setting of the Paris Mosque.

4 Dalloyau
2 place Edmond Rostand
75006
43 29 31 10
Across from the Jardins du Luxembourg: pastries, ice cream, and prepared meals.

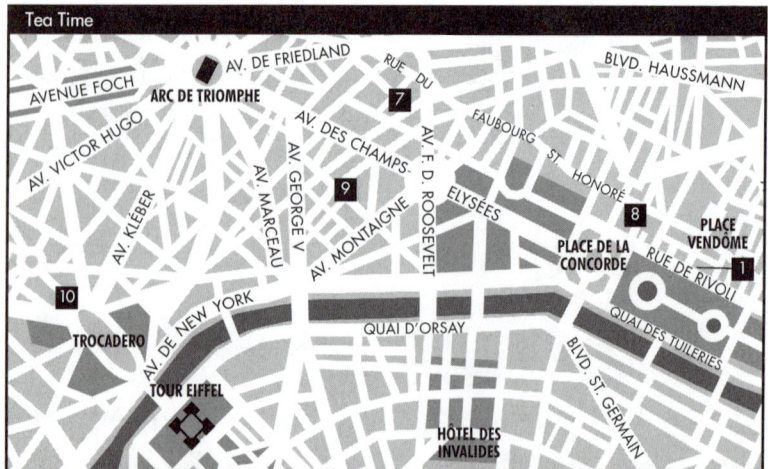

TEA TIME IN PARIS

5 Mariage Frères
*13 rue des Grands-Augustins
75006*
40 51 82 50
Near Saint-Germain-des-Prés.
An incredible selection of teas.

6 Tea and Tattered Pages
24 rue Mayet 75006
40 65 94 35
Stop in for a taste of typical British atmosphere: English tea, muffins, cheesecake, brownies, banana bread, and English books, new and secondhand.

7 Dalloyau
101 rue du Faubourg Saint-Honoré 75008
43 59 18 10
On Faubourg Saint-Honoré. Chocolate pastries and ice cream. Also take-out petits fours and prepared meals.

8 Ladurée
16 rue Royale 75008
42 60 21 79
Not far from Place de la Concorde. Tea, croissants, finger sandwiches, light lunches.

9 La Maison du Chocolat
52 rue François 1er 75008
47 23 38 25
A *salon de thé* exclusively reserved for lovers of chocolate. A delight just off the Champs-Elysées.

10 Carrette
4 place du Trocadéro 75016
47 27 88 56
Very stylish, very 16e arrondissement, and very good pastries.

IRRESISTIBLE ICE CREAMS

There's nothing like a stop for ice cream while sightseeing on a warm day. Paris has some of the world's best ice cream, and here are some of Paris' best.

On L'Ile Saint-Louis

1 Berthillon
31 rue Saint-Louis-en-l'Ile 75004
43 54 31 61
The best-known ice cream shop in Paris, where wise hostesses order their desserts. Sixty flavors of ice cream.

2 Coco Passion
17 rue des Deux Ponts 75004
43 25 50 93
Open until 2am.

3 Le Flore en l'Ile
42 quai d'Orléans 75004
43 29 82 79
Just across from Notre-Dame.

4 Pom'Cannelle
27 rue des Deux Ponts 75004
46 34 68 59
On Ile Saint-Louis, one of the favorite shops for tired and thirsty tourists.

On the Left Bank

5 La Chocolatière
5 rue Stanislas 75006
45 49 13 06
Chocolate, melon, and vanilla ice cream are the specialties in this very provincial *salon de thé*.

6 Dalloyau
2 place Edmond Rostand 75006
43 29 31 10
Excellent chocolate ice cream. Also pastries and take-out food.

7 Le Bac à Glaces
109 rue du Bac 75007
45 48 87 65
Across the street from Bon Marché. Thirty-five all-natural flavors, and sorbets for dieters.

8 Constant
26 rue du Bac 75007
47 03 30 00
Famous for its bitter chocolate ice cream.

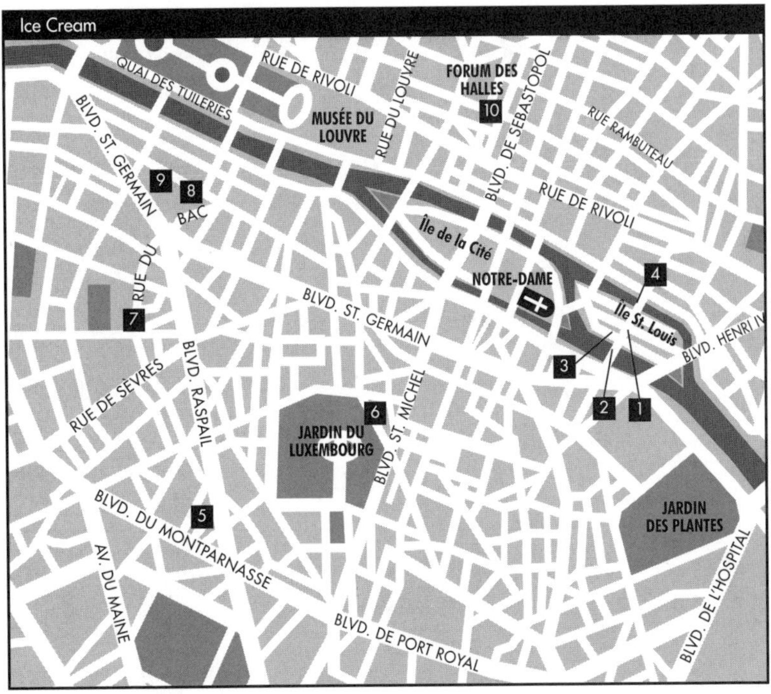

IRRESISTIBLE ICE CREAMS

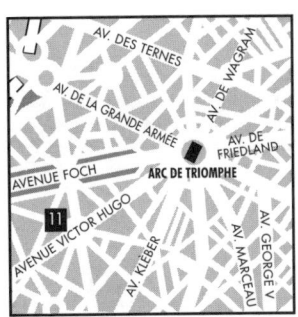

In the Marais

10 Gilles Vilfeu
3 rue de la Cossonerie 75001
40 26 36 40
On a street reserved for pedestrians. A host of innovative flavors: lichee, white cheese, tiramisu, and more.

9 Richart
258 boulevard Saint-Germain 75007
45 55 66 00
Specialist in super-bitter chocolate ice cream and cocoa sorbets.

On the Right Bank

11 Häagen-Dazs
5 place Victor Hugo 75016
45 00 95 65
For the real American ice cream.

12 GOURMET SHOPPING AND MORE WITH JEANNE MOREAU

"I have always enjoyed good food, but rather than go to a restaurant, I prefer to cook for friends at home. I am a careful shopper for the best fruits and vegetables, the best poultry and fish, the finest teas. Here are my most reliable sources."

JEANNE MOREAU, *actress* (Jules and Jim, Chimes at Midnight, La Femme Nikita, Until the End of the World), *film director* (Lumière, L'Adolescente), *and producer*

Food Shops

1 Au Jardin d'Espagne
8 rue du Marché Saint-Honoré
75001
42 61 02 91
To cook a fine dinner you need top-quality garden produce. Simone and Gilles Badier select the finest and freshest fruits and vegetables.

2 La Poularde Saint-Honoré
9 rue du Marché Saint-Honoré
75001
42 61 00 30
For poulardes, Bresse capons, ducks from Nantes, black-legged plump chickens from Challans—all their products are excellent. I have been a regular customer for 30 years.

3 Mariage Frères
13 rue des Grands-Augustins
75006
40 51 82 50
Excellent varied teas.

4 La Poissonnerie du Champ de Mars
145 rue Saint-Dominique
75007
47 05 03 52
Michel Lagriffoul specializes in the finest fish: sole, monkfish, turbot, brill. Fillets are cut in front of the customer.

5 Boucherie Renaissance-Marbeuf
10 rue Marbeuf 75008
47 20 72 07
The best chefs in Paris (Ledoyen, Maxim's, Le Ritz, La Tour d'Argent) buy their meat here. Baby veal, Simmenthal beef from Bavaria, pickled meats. It is important to have a close relationship with your butcher.

6 La Cave Vignon
16 rue Clément Marot 75008
47 20 16 18
One of the best wine cellars in Paris.

GOURMET SHOPPING AND MORE WITH JEANNE MOREAU

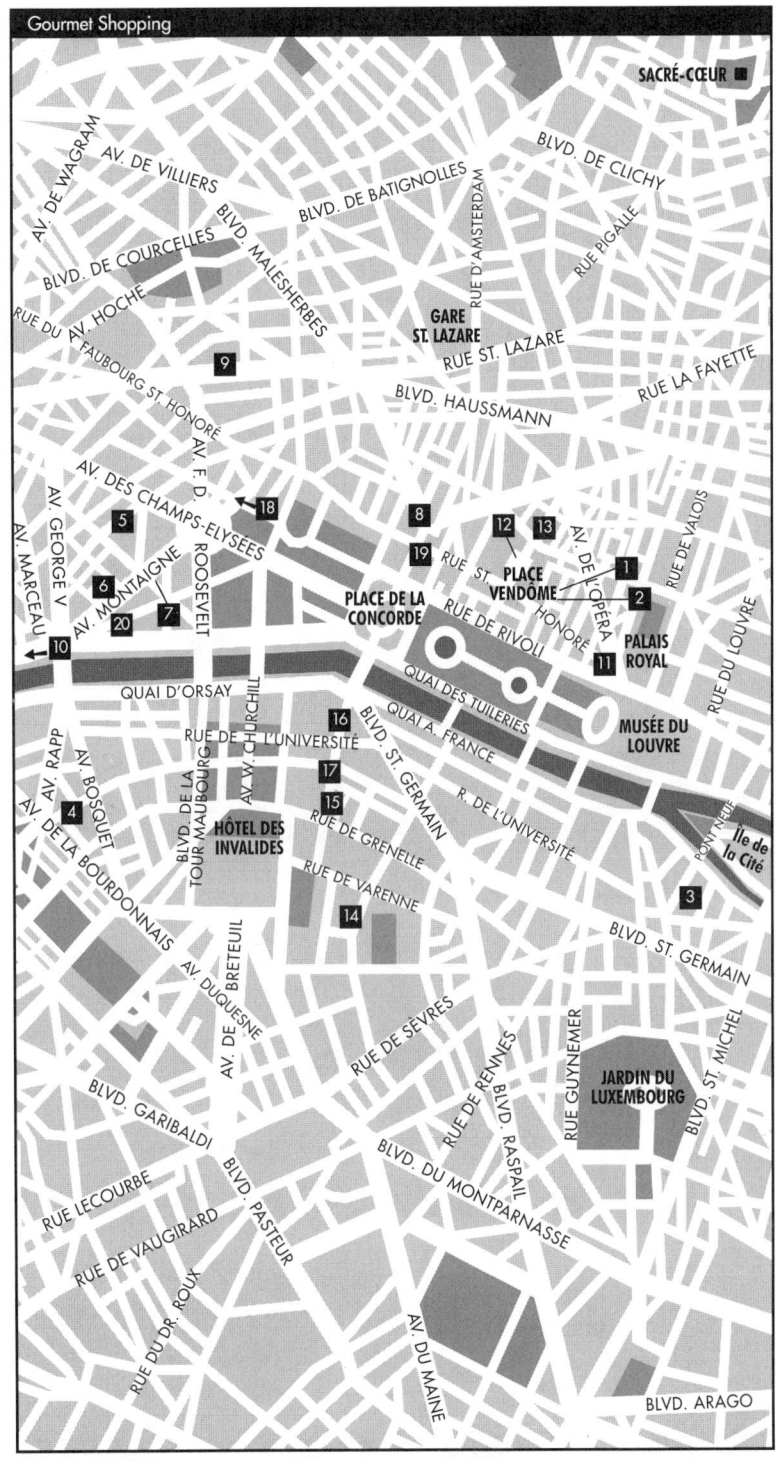

7 Fouquet
22 rue François 1er 75008
47 23 30 36

A chic clientele comes to this delightful century-old shop for fruit jams, lemon and thyme jams, and vegetables in vinegar from Saint-Céré. Also wonderful coffee—pure Arabica, roasted every day.

8 Hédiard
21 place de la Madeleine 75008
42 66 44 36

The most bountiful food shop in Paris—everything from 25-year-old wine vinegar to the famous *fruits confits* and Hédiard's truffle mustard. Open late.

9 Twinings of London
76 boulevard Haussmann 75008
43 87 39 84

Create your own personal mix from 80 different teas.

10 Lenôtre
44 rue d'Auteuil 75016
45 24 52 52

This marvelous caterer delivers and serves the finest meals for parties and receptions.

Miscellany

11 Goyard
233 rue Saint-Honoré 75001
42 60 57 04

Gorgeous luggage since 1853. I love beautiful bags, suitcases, trunks. So as not to lose my luggage, I hang a bicolored ribbon (white and red) on the handles.

12 Natori
7 place Vendôme 75001
42 96 22 94

Satin embroidery on linen, hand-made in the Philippines. Silk kimonos, cashmere dressing gowns.

13 Henri Maupiou
2 rue de la Paix 75002
42 61 08 27

Exclusive silks and woolens for dresses and suits. My seamstress sews my dresses according to my taste.

14 Cordonnerie Vaneau
44 rue Vaneau 75007
42 22 06 94

They stretch, shrink, or restore your boots, dye all leathers. Everything is hand-made by ancient techniques.

15 Louis G.
4 rue de Bourgogne 75007
45 51 30 39
Hairdresser. I rarely go to a hairdresser, but sometimes I have to change my hair color for a role. Pascal has some divine colorings.

16 Moulié-Savart
8 place du Palais-Bourbon 75007
45 51 78 43
A great florist.

17 Naïla de Montbrison
6 rue de Bourgogne 75007
47 05 11 15
A gallery for artists' jewelry. I do not like classical jewelry, but I love the rings and earrings designed by Martial Berro.

18 Artcurial
9 avenue Matignon 75008
42 99 16 16
For beautiful jewelry designed by Mme. Claude Lalanne.

19 Cassegrain
422 rue Saint-Honoré 75008
42 60 20 08
For stationery, small Smythson English notebooks with leather covers, and other sorts of notebooks of every color. Blue stationery is good for writing letters to depressed friends.

20 Harel
8 avenue Montaigne 75008
47 20 75 00
For their divine shoes and their adorable *vendeuses*.

13 RÉGINE'S PARISIAN CHOCOLATE ASSORTMENTS

"Just listen to me speak and you will understand how much I love Paris: I speak French with the Parisian accent. I have sung about my native city in a song called 'Paris.' Paris is everything to me: friends, bistros, shopping. I love to travel, but coming back to Paris is my greatest joy.

"Another great pleasure is to eat a piece of chocolate before I go to bed; otherwise I cannot sleep. During the day, as soon as I feel a bit tired I eat some bitter chocolate and all my energy returns. Bitter chocolate is the only chocolate I eat."

RÉGINE, *singer, actress, owner of restaurants and nightclubs, founder of S.O.S. Drogue International*

1 Hédiard
126 rue du Bac 75007
45 44 01 98
On a par with Fauchon, Hédiard is a superb *épicerie fine* in Paris, and has some of the best chocolates.

2 Fauchon
28 place de la Madeleine 75008
47 42 60 11
La crème de la crème source for everything related to fine edibles. Their chocolates and chocolate cakes are remarkable.

3 Hédiard
21 place de la Madeleine 75008
42 66 44 36
Great chocolates and fine groceries.

4 La Maison du Chocolat
225 rue du Faubourg Saint-Honoré 75008
42 27 39 44
Robert Linxe's chocolates are all hand-made, dark and strong, and shining with the glow of extra cocoa butter.

5 La Maison du Chocolat
56 rue Pierre Charron 75008
47 23 38 25
Dark and strong hand-made chocolates with the glow of extra cocoa butter.

6 Hédiard
70 avenue Paul Doumer 75016
45 04 51 92
Top-of-the-line groceries and delectables.

7 Hédiard
6 rue Donizetti 75016
40 50 71 94
Fine groceries and delectables.

8 Hédiard
106 boulevard de Courcelles
75017
47 63 32 14
Fine foods.

"One of my favorite brands of chocolate is Valhrona, probably the best in Paris. The chocolate has a strong taste, a blend of the finest ingredients. To be found in the following confiseries, *among others."*

9 Nezard-Lubré
3 rue Notre-Dame-des-Champs
75006
45 48 80 22

10 Peltier
66 rue de Sèvres 75007
47 83 66 12

11 Piousseau
208 bis rue de Grenelle 75007
45 51 29 28

12 Comptoir des Thés et Cafés
15 rue Le Marois 75016
42 88 62 79

Here are a few more "insider" suggestions to add to Régine's selection:

13 La Fontaine aux Chocolats
193 rue Saint-Honoré 75001
49 27 01 30
Here you will find 80 varieties of chocolate made from cocoa from Brazil, Ghana, Java, Ecuador, and Colombia, each with a different taste. Also *marrons glacés*, which mix deliciously with chocolate.

14 Dalloyau
2 place Edmond Rostand
75006
43 29 31 10
Since 1802, one of the best chocolatiers in Paris: ganaches, truffles, pralines.

15 Lenôtre
44 rue du Bac 75007
42 22 39 39
This famous caterer makes a remarkable variety of chocolates: *palets d'or*, truffles, pralines, orangettes, and last but not least, *noir intense*.

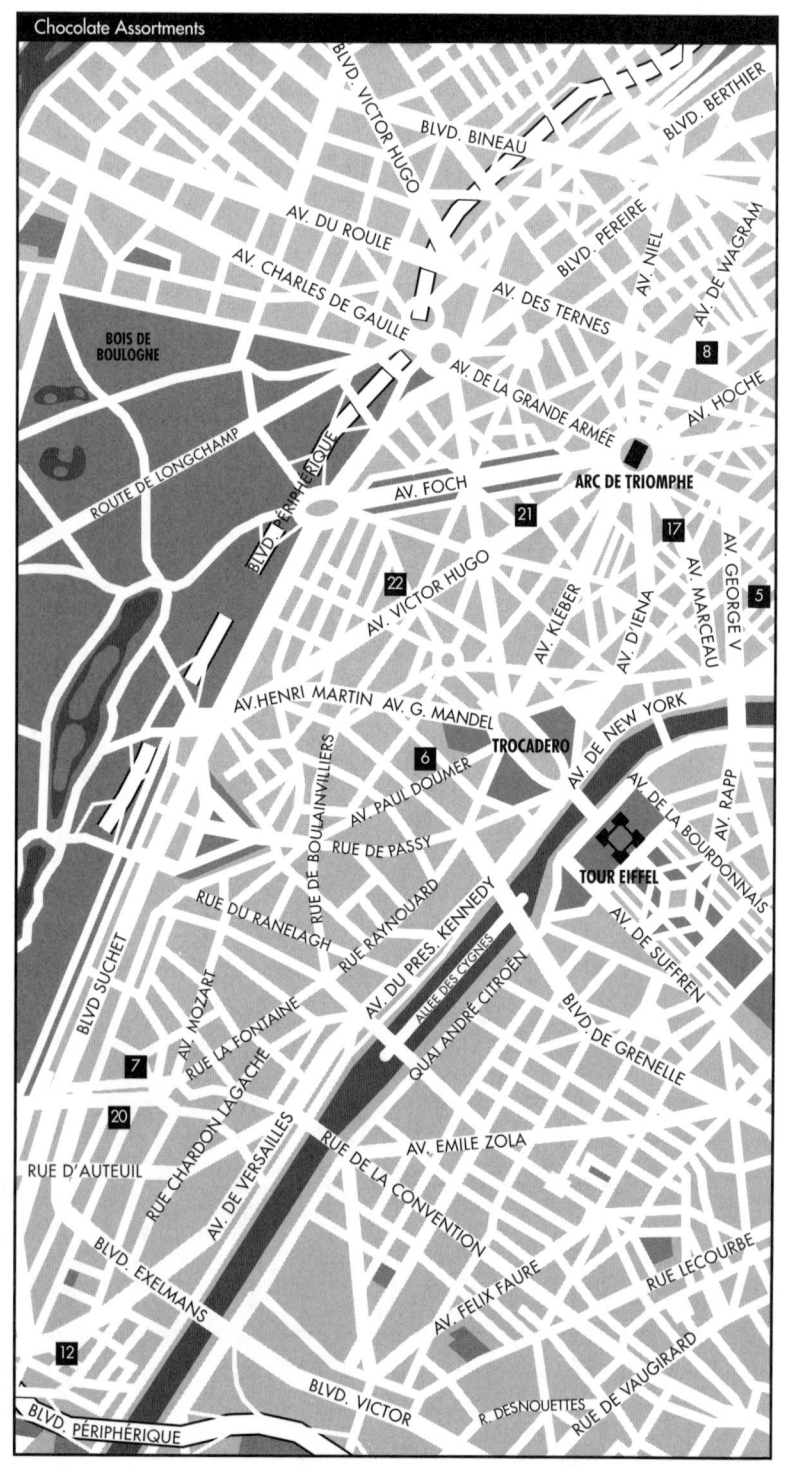

REGINE'S PARISIAN CHOCOLATE ASSORTMENTS

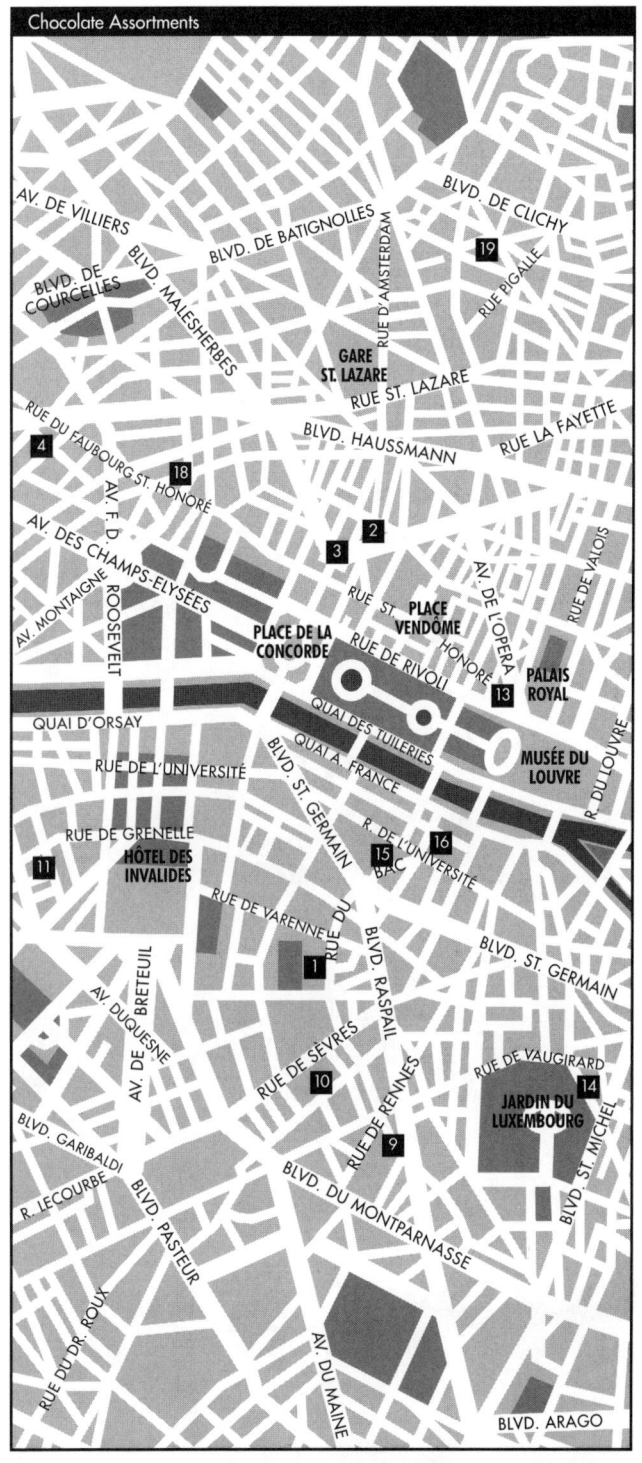

16 Christian Constant
26 rue du Bac 75007
42 96 53 53
Chocolat aux fleurs, aux epices, aux fruits. Made from pure cocoa, never too sweet.

17 Boissier
46 avenue Marceau 75008
47 20 31 31
Christmas tree decorations made of chocolate, letters in chocolate, very inventive creations.

18 Dalloyau
99 rue du Faubourg Saint-Honoré 75008
43 59 18 10
One of the best chocolatiers in Paris.

19 A l'Etoile d'Or
30 rue Fontaine 75009
48 74 59 55
Owner Denise Acabo sells an amazing collection of the choicest chocolates from all over France.

20 Lenôtre
44 rue d'Auteuil 75016
45 24 52 52
A remarkable variety of chocolates.

21 Lenôtre
49 avenue Victor Hugo 75016
45 01 71 71
Luscious chocolates of every variety.

22 Boissier
184 avenue Victor Hugo 75016
45 04 87 88
Inventions in chocolate.

ISABELLE ADJANI'S ORGANIC FOOD AND HEALTH SPOTS

"To stay alive and as healthy as possible, you must treat yourself as part of an ecological network. In a city which is so beautiful but, like any other city, so polluted, all the excesses of life in Paris must be counteracted. The following places can help you find the balance."

ISABELLE ADJANI, *actress* (The Story of Adèle H, Quartet, Camille Claudel, Les Sœurs Brontë, Toxic Affair, La Reine Margot)

Treatment Centers

1 Centre de Traitement de Cheveux Leonore Greyl
15 rue Tronchet 75008
42 65 32 26
Hair care, pollen and plant treatment only. Safe permanents, phytotherapy (cures through plants).

2 Institut Lancôme
29 rue du Faubourg Saint-Honoré 75008
42 65 30 74
Lymph drainage for face and body: massage without machines.

3 Jean-Michel Eté
7 rue Le Sueur 75016
45 00 45 08
Acupuncture and chiropractic *à la chinoise*.

Health Foods

4 Guenmaï
6 rue Cardinale 75006
43 26 03 24
Organic restaurant that specializes in health food, with a shop for teas and take-out food.

5 Veggie
38 rue de Verneuil 75007
42 61 28 61
The American owner prepares carrot juice and organic food throughout the day. Carry-out only.

6 Taghit
63 rue de l'Ouest 75014
43 20 25 57
Semolina, couscous, orange blossoms, weight-reducing bouillons, real food of the desert—the healthiest.

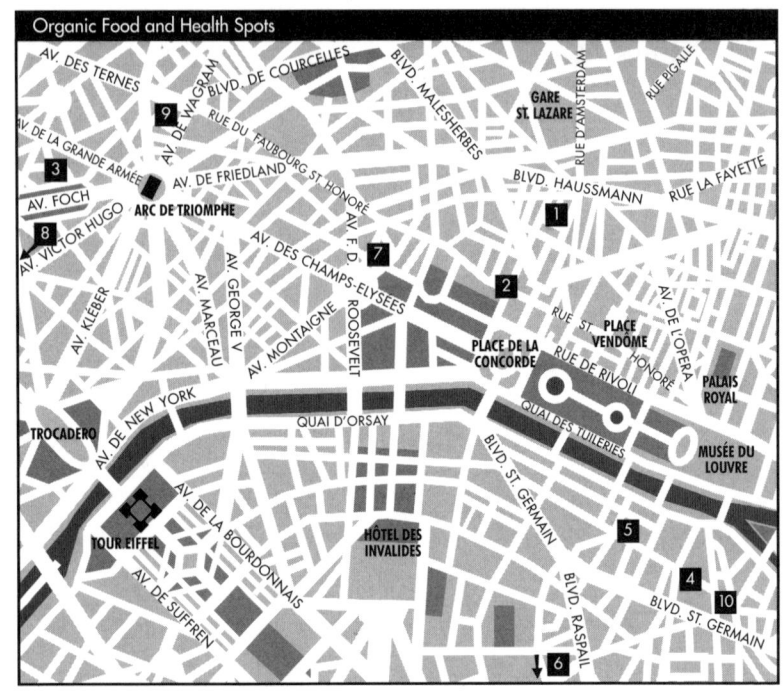

Phytotherapy and Homeopathy Pharmacies

7 Pharmacie Matignon
2 rue Jean Mermoz 75008
43 59 86 55

8 Pharmacie Basire
143 rue de la Pompe
118 bis avenue Victor Hugo
75016
47 27 88 49

9 Pharmacie de Wagram
49 avenue de Wagram 75017
43 80 42 78

Bookshop

10 L'Espace Bleu
91 rue de Seine 75006
43 54 99 00
An ecological and esoteric bookstore for the spirit, the body, and the soul.

GRAND HOTELS

One of the glories of Paris is its lavish abundance of grand hotels. Most of them have fine restaurants, too. Here are a few of the most prestigious:

1 Le Ritz
15 place Vendôme 75001
42 60 38 30
The emperor of all hotels, known the world over. Built in 1878 and still full of Second-Empire splendor, it overlooks the Place Vendôme and the rue de la Paix. An anachronistic but oh-how-pleasant *art de vivre*, which gave birth to the adjective *ritzy*. Several celebrities have had their own apartments here, including Coco Chanel. The Ritz is said to have the best breakfasts in Paris. Also a sumptuous health club in the basement: an 18-meter swimming pool, squash courts, and other facilities. A heliport on the roof!

Restaurant:
L'Espadon
42 60 38 30
Also decorated in Napoléon III style, it offers excellent cuisine (sea perch flambée, roasted kidneys) and one of the best wine lists in France. Garden service in summer.

2 Hôtel Meurice
228 rue de Rivoli 75001
44 58 10 10
This fabled hotel, known for its gracious beauty, was one of the heroes of the liberation of Paris. The film *Is Paris Burning?* depicted the recapture by the Resistance of the Meurice, where the Germans had set up headquarters in Paris. Be sure to ask for rooms overlooking the Tuileries Gardens.

3 Hôtel Intercontinental
3 rue de Castiglione 75001
44 77 11 11
A Second-Empire palace (circa 1860) adapted to modern standards. Fabulous drawing rooms, some overlooking the Tuileries.

4 Hôtel Lutetia
45 boulevard Raspail 75006
45 44 38 10
Built in 1910, it is a beautiful example of Art Déco style, with original frescoes. Within walking distance of both Saint-Germain-des-Prés and Mont-

parnasse, it is the grand hotel of choice for lovers of the Left Bank. Famous for the comfort of its suites and bathrooms.

Restaurant:
Le Paris
49 54 46 90
Slavik's contemporary version of Art Déco. Excellent cuisine: oysters with caviar, ravioli with cabbage, salmon with olives, duck cooked in honey, original desserts.

5 Le Bristol
112 rue du Faubourg Saint-Honoré 75008
42 66 91 45
Across the street from the Elysées Palace (residence of the President), the discreet façade of Le Bristol offers little indication of the splendor within: authentic Louis XV and XVI furniture in all rooms, old masters in the public rooms.

Restaurant:
A renowned *table* for connoisseurs: *filets de sole aux morels, turbot au sauternes.*

6 Le Crillon
10 place de la Concorde 75008
42 65 24 24
This former mansion dating back to the 18th century has views overlooking the most beautiful square in the world. Lavishly appointed suites and rooms.

Restaurants:
Les Ambassadeurs
42 65 13 14 – 42 65 11 12 – 44 71 16 16
Decorated by Sonia Rykiel. A must in high-quality French cuisine: gratin au lobster, *foie gras* with gingerbread and acacia honey, asparagus with scallops, Pauillac lamb, and staggering sorbets. A princely *table* . . . also a princely bill.

L'Obelisque
42 65 24 24
Less expensive fare in an elegant but more casual setting, where the same chef, Christian Constant, turns out *cuisine bourgeoise.*

7 Hôtel George V
31 avenue George V 75008
47 23 54 00
The palace of the Champs-Elysées: elegant, comfortable, a meeting place for American business travelers. A pleasant bar.

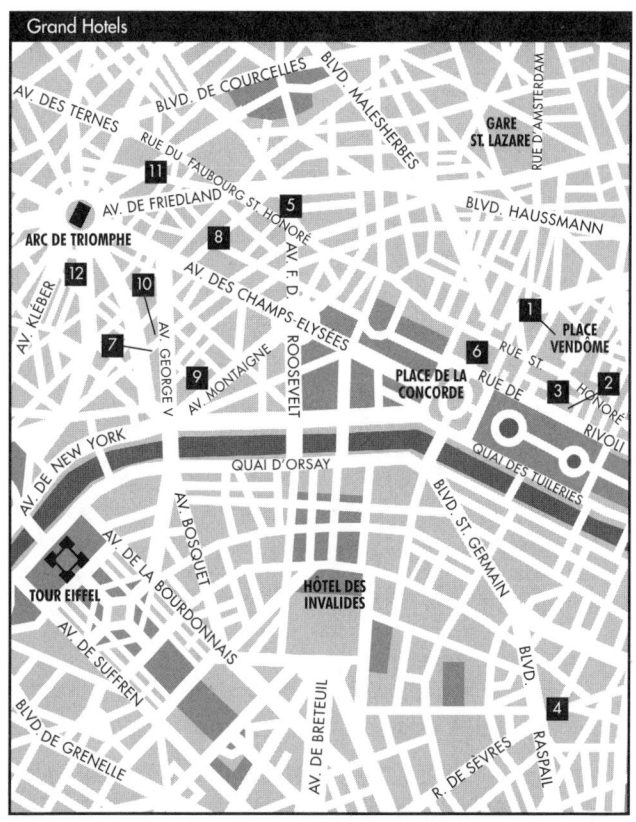

Restaurant:
Les Princes
47 23 54 00
1930s décor. Dining is especially pleasant in the summer under parasols on the flower-filled patio. Fine classical cuisine: lamb with coconut, soufflé with wild strawberries.

8 Hotel Lancaster
7 rue de Berri 75008
43 59 90 43
Not a palace, but better than a palace, just off the Champs-Elysées. Smaller than the other Champs-Elysées hotels mentioned above. Very discreet, very select, very British, a favorite with incognito British and American movie stars. Beautifully decorated suites, antique furniture, Persian carpets, marble fireplaces.

Restaurant:
This lovely small restaurant serves good French cuisine. There is garden dining among statues and flowers when weather permits.

9 Plaza-Athénée
25 avenue Montaigne 75008
47 23 78 33
Luxurious décor and service distinguish this palace favored by movie stars and the haute couture world of avenue Montaigne.

Restaurants:
Le Régence-Plaza
47 23 78 33
A superb interior terrace under Virginia creeper. Models come here for a quick lunch when the new collections are introduced.

Le Relais Plaza-Le Grill
21 avenue Montaigne 75008
47 23 46 36
This brasserie in the shape of a transatlantic liner offers typical "grill" before or after the shows at the nearby concert halls and theaters.

10 Le Prince de Galles (Marriott)
33 avenue George V 75008
47 23 55 11
Next door to the George V, just as refined, even closer to the Champs-Elysées.

Restaurant:
Not "palace" cuisine, but good French bourgeois food: *ris de veau, pot au feu, langoustines, turbot.* Amazing desserts.

11 Royal Monceau
37 avenue Hoche 75008
45 61 98 00
Luxury just off the Etoile: beautiful suites, a sauna, and Jacuzzi. Massages offered.

Restaurants:
Le Jardin
45 62 96 02
A faux rococo garden, full of floral scents and birds. Sea bream with peppers and artichokes, *sauté de foie à la rhubarbe.*

Le Carpaccio
45 62 76 87
One of the best Italian restaurants in Paris: carpaccio with black truffles, *loup de mer* with grilled eggplant.

12 Hôtel Raphaël
17 avenue Kléber 75016
44 28 00 28
Typical *Années Folles* (Roaring Twenties), frequented by Italian film and businesspeople.

Restaurant:
La Salle à Manger
44 28 00 17
An elegant meeting place for film people, especially those from Italy.

JEAN-PAUL RAPPENEAU'S FAVORITE LEFT BANK HOTELS

"When I am in the final stages of making a film, I feel the need to leave my home and find a quiet place to work. I have long lived in the provinces and therefore I look for a hotel with a provincial atmosphere, where one can feel the France of yesterday. Here are some hotels that have given me delight and satisfaction. Most of them are in my own neighborhood on the Left Bank and I feel at home in them."

JEAN-PAUL RAPPENEAU, *director* (La Vie de Château, Les Mariés de l'An II, Le Sauvage, Tout Feu Tout Flamme, Cyrano de Bergerac)

In order of preference:

1 L'Abbaye Saint-Germain
10 rue Cassette 75006
45 44 38 11
You enter the courtyard and find yourself miles from Paris. The rooms are small but refined. A few duplex suites.

2 Hôtel d'Angleterre
44 rue Jacob 75006
42 60 34 72
Calm and peaceful, on a charming patio in the heart of Saint-Germain-des-Prés. The staircase has been classified a historical monument.

3 Hôtel Esmeralda
4 rue Saint-Julien-le-Pauvre
75005
43 54 19 20
Simple but with a lot of atmosphere and a view overlooking Notre-Dame. The owner is an artist and a woman of good taste.

4 Relais Christine
3 rue Christine 75006
43 26 71 80
A precious treasure amid the gardens and lawns of a 16th-century Augustinian convent. The rooms and duplexes are beautifully decorated.

5 Hôtel Le Colbert
7 rue de l'Hôtel Colbert 75005
43 25 85 65
In an old neighborhood that has recently become fashionable, a classical but very comfortable hotel. President Mitterrand lives nearby.

6 Hôtel du Danube
58 rue Jacob 75006
42 60 94 07
Simple but full of charm, surrounded by antique shops.

7 Hôtel des Deux Continents
25 rue Jacob 75006
43 26 72 46
For several generations, this hotel in Saint-Germain-des-Prés has been managed by the same family, who provide a warm welcome to visitors.

8 Hôtel des Deux Iles
59 rue Saint-Louis-en-l'Ile 75004
43 26 13 35
L'Ile Saint-Louis is like a village in the heart of Paris, and at its center, this charming hotel has unexpected British colonial style.

9 Hôtel des Grands Hommes
17 place du Panthéon 75005
46 34 19 60
A recently renovated 18th-century hotel, celebrated for its view overlooking the Panthéon. There are wonderful views from the top floor.

10 L'Hôtel
13 rue des Beaux-Arts 75006
43 25 27 22
Famous in the 1970s when *tout Hollywood* used to drop in. The décor has aged a bit, but this hotel remains unique in Paris.

11 Hôtel Lenox Saint-Germain
9 rue de l'Université 75007
42 96 10 95
A charming modern hotel that is very well located in the heart of the Left Bank.

12 Hôtel Montalembert
3 rue de Montalembert 75007
45 48 68 11
In the center of literary Paris, this hotel dates back to the 1920s. Recently renovated in very refined taste.

13 Hôtel Sainte-Beuve
9 rue Sainte-Beuve 75006
45 48 20 07
This entirely redecorated, cozy establishment is on a small street in Montparnasse near the brasseries La Coupole and Le Dôme.

JEAN-PAUL RAPPENEAU'S FAVORITE LEFT BANK HOTELS

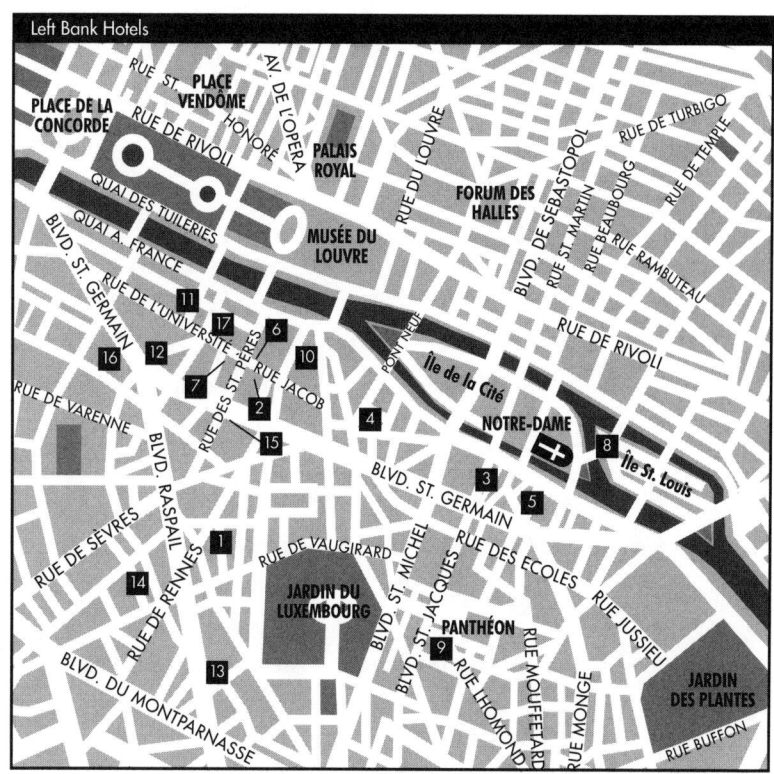

14 Hôtel Saint-Grégoire
43 rue de l'Abbé Grégoire 75006
45 48 23 23
Between Montparnasse and Saint-Germain-des-Prés, this comfortable hotel was recently renovated.

15 Hôtel des Saints-Pères
65 rue des Saints-Pères 75006
45 44 50 00
In Saint-Germain-des-Prés, this 17th-century house surrounds a peaceful interior garden.

16 Hôtel du Duc de Saint-Simon
14 rue Saint-Simon 75007
45 48 35 66
Luxury and sophistication in every detail with a lovely garden and courtyard views.

17 Hôtel de l'Université
22 rue de l'Université 75007
42 61 09 39
It is a voyage through time to be in this renovated 17th-century town house, so charming and dignified.

17 PARIS AT NIGHT

Paris is famous for its big cabarets and nightclubs, with their glorious *revues,* their "naked" women, their glitter and notoriety. Here is a selection where the legend lingers on, if sometimes with a dimmed luster.

1 Les Bains
7 rue du Bourg l'Abbé 75003
48 87 01 80
The "in" discotheque, in a former public bath.

2 Le Paradis Latin
28 rue du Cardinal Lemoine 75005
43 29 07 07
A few blocks from the Latin Quarter, the paradise of nonsense and amazing dancers. A certain knowledge of French is helpful.

3 Crazy Horse Saloon
12 avenue George V 75008
47 23 32 32
Famous for its extraordinary selection of *strip teaseuses,* just off the Champs-Elysées.

4 Le Lido
116 bis avenue des Champs-Elysées 75008
40 76 56 10
The cabaret of Paris, mostly for tourists.

5 Les Folies Bergères
32 rue Richer 75009
42 46 77 11
Its world-famous *revue* must not be missed. Dinner.

6 Le Moulin Rouge
Place Blanche
82 boulevard de Clichy 75018
40 06 00 19
Reminiscent of Toulouse-Lautrec, French cancan in a cardboard décor. Very good shows.

Paris also offers food shops, restaurants, drugstores, florists, and gas stations that are open at night:

Food Shops

7 Jo Goldenberg
7 rue des Rosiers 75004
48 87 20 16
Open until midnight.

8 La Boutique de Layrac
29 rue de Buci 75006
43 25 17 72
Open until 2am.

PARIS AT NIGHT

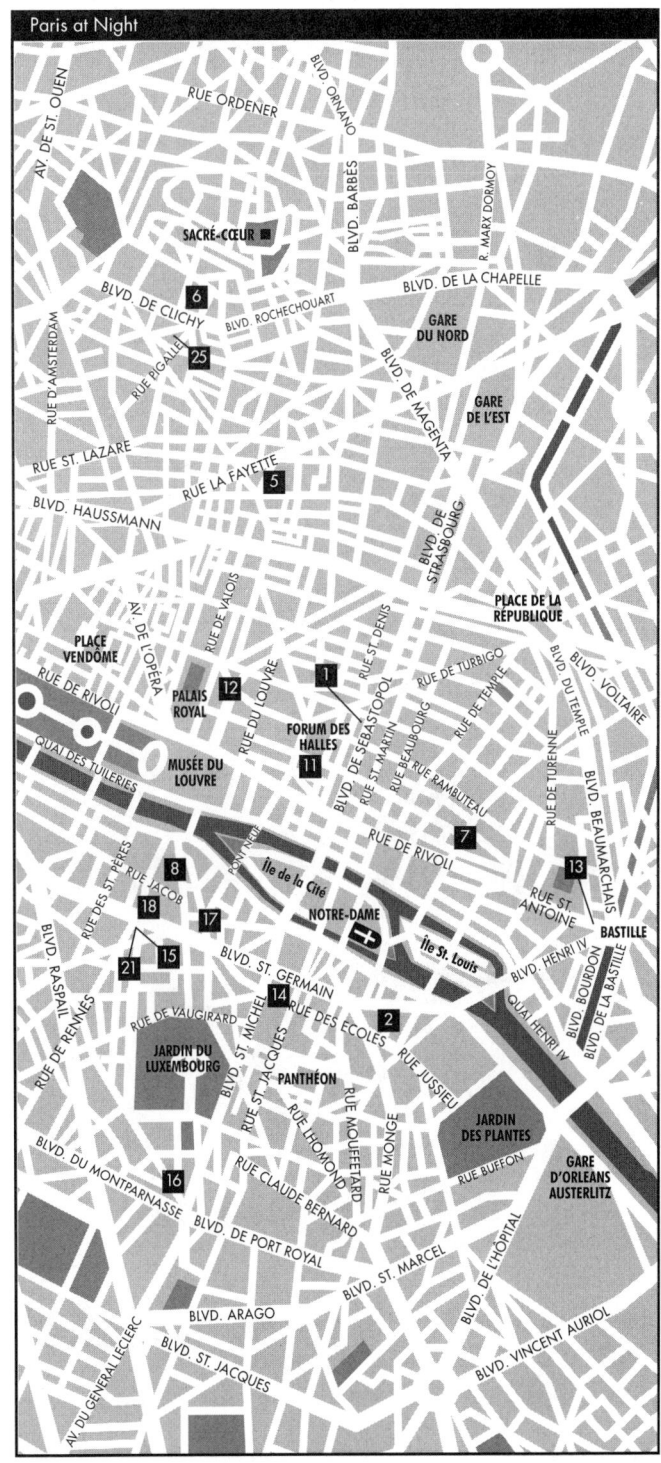

9 Le Marché Minute
44 boulevard Victor 75015
45 32 94 64
Open until 11:45pm.

10 L'An 2000
*82 boulevard des
Batignolles 75017*
43 87 24 67
Open until 1am.

Restaurants

11 Les Bouchons
19 rue des Halles 75001
42 33 28 73
Open until 2am.

12 Chicago Meatpackers
8 rue Coquillère 75001
40 28 02 33
Open until 1am.

13 Bofinger
5 rue de la Bastille 75004
42 72 87 82
Open until 12:45am.

14 Balzar
49 rue des Ecoles 75005
43 54 13 67
Open until 2am.

15 Chez Lipp
*151 boulevard
Saint-Germain 75006*
45 48 53 91
Open until 2am.

16 La Closerie des Lilas
*171 boulevard du
Montparnasse 75006*
43 54 21 68
Open until 1am.

17 Le Procope
*13 rue de l'Ancienne
Comédie 75006*
43 26 99 20
Open until midnight.

18 Le Vagenende
*142 boulevard
Saint-Germain 75006*
43 26 19 14
Open until 1am.

19 Le Bœuf sur le Toit
34 rue du Colisée 75008
43 59 83 80
Open until 2am.

20 Le Bar des Théâtres
6 avenue Montaigne 75008
47 23 34 63
Open until 2am.

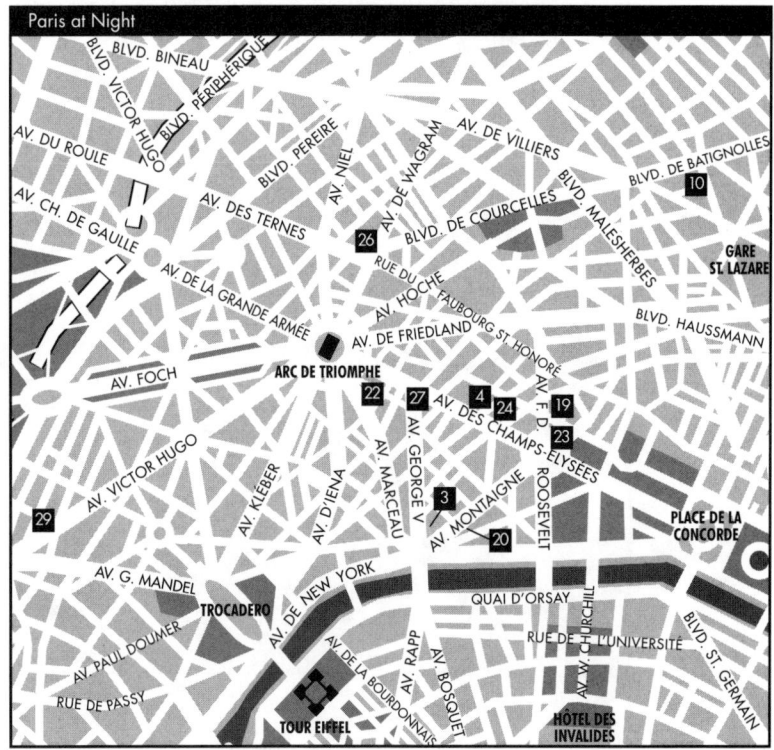

Drugstores and Pharmacies

21 Publicis Saint-Germain
*149 boulevard
Saint-Germain 75006*
42 22 92 50
Open until 2am.

22 Publicis Champs-Elysées
*133 avenue des
Champs-Elysées 75008*
47 20 94 40
Open until 2am.

23 Publicis Matignon
1 avenue Matignon 75008
43 59 38 70
Open until 2am.

24 Pharmacie des Champs-Elysées
*84 avenue des
Champs-Elysées 75008*
45 62 02 41
Open 24 hours a day.

25 Pharmacie Azoulay: La Grande
Pharmacie de la Place
5 place Pigalle 75009
48 78 38 12
Open until 1am.

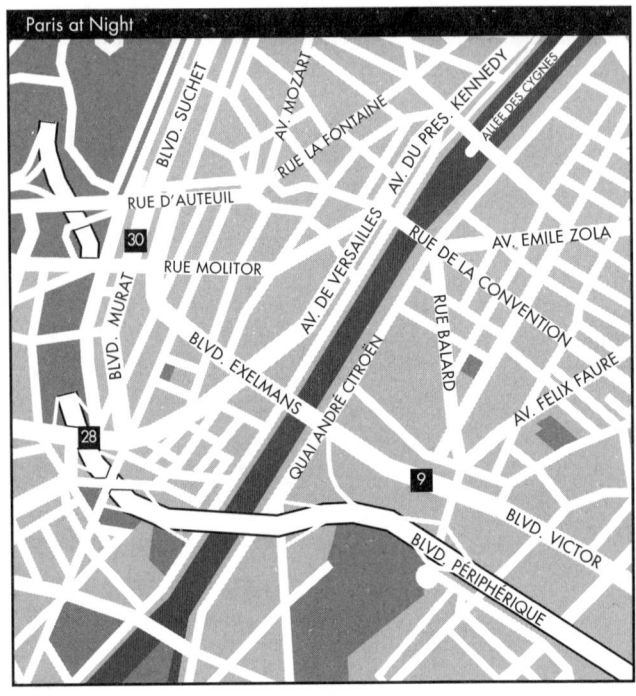

Florist

26 Elyfleurs
82 avenue de Wagram 75017
47 66 87 19
Open 24 hours a day.

Gas Stations

27 Parking George V
Corner Champs-Elysées and George V 75008
47 20 02 68
Open 24 hours a day.

28 Station Elf
2 avenue de la Porte-de-Saint-Cloud 75016
46 51 94 24
Open 24 hours a day.

29 Garage Lamartine
181 avenue Victor Hugo 75016
44 05 34 90
Open 24 hours a day.

30 Station Ciel Murat
105 boulevard Murat 75016
46 51 55 48
Open 6am–2am.

GIVENCHY'S PARIS

The name Hubert de Givenchy has long been synonymous with haute couture and with some of the most glamorous women of the world: Audrey Hepburn, Jacqueline Kennedy Onassis, Princess Grace, and the Duchess of Windsor. The Musée du Costume recently presented a retrospective of his career.

The following are some of his Paris preferences after a long lifetime in the City of Light.

Restaurants

1 L'Orangerie
*28 rue Saint-Louis-en-l'Ile
75004*
46 33 93 98
Especially popular on Sundays, when most Parisian restaurants are closed. Excellent welcome, excellent quality of food. L'Orangerie has existed for many years, and its praises cannot be sufficiently sung.

2 Le Stresa
7 rue Chambiges 75008
47 23 51 62
Delicious food and a very pleasant welcome. The quality and simplicity of the dishes are never disappointing. A warm and relaxed ambience.

Fabrics

3 Comoglio
22 rue Jacob 75006
43 54 65 86
A visit here will make you want to redecorate your Paris flat or country house. M. La Querrière re-creates antique fabrics with great artistry. The materials are impeccable, the printing is perfect.

4 Le Nouveau Musée de la Toile de Jouy
54 rue Charles de Gaulle
78350 Jouy-en-Josas
39 56 48 64
Here you can learn the historical background of the famous Toile de Jouy fabrics. The colors and materials are very contemporary.

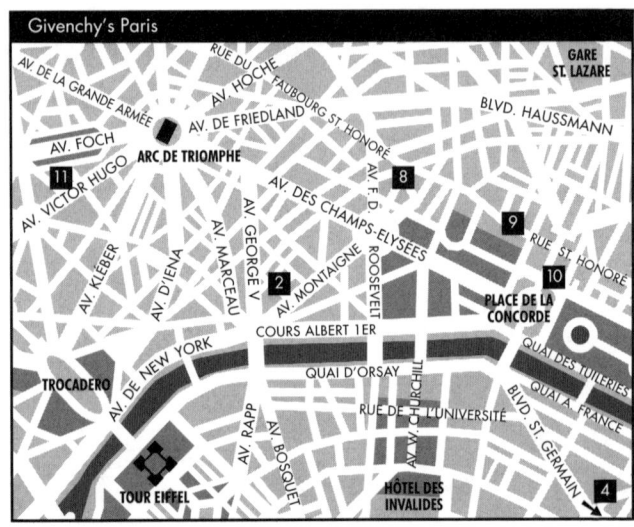

Museum

5 Musée de la Chasse et de la Nature
Hôtel Guénégaud
60 rue des Archives 75003
42 72 86 43
A charming 17th-century *hôtel particulier* houses this museum dedicated to the hunt and the outdoors with beautiful paintings, antique weapons, and stuffed trophies. Not to be missed.

Stationery

6 Papier Plus
9 rue du Pont Louis-Philippe
75004
42 77 70 49
Original stationery, all very modern and in fine taste. Photograph albums, scrapbooks, wrapping paper.

Antiques

7 Alain Demachy
9 quai Voltaire 75007
42 61 82 06
A great selection of fine-quality objects, mahogany furniture, old drawings, and paintings. (Equivalent to Mallett in London).

GIVENCHY'S PARIS

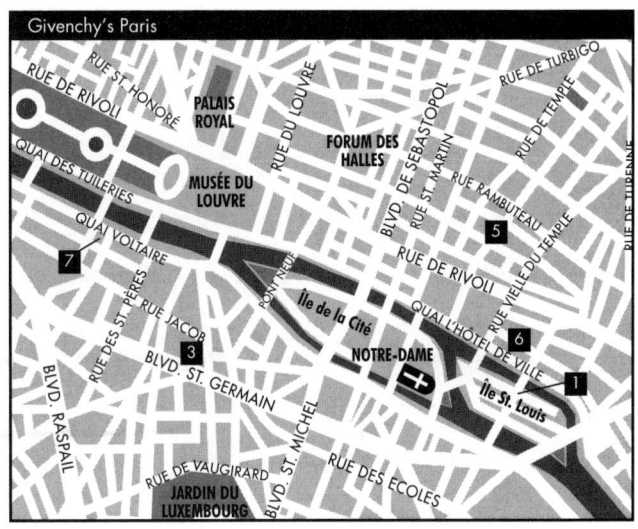

8 Didier Aaron
118 rue du Faubourg Saint-Honoré 75008
47 42 47 34
A large collection, constantly replenished, of antiques of high quality and originality.

9 Segoura
20 rue du Faubourg Saint-Honoré 75008
42 65 11 03
Beautiful 18th-century furniture and collectors' items.

Florists

10 Lachaume
10 rue Royale 75008
42 60 57 26
The best florist in Paris.

11 Mme. Lagautrière (Moreux)
72 avenue Victor Hugo 75016
45 00 58 55
A marvelous floral colorist creates superb bouquets and arrangements.

19 HERVÉ AARON'S PERSONAL CHOICES IN LE LOUVRE

"Le Louvre, a former palace of the kings of France, has been a museum since 1793. Today it is one of the world's greatest. To visit Le Louvre means to wander through its halls, to let your eyes satisfy their curiosity, their avidity, to stop at selected masterpieces. Here are my personal choices."

HERVÉ AARON, *art historian, president of Didier Aaron, New York*

Musée du Louvre
Palais du Louvre
Rue de Rivoli 75001
40 20 53 17– 40 20 51 11

The Richelieu Wing, opened at the end of 1993, features spectacular covered courtyards devoted to French sculpture. Major renovations are still under way; check for possible relocation of items.

1 *Amen and Tutankhamen*
Diorite, 1347–37 B.C.
Ground floor, Sully 5
Sculptural reflection of a profound and grandiose world that is still so near to us 3,500 years later.

2 Plaque from the Parthenon Frieze
Marble, ca. 440 B.C.
Ground floor
A supreme example of the harmony, rhythm, and simplicity of the great Greek art.

3 *Winged Victory of Samothrace*
Marble, 190 B.C.
Ground floor, Denon 3
She should have been chosen as the symbol of the Republic: "Vive la Liberté."

4 Eagle-shaped vase
(*Eagle of Suger*)
Porphyry, gilded silver, before 1147
First floor, Denon 3
An object of striking simplicity with a surprising balance. A marriage of antique and modern.

5 Uccello:
The Battle of San Romano
Tempera on wood, ca. 1455
First floor, Denon 6
The most modern painting in the whole museum. A masterpiece.

6 Mantegna: *Saint Sebastian*
Oil on canvas, ca. 1480
First floor, Denon 6
The apogee of the Renaissance, the dawn of our time.

HERVE AARON'S PERSONAL CHOICES IN LE LOUVRE 73

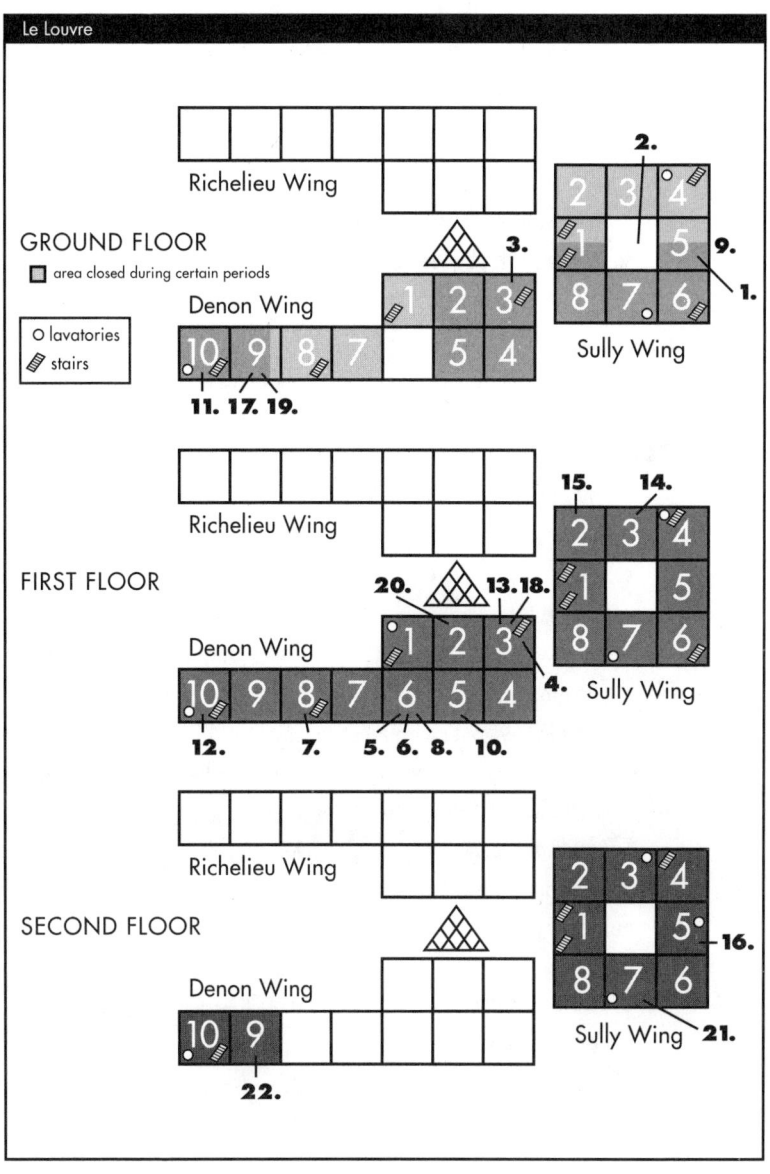

Map courtesy of Le Musée du Louvre

7 Jan Van Eyck: *The Madonna of Chancellor Rolin*
Oil on wood, 1435
First floor, Denon 8
I selected this work because it is so well painted. The Flemish Jan Van Eyck invented oil painting and proved that painting was not necessarily Italian.

8 Cimabue: *Madonna and Child in Majesty Surrounded by Angels*
Tempera and gold on wood, ca. 1270
First floor, Denon 6
The finesse and sweetness of the earthbound figures surrounded by gold ravish me.

9 The Old Moats of the Fortress
Ground floor, Sully
France and its history under our feet.

10 Titian: *The Pastoral Concert*
Oil on canvas, 1510–12
First floor, Denon 5
He took painting out of its harness, invented pure representation 350 years before Manet; the canvas vibrates.

11 Michelangelo: *The Dying Slave*
Marble, 1513–15
Ground floor, Denon 10
Genius, sensibility, intelligence.

12 Francisco de Zurbaran: *St. Bonaventura on His Deathbed*
Oil on canvas, 1629
First floor, Denon 10
A realist work of art but also how pictorial! The painting with its colors, its strength, speaks as loud as, if not louder than, history in words.

13 Rembrandt: *Bathsheba at Her Bath*
Oil on canvas, 1654
First floor, Denon 3
Rembrandt is the king of light, the king of realism. He created mystery and at the same time intimacy. How modern are his coloring and the stroke of his brush!

14 André-Charles Boulle: *Armoire*
Oak and pine, ebony, tortoise shell, brass and tin, gilt bronze, early 18th century
First floor, Sully 3
An exquisite piece from one of the best periods of French furniture. It shows great prowess in construction and in wood and metal work. A piece of *ébénisterie* (cabinetry) for the Sun King.

15 L. S. Boizot (sculptor), P. Ph. Thomire (bronzier): *Vase*
Porcelain with gilded bronze, manufactured by Sèvres, 1783
First floor, Sully 2
From the same period as the Boulle armoire. La Manufacture de Sèvres and Gauthière did incredible work in gilded bronze.

16 Chardin: *The Skate*
Oil on canvas, before 1728
Second floor, Cour Carrée, Room 39
A marvel in composition of masses and colors. And what a brush stroke!

17 Antonio Canova: *Eros and Psyche*
Marble, 1793
Ground floor, Denon 9
Neoclassical and yet romantic, this sculpture speaks of sweetness of gesture and sweetness of stone.

18 La Galerie d'Apollon
17th century
First floor, Denon 3
A superb space built by Le Vau and decorated by Le Brun, who later did the Galerie des Glaces in Versailles.

19 Augustin Pajou:
Psyche Abandoned
Marble, 1790
Ground floor, Denon 9
Sweetness and sensibility of the French 18th century condensed in one work.

20 Géricault: *The Raft of the Medusa*
Oil on canvas, 1819
First floor, Denon 2
Powerful, realistic 19th-century work.

21 Delacroix:
The Death of Sardanapalus
Oil on canvas, 1827
Second floor, Cour Carrée, Room 62
One of the keys to 19th-century art. He breaks with neoclassicism and embarks on romanticism. At the same time, he gives another meaning to composition and color.

22 Turner: *Landscape with a River and a Bay in the Background*
Oil on canvas, ca. 1845
Second floor, Denon 9
A painting that anticipates the entire explosion at the end of the 19th century.

ANDRÉ COURRÈGES' FAVORITE MUSEUMS

"For me, the museums of Paris are just as important as the Eiffel Tower; they represent the personality of France and all its richness."

ANDRÉ COURRÈGES, *the first avant-garde French haute couture designer, creates youthful fashions adapted to modern life.*

1 Centre Georges Pompidou ("Beaubourg")
19 rue Beaubourg 75004
44 78 12 33
The Georges Pompidou National Center of Art and Culture, which opened in 1977 to combined acclaim and criticism for its dramatic ectoskeletal architecture of glass, steel, and brightly colored pipes, is home to the National Museum of Modern Art. Here you'll find paintings and sculptures by the world's greatest 20th-century artists—Kandinsky, Pollock, Calder, and many more. It's a delight to ride the elevator in its glass tube toward the sky as Paris gradually spreads out below.

2 Musée Carnavalet
23 rue de Sévigné 75004
42 72 21 13
To wander through Musée Carnavalet in Mme. de Sévigné's former mansion is to pass through the history of Paris from the 16th century to today. Scale models (of the guillotine, for example), old relics, engravings, photos, and paintings by François Clouet and his school evoke high points in French history. You'll also see wonderful work by the craftspeople of yesteryear.

3 Musée Zadkine
100 bis rue d'Assas 75006
43 26 91 90
The charming garden and studio of Ossip Zadkine, a great Russian sculptor who should be more widely known. It is rare to see so complete a collection of an artist's works.

4 Musée d'Orsay
1 rue de Bellechasse 75007
40 49 48 14 – 45 49 11 11
The city's major museum of 19th-century French art, in a beautifully converted railway station. All the great Impressionists are here, with a stunning variety of Degas, sculptures and paintings by Gauguin, and van Gogh's marvelous suns.

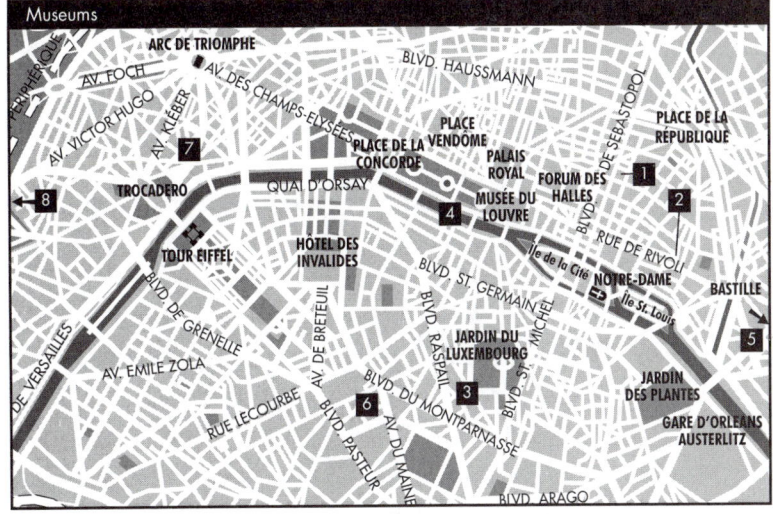

5 Musée des Arts Africains et d'Océanie
293 avenue Daumesnil 75012
43 43 14 54 – 44 74 84 80
This little-known museum with beautiful interior decoration houses a great wealth of African ritual art and Pacific artifacts. In the basement there are live creatures from the deep: crocodiles, piranhas, and giant turtles.

6 Musée Bourdelle
16 rue Antoine Bourdelle 75015
45 48 67 27
A museum filled with charm and *vérité:* the home and studio of Antoine Bourdelle, Rodin's great rival who produced sculpture of massiveness and power.

7 Musée Guimet
6 place d'Iéna 75016
47 23 61 65
To enter this museum is to open doors that lead to the mysteries of the East. There are wonderful Indian sculptures carved in Mathoura pink stone, 17th-century Japanese ceramics, and much more.

8 Musée Marmottan
2 rue Louis Boilly 75016
42 24 07 02
A magnificent collection of works by Monet, which often draws me back to Giverny to see once more the bridge he painted so well, with the pond and the water lilies.

UNUSUAL MUSEUMS

"Paris is a treasure trove of museums. There are literally dozens of them, often devoted to a specific theme such as fashion, French naval history, stamps, porcelain. Many museums are in beautiful houses and gardens worth a visit in their own right. The well-preserved homes of artists and writers have a particular fascination."

BRIDGET RESTIVO, *art historian, lives in New York and Paris.*

1 Musée Bricard
(Musée de la Serrure)
1 rue de la Perle 75003
42 77 79 62
Down the road from Musée Picasso *(see More Museums, Chapter 22)*, Eugène Bricard's private collection of locks and keys from Roman days to Versailles is handsomely displayed in a Marais *hôtel particulier*. The beautiful hardware is a decorator's delight.

2 Musée Cognacq-Jay
8 rue Elzévir 75003
40 27 07 21
A jewel of a museum on a tiny street in Le Marais, reopened in December 1991 after four years of restoration. It houses the collection of Ernest Cognacq, founder and owner of La Samaritaine department store, who collected exquisite small paintings and art objects. You'll find works by Watteau, Guardi, Greuze, Sir Thomas Lawrence, and a tiny floral gem by the Dutch master Cornelius van Spondeck tucked upstairs in Gallery 21.

3 Maison de Victor Hugo
Hôtel de Rohan-Guéménée
6 place des Vosges 75004
42 72 10 16
Victor Hugo wrote much of *Les Misérables* in these rooms overlooking the gardens and archways of the charming Place des Vosges. Satirical drawings by Daumier line the wooden stairs. My favorite little drawing is his friend Rodin's portrait of Hugo himself.

4 Musée National de la Légion d'Honneur et des Ordres de Chevalerie
Hôtel de Salm
2 rue de Bellechasse 75007
45 55 95 16

UNUSUAL MUSEUMS

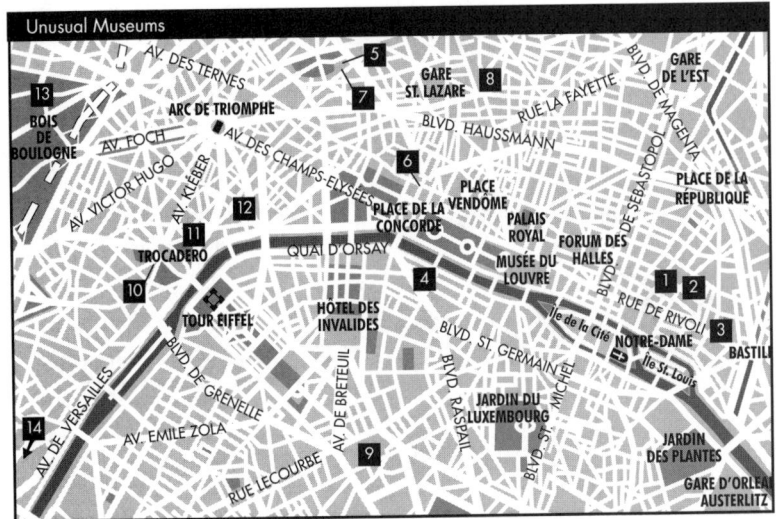

Uniforms, medals, military paintings, tapestries, and memorabilia. Founded by Napoléon, the Order of *La Légion d'Honneur* is France's most prized decoration, for both civilian and military achievements. If you love them like I do, you will be enthralled! The museum is across the street from the Musée D'Orsay.

5 Musée Cernuschi
(Musée d'Art Chinois de la Ville de Paris)
7 avenue Velasquez 75008
45 63 50 75
Home of Italian collector and financier Henri Cernuschi, who moved to Paris from Milan. A must for lovers of Chinese and Japanese art, artifacts, and bronzes in an elegant house at the entrance to Parc Monceau. Go for a stroll in the park afterward, one of the most beautiful parks in Paris.

6 Musée des Lunettes et Lorgnettes
380 rue Saint-Honoré 75008
(corner of rue Cambon)
40 20 06 98
A precious collection of eyeglasses, binoculars, and telescopes assembled over 40 years by the optician M. Pierre Marly. Recently relocated to this well-trodden fashion street made famous by Coco Chanel, who established her atelier a few doors away along the Rue

Cambon. My favorite is the plumed ostrich opera fan with a pair of *lunettes* attached. A fine catalog is available in English or French.

7 Musée Nissim-de-Camondo
63 rue de Monceau 75008
45 63 26 32
Count Moise de Camondo modeled this house after the Petit Trianon at Versailles and filled it with fine antiques and art objects from his favorite era, the 18th century. He bequeathed the house to the French government in honor of his only son, Nissim, who died in combat in World War I.

8 Musée Gustave Moreau
14 rue de La Rochefoucauld 75009
48 74 38 50
An intriguing house filled with works by the Symbolist painter, in an unexpected part of Paris filled with *hôtels particuliers* surrounded by private gardens.

9 Musée de la Poste
34 boulevard de Vaugirard 75015
43 20 15 30
What a stamp collection this is! All about the history of stamps from the Middle Ages to the present. The last galleries on the fifth floor present the modern technology used by the postal service.

10 Musée Georges Clemenceau
8 rue Franklin 75016
45 20 53 41
This house and garden abound with history. For 35 years it was the final home of Georges Clemenceau, statesman and Claude Monet's best friend. Don't miss his sensuously carved U-shaped desk and his collection of hats (he was never without one). Not far from the Place du Trocadéro.

11 Musée de la Marine
Palais de Chaillot
Place du Trocadéro 75016
45 53 31 70
If you love the sea as I do, this museum on French naval history is a labyrinthine treat for adults and children alike. There are models of Louis XV's fleet, sailing vessels, grand ocean liners, the first battleship *La Gloire,* nuclear submarines,

and *Le Valmy*, built of ivory, ebony, and silver. In between wandering about, watch one of the videos on a timely topic about the sea.

12 Musée de la Mode et du Costume
Palais Galliera, 10 avenue Pierre-1er-de-Serbie 75016
47 20 85 23
The history of French fashion from the 18th century to the present, with over 30,000 garments in its archives. It recently presented an exhibition in honor of 40 years of fashion by Givenchy.

13 Musée National des Arts et Traditions Populaires
6 route du Mahatma-Gandhi 75016
44 17 60 00
Take the Métro (ligne Vincennes—Défense) to Neuilly to find this museum in the Bois de Boulogne. Wonderful tableaux and other displays reviewing centuries of arts and crafts in preindustrial France. Rooms built as primitive huts, costumes from various regions, original tools to build with and till the land, all make for fascinating educational experiences for adults and children alike.

14 Musée National de la Céramique
Place de la Manufacture 92310 Sèvres
45 34 99 05
A simple Métro ride to the last stop on the Pont de Sèvres line and a walk across the bridge bring you to this imposing, elegant monument, a haven for anyone who loves porcelain. The finest examples of French, Italian, German, and Dutch porcelain and faïence line the sunny galleries. By appointment, you can visit the private library (in the afternoons only).

MORE MUSEUMS

Hervé Aaron, André Courrèges, and Bridget Restivo have guided you through their favorite Parisian museums. Many other museums are also well worth visiting. Here are a few:

1 Musée de la Serrure:
Musée Fontaine
190 rue de Rivoli 75001
42 61 51 53
Musée Fontaine is 300 years old and has always been the rival of Musée Bricard *(see Unusual Museums, Chapter 21)* in displaying locks and keys. It also has a vast collection of vases for staircases, and Art Nouveau and Art Déco locks. By appointment only.

2 Musée des Arts Décoratifs
107 rue de Rivoli 75001
42 60 32 14
Housed in a wing of the Louvre, this museum dedicated to the *art de vivre à la française* displays collections that show how the French lived from the Middle Ages to the 1920s: toys, furniture, tapestries, artifacts of everyday life. It also has a fine collection of Art Nouveau and Art Déco.

3 Musée de la Chasse et de la Nature
Hôtel Guénégaud
60 rue des Archives 75003
42 72 86 43
The superb Hôtel Guénégaud, built in 1638, is the last remaining complete *hôtel particulier* built by François Mansart. It includes a *jardin à la française* and the famous Mansart staircase.

Since 1964, it has housed everything related to the noble pursuits of hunting and falconry. It is dedicated to wildlife education and its importance in a modern world.

The museum houses ancient books and manuscripts related to hunting, as well as harquebuses, horse pistols, flintlocks, air pistols, a square-barreled rifle, a Napoleonic carbine rifle, knives and swords, crossbows, and hunting spears.

There are 500 engravings related to hunting and wildlife, as well as several paintings (Rubens, Tiepolo, Chardin,

MORE MUSEUMS

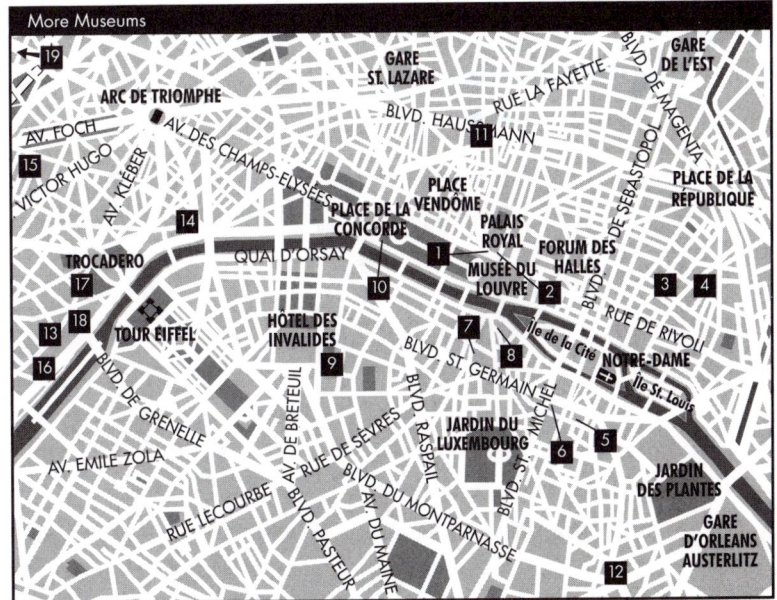

Corot), tapestries, trophies, and artifacts.

The Hotel Guénégaud also houses a club for hunters and protectors of wildlife with a bar, a restaurant, a library, a screening room, a shooting range, and a pool table.

4 Musée Picasso
Hôtel Salé
5 rue de Thorigny 75003
42 71 25 21
An elegant 17th-century mansion beautifully remodeled into a museum devoted to Pablo Picasso. Various periods of his work are splendidly displayed in sunlit rooms. Paintings by Cézanne, Matisse, Renoir, and others from his private collection are also displayed, along with photographs of Picasso with his family, mistresses, and friends.

5 Musée de la Police
1 bis rue des Carmes 75005
43 29 21 57
Houses the historical archives of the French police. A museum of crime and punishment: the guillotine blade of the Revolution and the Terror, a firing-squad post, the gun that shot President Doumer, burglars' tools, terrorists' bombs, and a rolling pin once used as a murder weapon.

6 Musée National du Moyen Age
Thermes de Cluny 61R
6 place Paul Painlevé 75005
43 25 62 00
This 16th-century mansion of the Cluny abbots in the heart of the Latin Quarter evokes the Middle Ages. The vaulted Gallo-Roman baths, 50 feet high, can still be visited. The collections cover all aspects of medieval life, with sculpture, paintings, stained glass, tapestries (including the famous *Lady with the Unicorn*), furniture, and metalwork.

7 Musée Delacroix
6 place de Furstenberg 75006
43 54 04 87
A tiny haven of peace on delightful Place de Furstenberg just a brief walk from the turmoil of Saint-Germain-des-Prés. Visit the apartment (three rooms), atelier, and garden of Eugène Delacroix, who settled here in 1857 to be nearer the Church of Saint-Sulpice, where he decorated the Chapel of the Angels. He died here in 1863.

8 Musée de la Monnaie
Hôtel des Monnaies
11 quai de Conti 75006
40 46 55 35 – 40 46 55 27
The museum of French numismatics is housed in the mint built in 1771. It recalls the history of the French people through their coins and medals, from the time of the Gauls around 300 B.C. to the present. The word *franc* appeared in the 14th century, and the decimal system was introduced during the Revolution at the end of the 18th century. Medals date to the 15th century. Some 2,000 coins and 450 medals are on display, as well as tokens and sculptures, the former coin-striking workshop, and historic minting equipment.

9 Musée Rodin
Hôtel de Brion
77 rue de Varenne 75007
47 05 01 34
In 1908, when he was 68 years old, Auguste Rodin was given this 18th-century *hôtel particulier*, a former convent, to live and work in as an exchange for donating his works to the state.

His most famous sculptures are here—*The Kiss, The Thinker, The Burghers of Calais, Balzac.* Many of the statues are in the lovely English-style garden. This museum is not far from Napoléon's tomb and Les Invalides.

10 Musée de l'Orangerie
*Place de la Concorde
Pavillon de l'Orangerie 75008
42 97 48 16*
Not to be missed are Monet's amazing *Nymphéas* (water lilies), and works by Cézanne, Renoir, Soutine, and Miró. Also, temporary art exhibitions.

11 Musée de la Parfumerie Fragonard
*9 rue Scribe 75009
47 42 93 40*
Just behind the Opéra this ravishing *hôtel particulier* is dedicated to perfume. Countless civilizations—from Egypt, Greece, Carthage, and Rome to the Middle Ages and the Renaissance—made great use of perfumes. Their popularity continues today. Perfume bottles are shown here as well as stills (alembics) and other tools of the perfume trade.

12 La Manufacture des Gobelins
*42 avenue des Gobelins 75013
43 37 12 60*
Founded in 1662 under Louis XIV, this factory is a must for tourists curious about the art of tapestry. On Tuesday, Wednesday, and Thursday from 2:00 to 3:30pm you can take a guided tour (in French or English) and watch how the world-renowned tapestries are made in a tradition that has been maintained since the 17th century. Great modern artists (Calder, Chagall, Delaunay, Miró, Picasso, Vasarély) sent their drawings here to be transformed into huge tapestries. La Manufacture des Gobelins works for the state, making tapestries for l'Elysée, ministries, museums, and embassies, but also for private individuals.

13 La Maison de Balzac
*47 rue Raynouard 75016
42 24 56 38*
A museum and library devoted to Honoré de Balzac, who lived here from 1840 to 1847. Here, he revised much of his *Human Comedy* and wrote some of his most

famous novels: *A Gloomy Affair, La Rabouilleuse, Splendors and Miseries of Courtesans, Cousin Bette, Cousin Pons.* It is said he lived here under a false name, as he was hounded by creditors and bailiffs. Now the museum with its preserved garden is an oasis of calm in the chic Passy district.

Several portraits of Balzac, along with sculptures, a turquoise-studded cane, and even an 1842 daguerreotype are on display. Balzac's study is preserved as in his time, including his coffee pot (he was a famous coffee addict) and the portrait of his beloved Mme. Hanska, to whom he wrote innumerable letters. The library houses copies of all of Balzac's works, along with drawings and illustrations by famous artists (Leonor Fini, Alechinsky).

14 Musée d'Art Moderne de la Ville de Paris
11 avenue du President Wilson 75016
47 23 61 27
While Centre Georges Pompidou is the national museum for modern art, this museum, which belongs to the city of Paris, displays its own collection of 20th-century art: Braque, Chagall, Derain, Dufy, Hartung, Matisse, Picasso. It also presents exhibitions by contemporary Parisian and European artists.

15 Musée de la Contrefaçon
16 rue de la Faisanderie 75016
45 01 51 11
This museum was founded in 1920 by the makers of famous brands, in order to protect their labels from counterfeiters. It's all about copies. Rums and cognacs bear names much like the originals: cognac from Henry Martin for Rémy Martin, Francine Ricard for Pastis Ricard, Perrenod for Pernot. Fake Lacoste garments, Cartier watches, Vuitton bags, and more.

16 Musée de Radio-France
116 avenue du Président Kennedy 75016
42 30 21 80
Some 600 types of radios are on display, from the first crystal sets to battery-powered radios. Ducretet's experiments

in wireless telegraphy gave birth to radio in the early 20th century. Exhibits include the first radio studio with its enormous microphone, the first TV studio (1935), the famous 1934 Philips radio sets, and one of the first TV sets.

17 Musée de l'Homme
17 place du Trocadéro 75016
44 05 72 00
Everything you always wanted to know about the human race. It has displays devoted to biological anthropology, human paleoanthropology, and prehistory, along with arts and artifacts of the peoples of Africa, the Arctic regions, Asia, the Pacific Islands, and America. Also an arts and crafts exhibition. Founded for the 1937 World Exhibition, it is a teaching and research center as well as a museum. It also houses temporary exhibitions and shows films on ethnography.

18 Musée du Vin
5–7 square Charles Dickens
75016
45 25 63 26
Vaulted caves from the 13th century display the vintner's art: how cognac is made, how wine is transformed from grapes. Wines from Ile de France (the region surrounding Paris) are exhibited here: Suresnes, Sucy en Brie, Argenteuil, Clamart, and Montmartre.

19 Musée de Neuilly
12 rue du Centre
92200 Neuilly-sur-Seine
47 45 29 40
Just off Bagatelle, in the mansion built by Arturo Lopez, a South American who made his fortune in guano, it houses a remarkable collection of antique wind-up figurines, on display every day at 3pm. Also objects that belonged to famous women, including a Marie Antoinette corset.

23 — MICHÈLE MORGAN'S SELECTION OF CONTEMPORARY ART GALLERIES

Unforgettable star of *Quai des Brumes*, *La Symphonie Pastorale*, *Joan of Paris*, and *Passage to Marseilles*, Michèle Morgan is also a talented painter who keeps up with the contemporary art scene. Here are her favorite Paris galleries, along with artists she admires.

In the Marais

1 Galerie Froment-Putman
33 rue Charlot 75003
42 76 03 50
James Turrel.

2 Galerie Daniel Templon
30 Rue Beaubourg 75003
42 72 14 10
Le Gac, Alberola, Cucci.

3 Galerie Karsten Greve
5 rue Debelleyme 75003
42 77 19 37
Pollock, Twombly.

4 Galerie Yvon Lambert
108 rue Vieille du Temple 75003
42 71 09 33
Blais, Combas, Toroni.

5 Galerie Adrien Maeght
12 rue Saint-Merri 75004
42 78 43 44
Delprat, Fiedler, Miró.

6 Galerie Beaubourg
23 rue du Renard 75004
42 71 20 50
Combas, Dado, Garouste.

7 Galerie de France
52 rue de la Verrerie 75004
42 74 38 00
Aillaud, Bram Van Velde, Soulages.

On the Left Bank

8 Galerie J.G.M. (Jean-Gabriel Mitterrand)
8 bis rue Jacques Callot 75006
43 26 12 05
Arman, Arp, Rauschenberg, Raynaud.

9 Galerie Prazan-Fitoussi
25 rue Guénégaud 75006
46 34 77 61
Abstract painters of the 1950s. Surrealists.

MICHÈLE MORGAN'S CONTEMPORARY ART GALLERIES

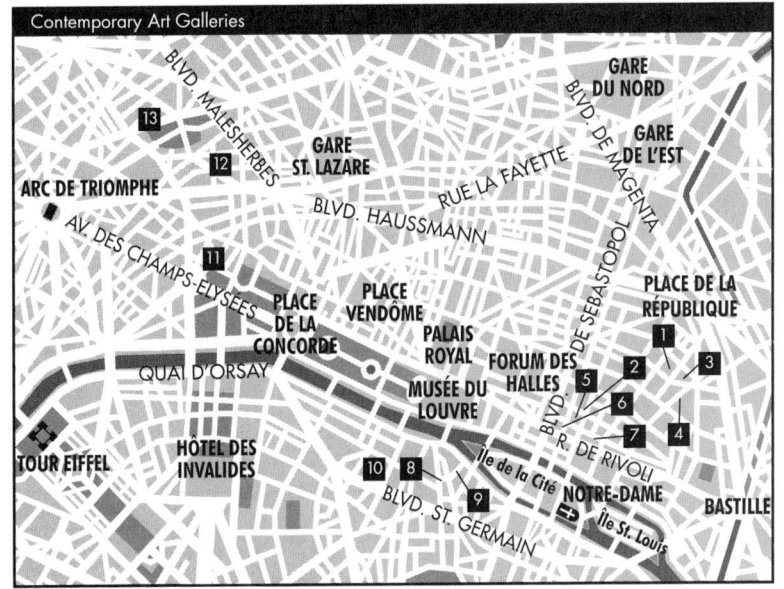

10 Galerie Denise René
*196 boulevard Saint-Germain
75007*
42 22 77 57
Vasarely, Takis, Soto.

*In the 8e and 17e
Arrondissements*

11 Artcurial
9 avenue Matignon 75008
42 99 16 04
César, Delaunay, Lalanne,
Arman, Saura.

12 Galerie Lelong
13 rue de Téhéran 75008
45 63 13 19 – 45 44 89 18
Adami, Alechinsky, Bacon,
Miró, Michaux.

13 Galerie Lahumière
*88 boulevard de Courcelles
75017*
47 63 03 95
Dewasne, Herbin, Masson.

CLAUDE LELOUCH OUT WITH THE KIDS

"I have six children, ranging from two to twenty-two years old. I take them out on Sundays to places that will entertain, interest, and at the same time educate them."

CLAUDE LELOUCH, *film director* (A Man and a Woman, The Crook, Happy New Year, Cat and Mouse, And Now My Love, La Belle Histoire, Tout Ça Pour Ça?)

1 Vidéothèque de Paris
Forum des Halles
Porte Saint-Eustache
2 Grande Galerie 75001
44 76 62 00
A retrospective of Paris on video, with special screenings for children on Wednesdays.

2 Centre de la Mer et des Eaux
195 rue Saint-Jacques 75005
46 33 08 61
Everything about the sea, including tropical aquariums and films by Jacques Cousteau.

3 Le Muséum d'Histoire Naturelle
Jardin des Plantes
57 rue Cuvier 75005
40 79 30 00
Everything about the animal kingdom from prehistory to today, including a zoo.

4 Palais de la Découverte
Avenue Franklin Roosevelt
75008
40 74 80 00 – 43 59 18 21
Features the discoveries of modern science, a planetarium and scientific films.

5 Le Musée Grévin
10 boulevard Montmartre
75009
42 46 13 26
The story of mankind in wax from historical figures to screen stars.

6 La Ferme Georges Ville
Bois de Vincennes
Route du Pesage 75012
43 28 47 63
A working farm with domestic animals, vegetable gardens, and orchards.

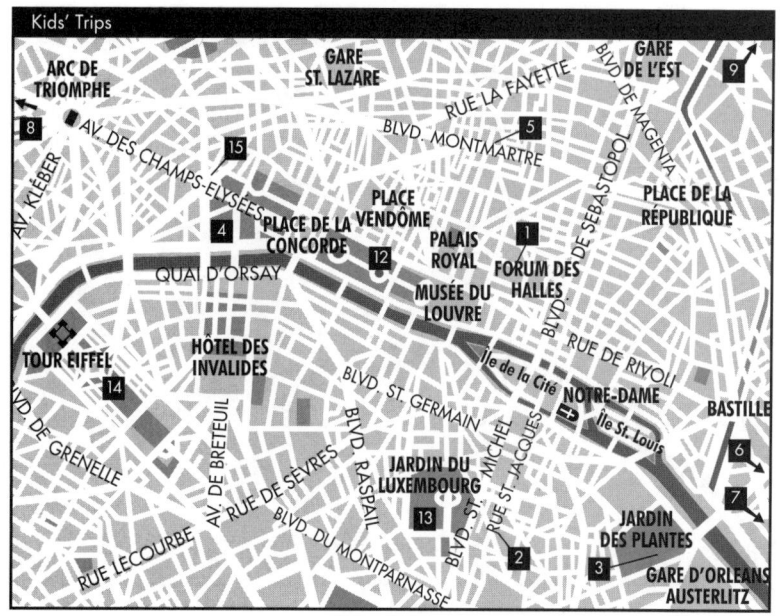

7 Le Parc Zoologique de Paris
Bois de Vincennes
53 avenue de Saint-Maurice
75012
43 43 84 95
Over 1,000 animals: 110 species of mammals and 150 species of birds in 500,000 square feet of nature at the gates of Paris.

8 Le Jardin d'Acclimatation
Bois de Boulogne
Boulevard des Sablons 75016
40 67 90 80
A zoo, an enchanted river, a miniature train, a puppet show, and more.

9 Cité des Sciences et de l'Industrie
Parc de la Villette
30 avenue Corentin Cariou
75019
40 05 70 00
An enormous museum relating the adventure of space, of life, of communication. Planetarium, 3-D films at La Géode.

10 La Mer de Sable
Parc d'Ermenonville
Autoroute du Nord A1—sortie Ermenonville
Route Nationale 330
60950 Ermenonville
(16) 44 54 00 96
Games, merry-go-rounds, and shows.

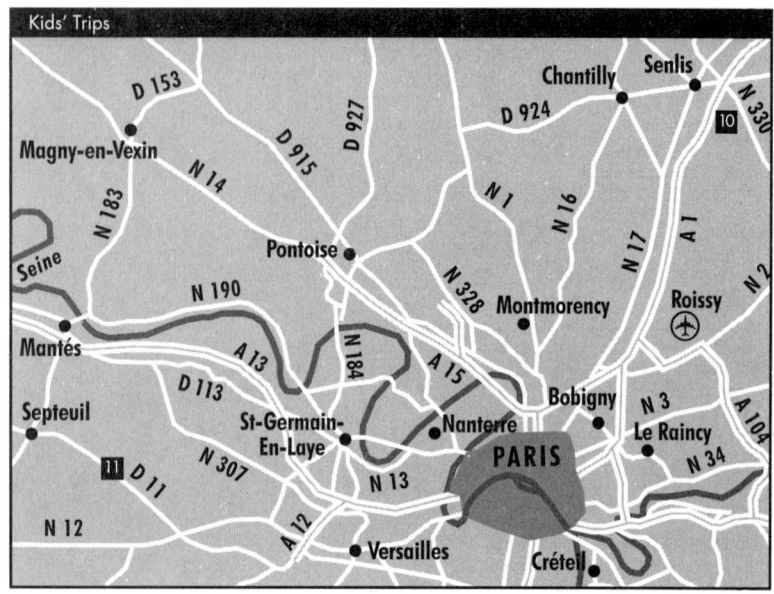

11 Le Parc Zoologique de Thoiry
78770 Thoiry
34 87 40 67
A huge safari park where lions and other animals roam free.

Puppet Shows

12 Théâtre de la Petite Ourse
Jardin des Tuileries 75001
42 64 05 19
Puppet shows for children over five years old.

13 Marionnettes du Luxembourg
Jardin du Luxembourg 75006
43 26 46 47 – 43 29 50 97

14 Marionnettes du Champ de Mars
Avenue du Général Marguerite 75007
48 56 01 44

15 Marionnettes des Champs-Elysées
Rond-Point des Champs-Elysées 75008
45 79 08 68 – 42 57 43 34

DAY TRIPS AROUND PARIS

The treasures of Paris are inexhaustible, but if you suddenly get tired of its hustle and bustle, why not take a day trip to some of the wonderful places that surround the capital?

1 Auvers-sur-Oise
95430 (Val d'Oise)
About 25 miles from Paris
Vincent van Gogh painted his last masterpieces in this lovely town and countryside, and died here. Other artists, too, came here to paint: Corot, Daumier, Pissarro, Cézanne, Monet, Renoir. Visit the cemetery with the tombs of the brothers Vincent and Théo. Other places of interest include la Maison Daubigny, la Maison du Dr. Gachet, and l'Auberge Ravoux.

Top off your day with a fine dinner of classical cuisine on a beautiful terrace:
Hostellerie du Nord
6 rue du Général de Gaulle
30 36 70 74

2 Blérancourt
02300 Chauny (Oise)
About 70 miles from Paris on the border of the Ile de France between Compiègne and Coucy

The Château de Blérancourt is an early-17th-century castle that houses a fascinating museum of artifacts illustrating the history of the friendship between France and the United States. There are paintings of great battles (such as *Yorktown*, painted by Siméon Fort, Maréchal de France), a bust of Lafayette, a painting of Lafayette on his deathbed by Ary Scheffer, watercolors of French mansions in the U.S. (such as Du Pont de Nemours' mansion, "Angelica"). The beautiful gardens are filled with plants and trees from the U.S. The Anne Morgan Pavilion in the gardens is dedicated to the friendship between France and the U.S. It was founded by the American banker J. P. Morgan's daughter, who organized a military hospital here in 1917. On display are Ford ambulances sent during World War I and a portrait of Peggy Guggenheim by Courmes.

For a good meal, you must go to Compiègne (about 10 miles):
La Rotisserie du Chat qui Tourne
17 rue Eugéne Floquet 60200
(16) 44 40 02 74

3 Champs-sur-Marne
77420 (Seine et Marne)
About 14 miles from Paris
Famous for its château (60 05 24 43) built in the 18th century. Mme. de Pompadour, one of Louis XV's innumerable paramours, lived there. She designed a classical *jardin à la française*, drawn up by a nephew of Le Nôtre. It was remodeled *à l'anglaise* in 1820. With glades and groves, it covers over 200 acres and is one of the most beautiful promenades near Paris.

A restaurant in Chennevières (less than 10 miles away):
L'Ecu de France
31 rue de Champigny 94430
45 76 00 03
Good food on a beautiful terrace overlooking the Marne. An old post relay.

4 Chantilly
60631 (Oise)
About 30 miles from Paris
Originally a Renaissance castle built in 1528, it was remodeled by Mansard, again in the 18th century, then again in the 19th. The Petit Château is filled with memorabilia of the Condé family, who have owned the premises since the 17th century. The Musée Condé, (16) 44 57 08 00, is considered one of the richest museums in France; don't miss the sumptuously illuminated *Book of Hours* of the Duke of Berry (1415), the library, and the numerous works of art (Poussin and others). The superb gardens designed by Lenôtre include a pond with 100-year-old carp. The Great Stables, (16) 44 57 40 40, built in 1721, arguably the most beautiful stables in the world, include a horse and pony museum with costumed riding shows. Some 3,000 horses are trained in and around Chantilly, which has a famous racetrack.

DAY TRIPS AROUND PARIS

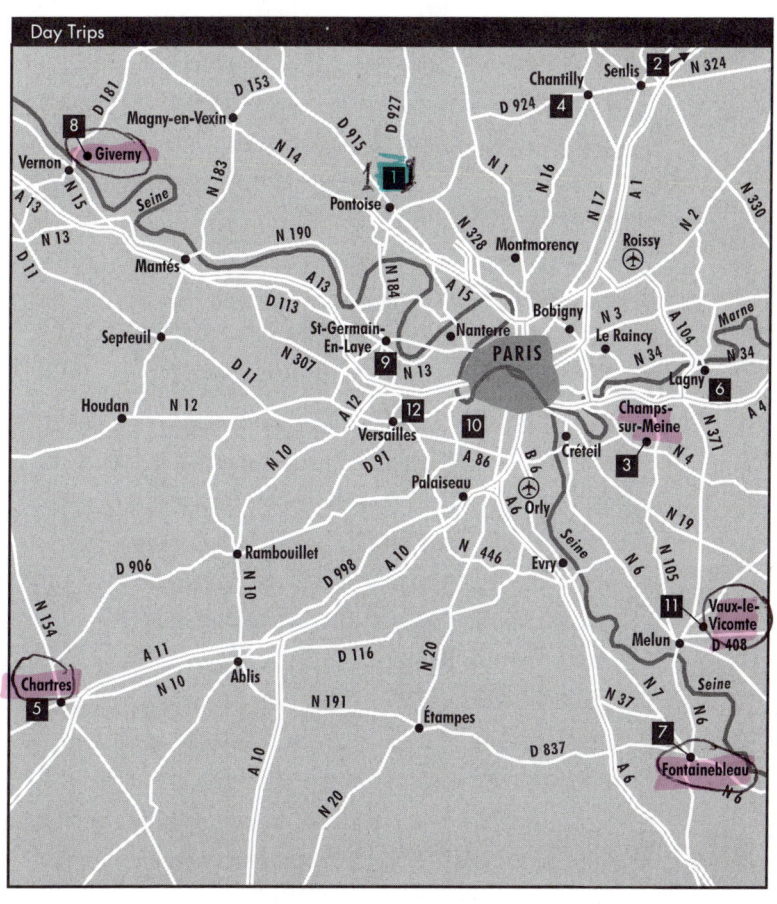

A restaurant about 5 miles away:
Les Etangs
1 rue du Clos des Vignes 60580
Coye La Forêt
(16) 44 58 60 15
A pleasant *auberge* in beautiful surroundings at the edge of the forest.

5 Chartres
28000 (Eure et Loir)
55 miles from Paris
Dominating this small town is one of the world's most famous cathedrals. Chartres remains true to its Romanesque and Gothic origins dating back to the 12th century. Its two dissimilar spires rise magnificently above the plain of Beauce: the Old Bell Tower *(Clocher Vieux)* is somber, simple Romanesque, while the taller New Bell Tower *(Clocher Neuf)* is pure flamboyant Gothic. The Royal Doorway *(Portail Royal)* is Romanesque with its elongated Old Testament figures, while the sculptures of religious scenes on the north and south porticos are in the more vigorous Gothic style. The enormous nave is a perfection of Gothic architecture. The stained-glass windows (25,000 square feet, with 5,000 figures) are astonishingly beautiful.

Restaurant:
Le Grand Monarque
22 place des Epars
(16) 37 21 00 72
Remarkable *menu à la carte* and wine list, specializing in wines from the Loire Valley.

6 Château de Ferrières
Ferrières en Brie
77164 (Seine et Marne)
About 20 miles from Paris
The Château de Ferrières was built for Baron James Rothschild in 1855 by English architect Joseph Paxton, designer of the Crystal Palace for the London Exhibition of 1851. This Renaissance-style building sports towers at each of its four corners. Eugène Lami decorated the interiors in Second Empire style. There is a superb *parc à l'anglaise* of over 300 acres with beautiful lawns, rare plants, and an *orangerie*. The castle can be visited on Sunday afternoons in winter, and Wednesday

through Sunday from May 1 on. It is advisable to phone in advance (64 66 31 25), as the castle is often reserved for on-location historical films.

Restaurant:
Hostellerie de l'Aigle d'Or
8 rue de Paris 77183
Croissy-Beaubourg
60 05 31 33
Very pleasant dining at the forest's edge.

7 Fontainebleau
77300 (Seine et Marne)
64 22 27 40
About 40 miles from Paris
The magnificent castle, one of the three great Royal Palaces in France, has been a royal residence since the 12th century. Up to the time of Napoléon III (1852-1870), it was altered to some degree by practically all the sovereigns of France. François I replaced the original medieval buildings with Renaissance construction, calling upon several Italian artists for the decoration. A Museum of Military Art and History, devoted to the Napoleonic cult, reminds us that it was at the foot of the castle's horse-shoe staircase that Napoleon bade farewell to his faithful Guard in April 1814, following his first resignation.

After touring the castle, go for a stroll in the network of footpaths through the famous 62,000-acre Forest of Fontainebleau. Rock climbers will find some delightful challenges.

Restaurant:
Le Beauharnais
27 place Napoléon Bonaparte
64 22 32 65
Classic cuisine and wines of great vintages in a beautiful décor around a charming indoor patio.

8 Giverny
27620 (Eure)
(16) 32 51 28 21
About 45 miles from Paris
The house where Claude Monet lived from 1883 until his death in 1926 is now a museum open from April 1 to October 31. Explore the gardens where innumerable flowers evoke his paintings, the garden filled with bamboo and rhododendrons; the ponds

with the famous water lilies; the Japanese bridge; and, in the museum, the Japanese etchings. Monet had three passions: painting, gardening, and photography: they are still present here in Giverny.

Do not miss the recently opened American Museum nearby, at 99 Rue Claude Monet, 27620 Gasny, (16) 32 51 94 65. Open from April 1 to October 31, the museum celebrates American artistic achievements from 1865 to 1915 in the land that gave birth to impressionism. It houses a permanent exhibition of American painters who came to France in the 19th century, and a yearly exhibition which features American art from the 18th to the 20th centuries.

Restaurant:
Les Jardins de Giverny
Chemin du Roy
(16) 32 21 60 80
Roses in the garden, an elegant dining room, a simple cuisine, good Bordeaux wines.

9 Saint-Germain-en-Laye
78100 (Yvelines)
About 18 miles from Paris
A town as old as the French line of kings: many were born here, including Louis XIV. The château remains much as it was when François I had it remodeled in the 16th century. Its Grande Terrasse overlooks the Seine and the famous Saint-Germain Forest, which is regularly threatened by plans for a highway. The castle houses the Museum of National Antiquities with its priceless collection of archeological specimens from the Paleolithic period to the Middle Ages.

Also:
Le Musée Départemental du Prieuré
2 bis rue Maurice Denis
39 73 77 87
One of the oldest mansions in Saint-Germain-en-Laye, it belonged to Mme. de Montespan, the favorite mistress of Louis XIV, and much later (1914) to Maurice Denis, the initiator of the "Nabi" movement. He painted here and drew the frescoes for the Théâtre des Champs-

Elysées. His atelier displays his sketches and works by painters of the Pont Aven and Pouldu Group (Gauguin, Sérusier) and the Postimpressionists (Odilon Redon, Mucha, Theo Van Rysselberghe).

Restaurant:
Cazaudehore
1 avenue du Président Kennedy
34 51 93 80
Meals are served in the garden, a generous cuisine with a whiff of southwestern France and a magnificent wine list. The beautiful interior opens onto a terrace.

10 La Vallée aux Loups
Chatenay-Malabry
92290 (Hauts de Seine)
L'Ermitage
87 rue de Chateaubriand
47 02 08 62
(The house is open to the public on some days; phone in advance.)
L'Ermitage, where François René de Chateaubriand lived from 1807 to 1817, was the home of the Romantic movement. Mme. Recamier came here, as did painters, writers, and musicians. With its authentic furniture, engravings, and personal memorabilia of the famous author and politician, L'Ermitage captures the whole atmosphere of the early 19th century. It is nestled in a *parc à l'anglaise* conceived and planted by Count René, with cypresses from Louisiana, cedars from Lebanon, and magnolias, catalpas, rhododendrons, and copper beeches.

A restaurant about 1,600 feet away offers a flowered terrace with a superb view up to 30 miles:
Le Panoramic
Le Plessis-Robinson
32 rue de Malabry 92350
46 61 02 73

11 Vaux-le-Vicomte
77950 Maincy (Seine et Marne)
About 30 miles from Paris
60 66 97 09
The celebrated château, built between 1656 and 1661 by Nicolas Fouquet, Superintendent of Finances, so enraged Louis XIV with its extravagance that he had Fouquet imprisoned for the rest of his life. Louis then put architect Le Vau, interior decorator

Le Brun, and landscaper Le Nôtre to work on Versailles. Like Versailles, Vaux-le-Vicomte is an exquisite example of 17th-century classical architecture; the park and the gardens are magnificent.

Also see the Musée des Equipages, devoted to the art of coach-making and horse-drawn carriages.

There is a terrace and a cafeteria here. But for a good restaurant, travel a few miles more to Samois:
L'Hostellerie du
Country Club Samois
Quai Franklin Roosevelt 77920
64 24 60 34
Very good food on a terrace with a magnificent view of the Seine Valley.

12 Versailles
78000 (Yvelines)
About 14 miles from Paris
30 84 74 00
The world-famous palace with its magnificent gardens is a perfection of French classicism, the symbol of the French monarchy at its peak. On the site of a modest hunting lodge built by his father, Louis XIV erected the most sumptuous of royal dwellings, copied many times throughout Europe. See the *Grands Appartements* of the King and Queen; the famous *Galerie des Glaces* (Hall of Mirrors), where the Treaty of Versailles was signed in 1919; the apartments of Mme. de Maintenon, Mme. du Barry, and Mme. de Pompadour; the Opera and the Chapel; and the Grand et Petit Trianons, where Marie Antoinette played the shepherdess. But most of all, wander through the park, with its ponds and sculptures. Finally, don't miss the *Son et Lumière* show, which tells the story of Versailles with fireworks and lights.

Restaurant in Versailles:
Les Trois Marches
1 boulevard de la Reine
39 50 13 21
Inside the gorgeous Trianon Palace Hôtel is one of the finest restaurants in France, with a splendid glass roof and wall overlooking the park and its sheep. Simple but subtle and refined cuisine. Surprising pastry and a very good wine list.

MSTISLAV ROSTROPOVICH'S SURVEY OF THE CONCERT HALLS

"When you love a woman, you love every detail of her being. A poet takes inspiration from each and every aspect of his beloved. The same is true of my love for Paris. I have traveled all over the world. There are cities I respect, like London. There are cities I like, such as smaller cities in Italy whose beauty reminds me of chamber music. But in Paris, I feel like a man in love; in love and at home.

"In some bistros, admittedly after a few drinks, I often wonder why everyone is not speaking Russian. I have the feeling that Paris is my city, so it surprises me not to hear my own language. When my wife and I were forced to leave the USSR, the first city where we bought an apartment was Paris."

MSTISLAV ROSTROPOVICH, *violoncellist, conductor*

1 L'Auditorium du Musée du Louvre
Cour Napoleon 75001
40 20 52 99
Built under I. M. Pei's Pyramid in the renovated Musée du Louvre, this is a concert hall for chamber music, not for opera. Music should be appropriate to the concert halls it is played in. Schubert and Chopin belong in romantic concert halls. For modern music like Boulez's (he is a genius), a more neutral hall is required.

2 Châtelet Théâtre Musical de Paris
Place du Châtelet 75001
42 33 00 00 – 40 28 28 40
I played with the Leningrad Philharmonic Orchestra in this huge concert hall. For solos with my wife, Galina Vishnevskaya, I found the acoustics to be less than perfect. But I think of this hall with pleasure, for when you come out of it, you are in old Paris, with the Fontaine du Châtelet just across the street.

3 Eglise Saint-Eustache
2 rue du Jour 75001
In a charity concert for the fight against multiple sclerosis, I played Bach in this Gothic church with a Renaissance décor.

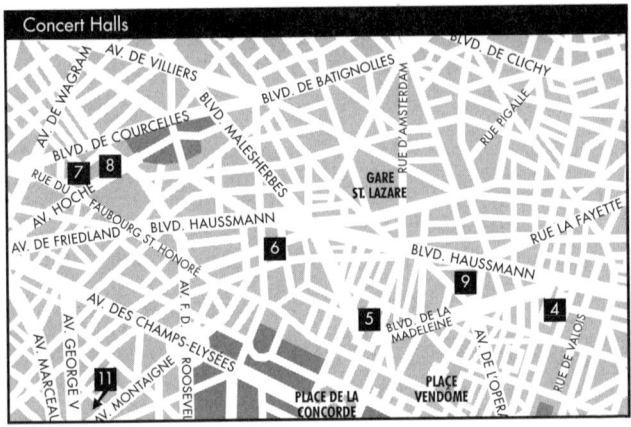

Concert Halls

4 Opéra Comique
Salle Favart
5 rue Favart 75002
42 86 88 83 – 42 96 12 20
A charming 19th-century (1898) building where I played three Bach suites for cello in a charity concert for the Opéra Comique. It is a lovely concert hall. I remember listening to Prokofiev's *L'Ange de Feu* here.

5 Eglise de la Madeleine
Place de la Madeleine 75008
I remember with pleasure a charity concert I gave in this imitation of a Greek temple, built in the late 18th and early 19th centuries—three Bach suites in support of Professor Hamburger's medical research.

6 Salle Gaveau
45 rue La Boétie 75008
49 53 05 07
I have played in so many concert halls. The atmosphere of each depends on a variety of small details. My first Paris concert was given in Gaveau. The program, two suites by Bach as well as music by Prokofiev and Shostakovich, was very heavy. My fear was physical and prevented me from feeling any love for the concert hall. But I remember that the public was fantastic.

7 Salle Pleyel
252 rue du Faubourg Saint-Honoré 75008
45 61 06 30
One of the best concert halls in Paris. I have played there with some very dear friends:

MSTISLAV ROSTROPOVICH'S SURVEY OF THE CONCERT HALLS

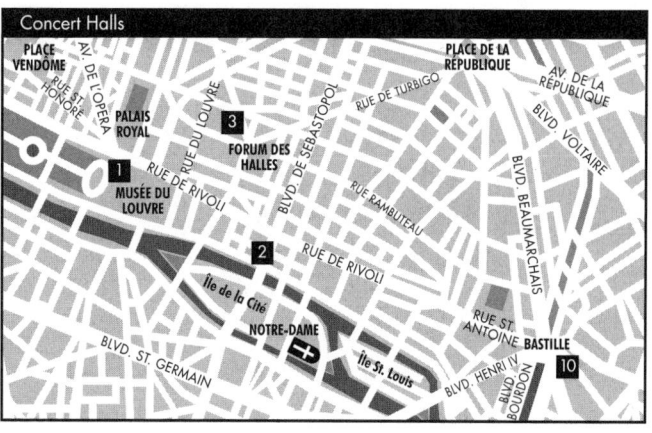

Jean-Pierre Rampal, Yehudi Menuhin, Isaac Stern. My relationship with any concert hall is different from that of a tourist. For a performer, it has to do with the walls, the chairs, the soul, and the sound of the place—not just its beauty.

8 The Russian Church
12 rue Daru 75008
46 22 38 91
I played on the steps outside for the funeral of Andrei Tarkowski, as only choirs are permitted to perform in Russian churches. Even my passion for Bach could not keep my hands from going numb on the bitterly cold morning of January 5, 1987. I was saved by half a bottle of vodka, which I gratefully consumed in the Café Petrograd across the street.

9 Opéra Garnier
Place de l'Opéra 75009
47 42 53 71
I love the Opéra Garnier, a marvel of Napoléon III architecture. The moment you enter the place, you are overcome by the sensation that something special is about to happen. Opera is so different from real life—it is a fairy tale. So it is fitting that opera houses should have a grandeur and a magic not to be found in other buildings. Opéra Garnier holds a special place in my heart, for it was there that I conducted Tchaikovsky's *Eugene Onéguine,* while my wife sang Tatiana. It was her farewell to the stage.

10 Opéra Bastille
120 rue de Lyon
Place de la Bastille 75011
44 73 13 00 – 43 43 96 96
This is the architecture of the Mitterrand era. Although I have not played or conducted here, I have visited the building and I think that the controversial architecture makes some sense. However, its façade is unusual and disturbing for an opera house. One can be forgiven for wondering if it is an office or an apartment building or a department store. I confess to preferring the Opéra Garnier.

11 Studio 106
Maison de la Radio
116 avenue du Président Kennedy 75016
42 30 23 08
I often played and conducted in this studio. It is a very good place for recording and for radio broadcasts. I recorded Tchaikovsky's opera *The Queen of Spades,* Puccini's *Tosca,* and Prokofiev's opera *War and Peace* here.

27 MICHEL LEGRAND'S FAVORITE JAZZ SPOTS

"Jazz is alive and well and living in Paris. Many great American jazz artists love to come here and participate in jam sessions (in French, *faire un boeuf*). There are only a handful of good jazz clubs in Paris—no more—but then I am not sure there are more than a handful of good jazz clubs in New York."

MICHEL LEGRAND, *composer and three-time Academy Award winner for musical scores of* The Thomas Crown Affair, Summer of '42, *and* Yentl

In order of preference:

1 Le Petit Journal Montparnasse
13 rue du Commandant Mouchotte 75014
43 21 56 70
Old Parisian mood, café-style, music, food, and drinks.

2 The New Morning
7–9 rue des Petites-Ecuries 75010
45 23 51 41
The biggest and most important jazz club in Paris. For big stars.

3 Club Lionel Hampton
Hôtel Meridien
81 boulevard Gouvion Saint-Cyr 75017
40 68 30 42
Don't think it's only "lobby music." Great players, drinks.

4 Le Petit Opportun
15 rue des Lavandières Sainte-Opportune 75001
42 36 01 36
Intimate jazz club. Old "Saint-Germain-des-Prés" *cave*-style. Great ambience guaranteed. People have to sit on each other's laps.

5 La Villa
29 rue Jacob 75006
43 26 60 00
Classy new place for jazz buffs.

6 Le Duc des Lombards
42 rue des Lombards 75001
42 33 22 88
Café concert, restaurant upstairs. Popular place with younger jazz buffs.

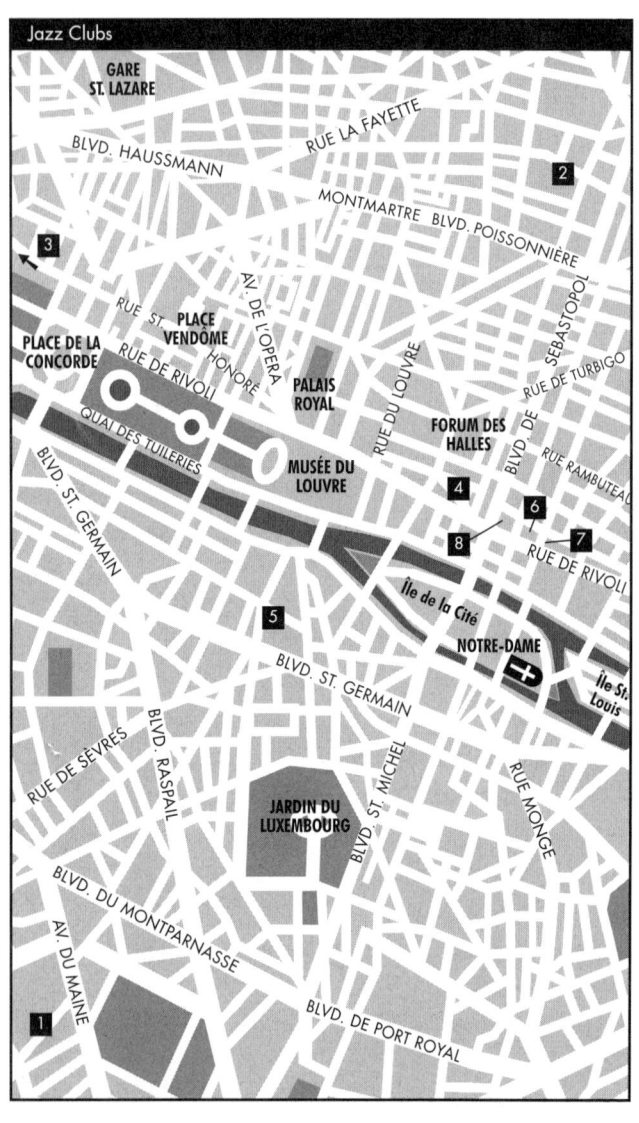

7 Le Sunset
60 rue des Lombards 75001
40 26 46 60
Good restaurant, with jazz in the basement. You will have a great time.

8 Le Baiser Salé
58 rue des Lombards 75001
42 33 37 71
Fusion, modern jazz, the Brazilian sound, video bar. A fun place.

COSTA-GAVRAS' CINEPHILIA

"Paris dreams and inspires dreams. Cinema is part of that dream. The cinephile as well as the average moviegoer will find in Paris the greatest number of cinemas and the widest choice of films from all over the world. Old and new films, forgotten masterpieces, and works from obscure countries can be seen all year round, all day long. The cinephile must not miss the Musée Henri Langlois. It is a voyage through the history of cinema, an initiation into the magic, poetry, and pleasure of film."

COSTA-GAVRAS, *director* (Z, The Confession, Missing, Music Box) *and former president of the Cinémathèque Française, the official French film archive*

Biggest Cinemas, Biggest Screens

1 Forum Horizon
*7 place de la Rotonde
Forum des Halles 75001
45 08 57 57*

2 Gaumont Opéra
*31 boulevard des Italiens 75002
47 42 60 33*

3 Le Rex
*1 boulevard Poissonnière 75002
42 36 83 93*

4 Gaumont Rama Ambassade
*50 avenue des Champs-Elysées 75008
43 59 19 08*

5 U.G.C. Normandie
*116 avenue des Champs-Elysées 75008
45 63 16 16*

6 Gaumont Grand Ecran
*30 place d'Italie 75013
45 80 77 00*
The last of the huge Gaumont movie palaces, with three theaters. One of them has 652 seats and the biggest screen in France.

7 Gaumont Grand Ecran Grenelle
*60 avenue de La Motte-Picquet 75015
43 06 50 50*

8 Le Grand Pavois
*364 rue Lecourbe 75015
45 54 46 85*

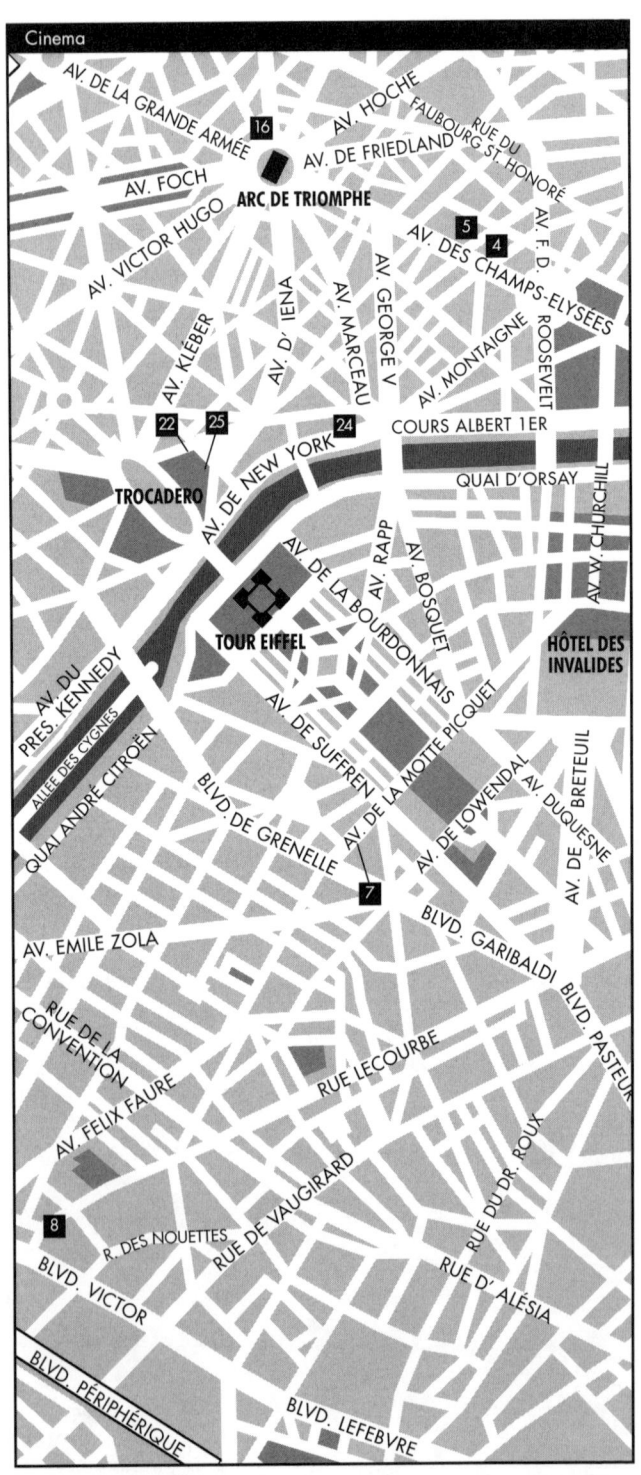

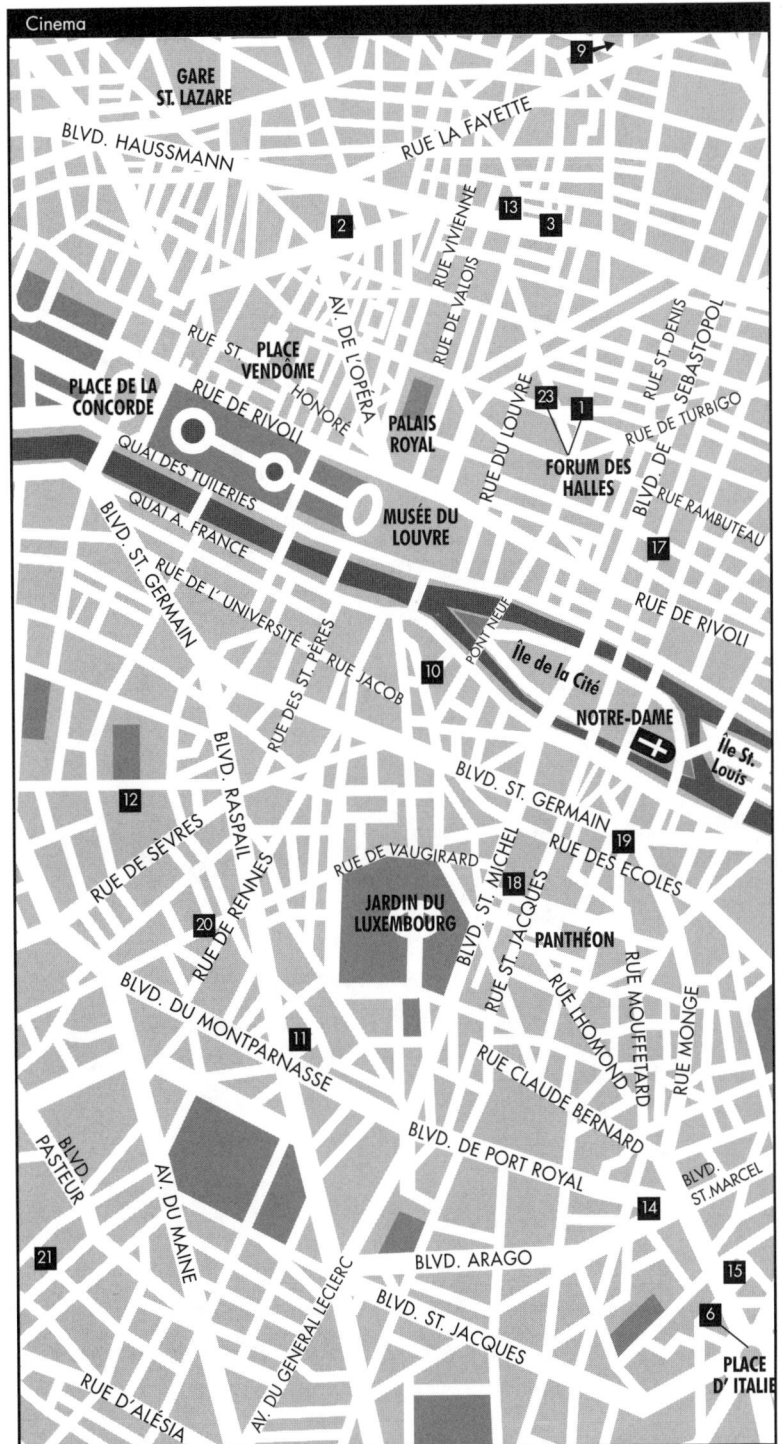

9 La Géode
Cité des Sciences et de l'Industrie
Parc de la Villette
26 avenue Corentin Cariou
75019
40 05 80 00

New Cinemas in Old Buildings

10 Action Christine
4 rue Christine 75006
43 29 11 30

11 Quatorze Juillet Parnasse
11 rue Jules Chaplain 75006
43 26 58 00

12 La Pagode
57 bis rue de Babylone 75007
47 05 12 15

13 Max Linder
24 boulevard Poissonnière
75009
48 24 88 88

14 Escurial
11 boulevard de Port-Royal
75013
47 07 28 04

15 La Fauvette-Gaumont Gobelins
58 avenue des Gobelins 75013
47 07 55 88

16 Le Mac-Mahon
5 avenue Mac-Mahon 75017
43 29 79 89

Special Programs

17 Centre Georges Pompidou
Salle Garance
Rue Saint-Merri 75004
44 78 12 33

18 Accatone
20 rue Cujas 75005
46 33 86 86

19 Grand Action
5 rue des Ecoles 75005
43 29 44 40

20 L'Arlequin
76 rue de Rennes 75006
45 44 28 80
Great classics.

21 L'Entrepôt
7–9 rue Francis de Pressensé
75014
45 43 41 63

22 Musée Henri Langlois
Palais de Chaillot
Place du Trocadéro 75016
47 04 24 24
English-language tours available.

Cinémathèques

These film archives offer admission and public screenings at a nominal fee:

23 La Vidéothèque de Paris
Porte Saint-Eustache
2 Grande Galerie 75001
40 26 34 30

24 La Cinémathèque Française
Salle du Palais de Tokyo
13 avenue du Président Wilson
75016
47 04 24 24

25 Salle du Palais de Chaillot
Avenue Albert de Mun 75016
47 04 24 24 – 47 20 13 50

GERARD OURY'S WALKING TOUR OF MONTMARTRE

"In the third century, Saint Denis was beheaded here. He is supposed to have then climbed the path to the top of the hill, carrying his head under his arm and washing it in one of the numerous fountains on his way. *Montmartre* means *Mont des Martyrs*. I remember this sad tale every evening when I come home through avenue Junot and rue Lepic: it reminds me I must be careful not to lose my head. Instead, I keep my eyes on Basilique Saint-Denis and this beautiful city of Paris, where I was born."

GÉRARD OURY, *director* (La Grande Vadrouille, The Adventures of Rabbi Jacob, L'As des As, La Soif de L'Or) *and modern art collector*

Sights and Sounds

1 Le Sacré-Cœur
Rue du Chevalier de la Barre
Construction of this spectacular white basilica at the top of Montmartre began in 1876, after the harsh defeat of France by Prussia, and was completed in 1914. It is Paris' most controversial monument—favored by tourists and deplored by the intelligentsia. Everyone agrees that the views from the dome are magnificent.

2 Eglise Saint-Pierre-de-Montmartre
2 rue du Mont Cenis
46 06 57 63
One of the oldest Gothic churches in Paris, built in the 12th century on the ruins of a Gallo-Roman temple. Ignatius Loyola founded the order of Jesuits here in 1534.

3 Le Musée du Vieux Montmartre
12 rue Cortot
46 06 61 11
A must: its exhibitions are worthy of the best museums. Built in the 17th century, it is surrounded by beautiful gardens. Auguste Renoir, Raoul Dufy, and Suzanne Valadon worked here.

4 *La rue des Saules*
The famous cabaret Lapin Agile is still here. The satirist Aristide Bruant made its reputation. It was originally called *Aux Assassins*. A lot of hoodlums came here, along with

GERARD OURY'S WALKING TOUR OF MONTMARTRE

artists and high-society people who wanted to get a glimpse of the underworld. A whiff of *vie de bohème*, now gone.

5 *Rue Saint-Vincent*
Famous popular songs were born here. "La Goualante du Pauvre Jean" and the sad story of Rose and rue Saint-Vincent are still sung today with melancholy. But its wine is cheerful and the Clos Montmartre still alive. On the first Saturday of October, at the corner of rue Saint-Vincent and rue des Saules, the 3,250 grapevines of Thomery Wine are picked.

They make a remarkable wine, even more appreciated because there are so few bottles; it is the only wine of Paris.

6 A. Beauvilliers
52 rue Lamarck
42 54 54 42
A former bakery decorated with hundreds of flowers all year round. One of the best restaurants in Montmartre or in Paris.

7 *La Place du Tertre*
Good old Place du Tertre, where the painters of today dream of the painters of

yesterday. When they sell their canvases to the Japanese, Americans, or Dutch, do they see an auctioneer in the future crying "Ten million dollars! Sold!"? Neither Gauguin nor van Gogh dared to dream such a dream.

8 La Mère Catherine
6 place du Tertre
46 06 32 69
Mother Catherine's omelettes are a tradition and a ceremony of initiation. Eating them gives tourists the impression they have become, if not Parisians, at least citizens of Montmartre.

9 Le Château des Brouillards
There is no château and very rarely *brouillard* (fog), but this is a place where one can dream. It is like drinking a sip of pleasure to think that Gérard de Nerval, a 19th-century poet, used to live here.

10 *La rue Norvins*
This street, named after a historian of Napoléon, is famous because the actor Jean Marais lives in the "*Folie Sandrine*." So do I. "*Folie*": that was the name in the 18th century for pleasant and discreet houses in which follies were committed. Perhaps it is still true?

11 La Pomponnette
42 rue Lepic
46 06 08 36
The food is excellent, and the walls are covered with portraits of stars and boxers. It is difficult to climb the hill after a meal here.

12 *Avenue Junot*
Every day I go up and down this avenue, which is paved with souvenirs. Film director Claude Lelouch gives private screenings at his Club 13. To get there, you pass the house of the turn-of-the-century artist Poulbot, whose depictions of street urchins of Montmartre have come to be called "*les petits poulbots*."

13 Le Clodenis
57 rue Caulaincourt
46 06 20 26
A wonderful actress, Nicole Courcel, recently opened this restaurant and offers excellent provençal cuisine. Here I meet

14 *La rue Lepic*

A market street lined with outdoor stands where merchants shout to sell their produce during all four seasons. As you climb higher, things quiet down. Vincent and Théo van Gogh lived at no. 51 and Georges Courteline, writer of comedies, at no. 89. Every time I pass there, I feel inspired to go to work.

15 Le Cimetière de Montmartre
Avenue Rachel
A very touching cemetery. Every day people cross its iron bridge on foot or by car, bus, or tourist coach. Do they realize that Stendhal, Zola, and Dumas are lying here? Do they think of Heinrich Heine, Nijinsky, Marie Duplessis ("Camille"), and François Truffaut?

16 Moulin de la Galette
83 rue Lepic
In 1990, Renoir's masterpiece *Le Moulin de la Galette* was auctioned at Sotheby's in New York for $78 million. The original building, or what is left of it, between avenue Junot and rue Lepic, no longer hosts popular balls. The mill is still here, though, on rue Lepic, on top of Graziano's (46 06 84 77), one of the best Italian restaurants in Paris.

17 Moulin Rouge
82 boulevard de Clichy
46 06 00 19
Moulin Rouge brings to mind Toulouse-Lautrec, the cancan, La Goulue, Grille d'Egout, and Valentin le Désossé, a century ago.

18 Le Bateau Lavoir
Place Emile Goudeau at the bottom of rue Ravignan
Renovation to turn this wooden structure into a museum was going to begin on the very day it burned down. There remains only a glass window filled with photographs of famous people. Picasso, Braque, Juan Gris, and Modigliani worked here. They ate little and made love a lot. Between sessions, Picasso painted *Les Demoiselles d'Avignon*.

my friends from the theater and cinema.

19 *La Place des Abbesses*
Many a film was shot on this quintessential Paris *place*. It has everything—an Art Nouveau Métro station, public benches where old people pass the time, children on rollerskates, an ultra-modern church, accordion players, and very pretty young women—one of those combinations that the 20th-century poet Jacques Prévert loved.

20 Le Petit Train de Montmartre
It stops at red lights! Children love it. It crosses Place du Tertre, rue Saint-Vincent, and goes on to Place Pigalle—the most poetic train trip one can take in Paris.

21 *La Place Charles Dullin*
Place Charles Dullin means the Théâtre de l'Atelier. Dullin, who had a falsetto voice and was a hunchback, was also a great actor and stage director. With Jouvet, Baty, Copeau, and Pitoëff, he was part of the "Cartel," a group of theater directors who shaped the Parisian stage between the two world wars. In his workshop, a whole generation of actors was formed, many of whom are still active.

22 Le Marché Saint-Pierre
2 rue Charles Nodier
A shopping paradise for the home. Every material from flannel to "zenana," miles of draperies, flowered prints, canvas for mattresses, at incredible prices. Here, as in heaven, people wait in line to be admitted.

TOURING L'ILE DE LA CITÉ
WITH CHARLOTTE RAMPLING

"Paris is for me one of the most beautiful cities in the world. I have lived in France for 15 years, and if I had to live in the heart of the city, I would certainly choose an island—either L'Ile de la Cité or L'Ile Saint-Louis. I love to walk in their little streets, which were not meant for cars, and to discover there the history of this city that I love and the history of its inhabitants."

CHARLOTTE RAMPLING, *actress* (The Damned, Night Porter, Stardust Memories, The Verdict)

L'Ile de la Cité is the starting place of the history of Paris, point zero for all distances measured in France. It was the seat of royal power, the seat of Christendom in France, and also the nation's first academic center.

1 Notre-Dame de Paris
The Cathedral of the Archbishopric of Paris was built between 1160 and 1350 in early Gothic style. It was defaced several times, and "restored" in the 19th century by Viollet-le-Duc, who had the sculptures of the façade "remodeled." Climb to the top of the South Tower for a superb view of Paris.

2 Le Parvis
Remodeled in the 19th century by Préfet Haussmann, this huge square in front of Notre-Dame de Paris is four times bigger than it was in the Middle Ages. A recently dug parking lot under the Place du Parvis revealed a Gallo-Roman enclosure and a Merovingian cathedral. An archeological crypt is open to the public. In Notre-Dame and on Le Parvis float the ghosts of Victor Hugo's characters: the Hunchback of Notre-Dame and the gypsy Esmeralda.

3 Le Marché aux Fleurs
Quai de la Corse
Located between the Hôtel-Dieu hospital, the Préfecture de Police, and the Tribunal de Commerce, three uninteresting buildings which I hope you never have to visit, the flower market has existed since 1808.

You can find here, at good prices, every variety of flower. On Sundays it is a bird market.

4 La Sainte Chapelle
4 boulevard du Palais
43 54 30 09
A marvel of Gothic architecture, also known for the splendor of its 13th-century stained-glass windows, the oldest in Paris. The famous Grande Rosace (Rose Window) dates back to the 15th century.

5 La Conciergerie
1 quai de l'Horloge
43 54 30 06
Built in the 14th century, it was a wing of the Royal Palace, which was abandoned by the kings after one of the many insurrections of the people of Paris. It consists of three superb Gothic halls, and also the Tour de l'Horloge, which received the first Parisian clock in 1370. Among the many famous people who were imprisoned here was Queen Marie Antoinette, who was sent from here to the guillotine.

6 *Place Dauphine*
Created by Henri IV, it was one of the five Royal Places of Paris, along with the Place des Vosges, the Place des Victoires, the Place Vendôme, and the Place de la Concorde. After World War II, several rows of sycamore trees were planted here to create a pleasant walkway. Simone Signoret and Yves Montand lived here in a flat they called "La Roulotte."

7 Le Pont Neuf
Despite its name, this is the oldest bridge in Paris. Also the most famous. Built from 1578 to 1604, it is surprisingly wide and allows automobile traffic without too many problems. No houses were ever built on it, which is exceptional for Parisian bridges. It had sidewalks from the beginning, at a time when they were unknown in Paris. At its center a statue of King Henri IV was erected in 1614, four years after his assassination; it was recast in 1818 by a Bonapartist foundryman who, it is said, placed several statuettes of the emperor inside the larger figure.

TOURING L'ILE DE LA CITE WITH CHARLOTTE RAMPLING

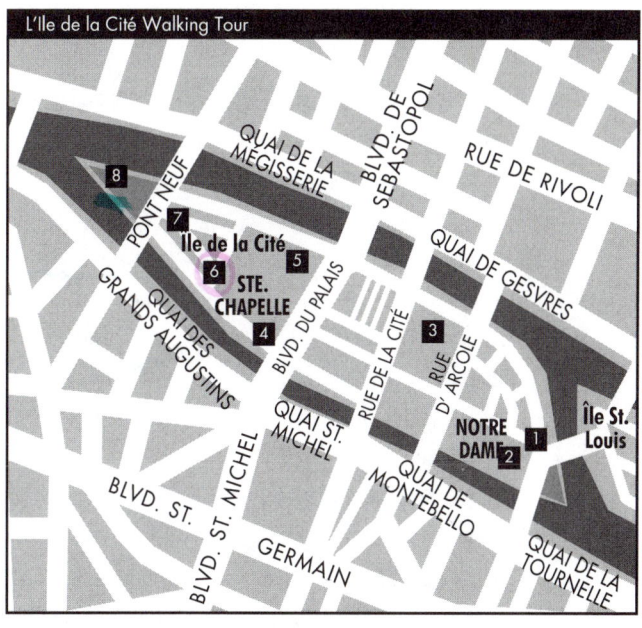

8. *Le Square du Vert Galant*
A lovely garden at the end of L'Ile de la Cité where Parisians come to stroll in the shade of its beautiful trees and to sunbathe in summer. Jacques de Molay, Great Master of the Order of the Temple, was burned alive here during the reign of Philippe le Bel in the 14th century.

TOURING L'ILE SAINT-LOUIS WITH CHARLOTTE RAMPLING

This tiny island is one of the curiosities of Paris and one of its most charming districts. A number of *hôtels particuliers,* former private mansions of the aristocracy, are preserved here, the majority dating to the 17th century.

1 L'Hôtel Lambert
1 quai d'Anjou
At the end of the quai. The mansion was built in 1642 by Le Vau and decorated by Le Sueur and Le Brun for Lambert, Superintendent of Finances for Louis XIII. Voltaire's friend Mme. du Châtelet lived here. And, more recently, actress Michèle Morgan.

2 L'Hôtel de Lauzun
17 quai d'Anjou
Built in 1657 for the lover of the Grande Mademoiselle, first cousin to Louis XIV. He was imprisoned before he could move in. Baudelaire and Théophile Gautier lived here.

3 L'Eglise Saint-Louis-en-l'Ile
19 rue Saint-Louis-en-l'Ile
46 34 11 60
Built between 1664 and 1726 in "Jesuit" style, it is one of the finest examples of French baroque churches. It houses several works of art and a collection of embroidery.

4 *Rue Saint-Louis-en-l'Ile*
Many 17th-century *hôtels particuliers* are to be found on this street. At no. 28 is L'Orangerie restaurant (46 33 93 98) owned by Jean-Claude Brialy, an actor and theater director whose warm welcome and kindness are equal to his cuisine. At no. 35 the Ulysses Book Shop offers every book and every map on all the voyages you have ever dreamed of, and more. At no. 31 the famous Berthillon (43 54 31 61) offers simply the best ice cream in Paris—60 different flavors. Also famous for its waiting lines.

5 *Rue des Deux Ponts*
At no. 12 a plaque commemorates the arrest during the Nazi occupation of 112 Jewish inhabitants of the building, including 40 children. None ever returned.

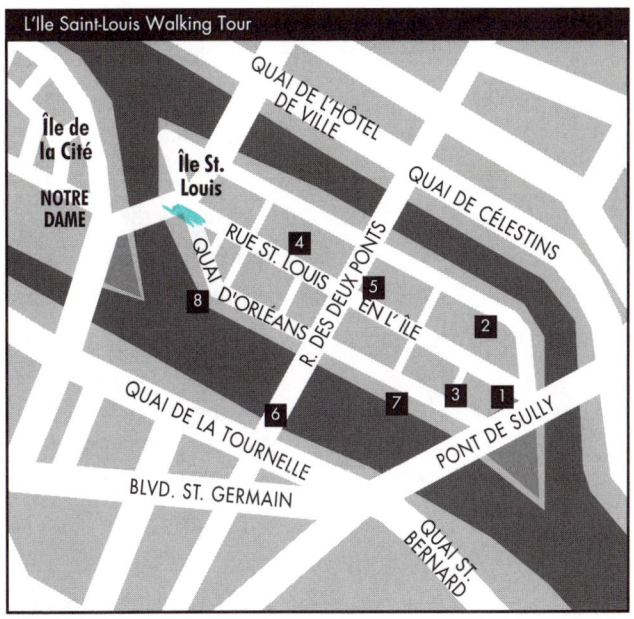

L'Ile Saint-Louis Walking Tour

6. Le Pont de la Tournelle
   This bridge was built in 1645. In 1923 a statue of Sainte Geneviève, Patron of Paris, by Marcel Landowski was erected here. In the 5th century she saved the Parisians from an invasion of Attila's Huns.

7. *Le Quai de Bethune*
   A long succession of beautiful façades. No. 36 is the Hôtel du Conseiller au Parlement Pierre Vuole, where Marie Curie died. At no. 24 Helena Rubinstein ordered the superb Hôtel Hesselin torn down in 1935; it was replaced by the present building where President Georges Pompidou died and where Mme. Pompidou still lives.

8. *Le Quai d'Orléans*
   At no. 6, the Polish Library and the Adam Mickiewicz Museum. At no. 12 lived the poet Félix Arvers, who penned the famous sonnet "To the Unknown Woman." It is engraved on the façade: "*Mon âme a son secret, ma vie a son mystère . . .*" (My soul has its secret, my life its mystery). The lady never knew that the poet was in love with her.

A WALK THROUGH THE MARAIS WITH SOPHIE MARCEAU

"To live in the Marais is an enchantment. At the beginning, in the 13th century, the Marais (the Marsh) was . . . a swamp. Then, slowly, kings, marquises, and Jewish tradespeople started to build castles, *hôtels particuliers*, gardens, and squares. Many of the structures were destroyed during the Revolution. Fortunately, some survived and document the upheavals of history. Today, there are no more destructions. The old sites are protected. Le Marais dreams of peace and of pedestrians. So do I!"

SOPHIE MARCEAU, *film actress* (La Boum, Fort Saganne, For Sasha, La Note Bleue, Fan Fan) *and stage star (George Bernard Shaw's* Pygmalion)

1 *Rue Saint-Paul*
Great antiques shops. Excellent bread in the *boulangerie* at the corner of rue de Rivoli.

2 Le Petit Sully
Orangerie of Hôtel de Sully
62 rue Saint-Antoine
44 61 20 00 – 48 87 24 15
In this unexpected smaller 17th-century *hôtel particulier*, orange trees were grown to enhance the grounds of the neighboring Grand Hôtel de Sully.

3 *Place des Vosges*
You never know where to look to absorb everything on the Place des Vosges, with all the grandeur of 17th-century French taste. In fact, unless you manage to live here, you can see only parts of it. It is beautifully lit at night.

4 *Rue des Francs-Bourgeois*
Fashion, fashion: chic expensive shoes, clothes, fake jewelry—not one bookstore has survived, not one bakery. This is the kingdom of useless chic.

5 *Rue des Rosiers*
Strolling here on a Sunday morning is like walking through a *shtetl* (Jewish village).

6 *Rue des Hospices Saint-Gervais*
A simple plaque on a school wall commemorates the spot where several dozen Jewish children were taken to Auschwitz to be exterminated.

7 Le Musée Carnavalet
23 rue de Sévigné
42 72 21 13
Everything you always wanted to know about Paris can be

A WALK THROUGH THE MARAIS WITH SOPHIE MARCEAU

found here; it is the historical museum of the city. I would love to have a house like this. In the 17th century it was the home where Mme. de Sévigné wrote her famous letters.

8 *Rue Payenne*
A collection of *hôtels particuliers*, full of charm. Hôtel Marle (no. 11) and Hôtel Chatignon (no. 13) with their little gardens are divine.

9 Hôtel Aubert de Fontenay (Hôtel Salé—Musée Picasso)
5 rue de Thorigny
42 71 25 21

Where Picasso's paintings have taken refuge and the 17th and 20th centuries come together. This is the spirit of Paris!

10 *Rue Quincampoix*
This street is supposed to bring bad luck. In 1719, at no. 65, a Scottish adventurer named Law invented his famous "system" of exchanging gold coin against paper currency. When Law went bankrupt, a few French speculators (mainly aristocrats) made a fortune, but hundreds were ruined. A seed of the Revolution is thought to lie here.

33 19TH-CENTURY MONUMENTS WITH ANDRZEJ ZULAWSKI

"Monuments have the same effects on cities that tenants have on apartments: they define them. Without them, a city is like a documentary film. With them, it becomes a fiction film. French monuments were mainly created in the 19th century. You can climb many of the Parisian monuments, and then you are at the center of the show!"

ANDRZEJ ZULAWSKI, *film director* (La Troisième Partie de la Nuit, L'Important c'est d'Aimer, Possession, La Note Bleue)

In order of preference:

1 La Tour Eiffel
Champ de Mars 75007
45 50 34 56
This is not quite as obvious as you might think. I know of no Parisian who has ever climbed higher than the restaurant on the first floor, but the views from the top are breathtaking.

2 La Sacré-Cœur de Montmarte
35 rue du Chevalier-de-la-Barre 75018
42 51 17 02
Most likely the ugliest church in the world, but to climb up here is to get the widest view of Paris.

3 L'Arc de Triomphe
Place Charles de Gaulle 75008
When you reach the top, you understand that Paris is not a heart, but a straight line. The bas-reliefs are ferocious; Rude's *Marseillaise* is the best known. The Arch of Triumph is also the Tomb of the Unknown Soldier.

4 Le Pont Alexandre III
75008
Everything here is flamboyant. You can admire the bridge from above and from below. The bronze and copper statues have recently been regilded. This is the epitome of the nouveau-riche monument.

5 Le Pont de Bir Hakeim
75015/75106
Where Marlon Brando chased Maria Schneider in Bertolucci's *Last Tango in Paris*. A horizontal Eiffel Tower spanning the Seine, a prime example of the romanticism of the industrial age. At night you can hear the nostalgic rumble of the elevated Métro.

6 Le Pont Neuf
75004
For me, the most beautiful bridge in Paris. It was even more attractive a couple of years ago, when Christo wrapped it in beige canvas. It is also the oldest bridge in Paris.

7 Statue of Henri IV
75004
This statue in the middle of the Pont Neuf was destroyed during the Revolution and replaced in 1818. Small statues of Napoléon were nestled in its belly. Too bad you cannot open it to see them.

8 Le Pont de l'Alma
75008/75016
One of its arches reveals the statue of the famous Zouave (a French soldier in Arab dress who fought in the Napoléon III wars). It is used by Parisians to measure the height of the Seine in times of flood. From this bridge you move on to the statue of Adam Mickiewicz.

9 Statue of Adam Mickiewicz
Under the chestnut trees of Cours Albert Ier 75008
Few people have read Mickiewicz except the Poles, but I can assure you he was the greatest Romantic poet in the world. Bourdelle, who sculpted this statue, caught a cold during its unveiling and died.

10 Le Grand Palais
Avenue du Général Eisenhower 75008
44 13 17 17
and

11 Le Petit Palais
Avenue Winston Churchill 75008
42 65 12 73
Because they were shy people, the architects of the two *Palais* saw fit to wrap steel in stone, just as women of the time were wrapped in corsets. Pure 1900, a dozen sculptures in a delicious kitsch style. On the roof of the Grand Palais you can see Récipon's quadriga (a chariot drawn by four horses abreast), a sublime view of the Hôtel des Invalides, and the palace of the President of the French Republic. Check visiting hours or bribe the watchman.

12 L'Arc de Triomphe du Carrousel
Cour du Louvre 75001
At the base of the famous straight line leading to the

126 SECRETS OF PARIS

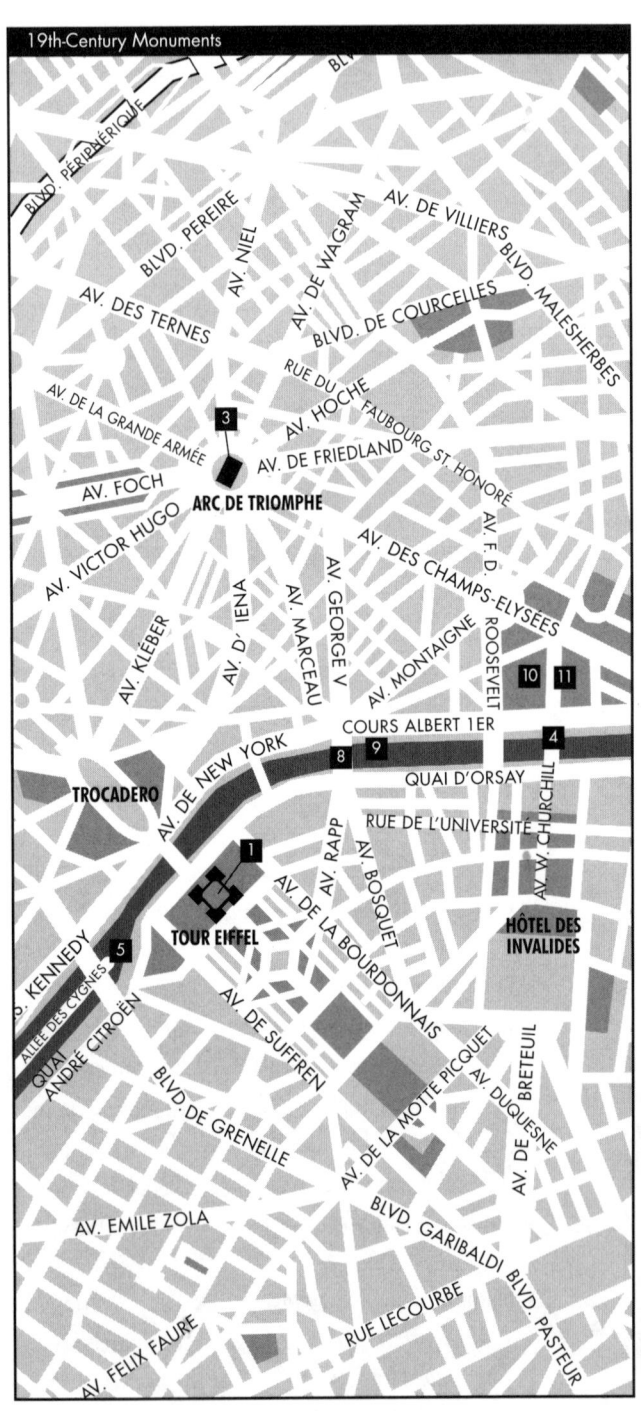

19TH-CENTURY MONUMENTS WITH ANDRZEJ ZULAWSKI

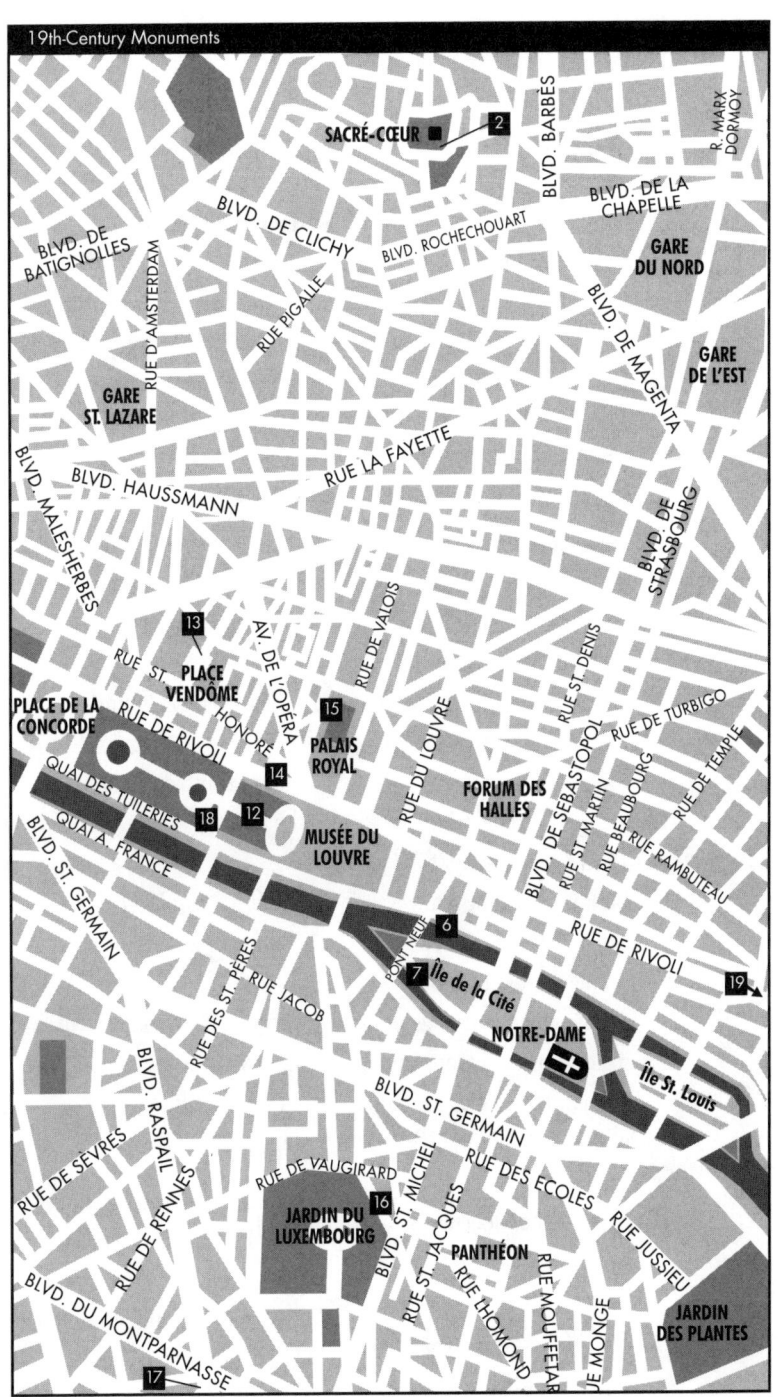

Place de la Concorde and the Arc de Triomphe at the Place de l'Etoile. The quadriga on top was "borrowed" by Napoléon during his Italian campaign. It proves how much Paris owes to the plundering of Italy.

13 La Colonne Vendôme
Place Vendôme 75001
Climb to the top of the column and meet Napoléon dressed up as Caesar (see Billy Wilder's *Love in the Afternoon*). Watchman often impossible to find; bribing difficult. View overlooking the Ritz and the most beautiful *place* in Paris.

14 Statue of Jeanne d'Arc
Place des Pyramides 75001
Built in 1903, the statue was regilded by the Germans during the Occupation. Today the site is used as a rostrum by the Front National neo-fascists—a major example of distortion of meaning.

15 La Fontaine Molière
Rue de Richelieu (angle rue Molière) 75001
An 1869 piece of cake in an orgy of marble: Molière mopes seated on the "*Malade Imaginaire's*" armchair. In France, grandeur is often sad.

16 La Fontaine Médicis
Luxembourg Gardens 75006
In the greenest part of the Luxembourg, you cannot climb the fountain, but you can rest in its shade.

17 *Balzac*, by Rodin
Carrefour Vavin 75014
For me, the only good sculpture in Paris.

18 The Maillol sculptures
In front of Le Louvre 75001
Just to contradict what I just said.

19 *La Grisette de 1830*
Boulevard Richard Lenoir 75011
La grisette—a young woman of easy virtue—was a favorite subject of 19th-century literature and art.

And across the street,
Statue of Frédéric Lemaître
Lemaître was a 19th-century theatrical star and one of the characters in Carné and Prévert's film *Les Enfants du Paradis*, a masterpiece.

A TOUR OF THE SHOPS OF
SAINT-GERMAIN-DES-PRÉS

First, Saint-Germain-des-Prés was a famous Left Bank church. After World War II the neighborhood became the nucleus of the existentialist movement. In the late 1940s and 1950s, a whole generation discovered its cafés—Les Deux Magots and Café de Flore—and its *caves* (cellars), where New Orleans jazz reigned and jitterbug was king.

Today, Saint-Germain-des-Prés offers some of the smartest shopping in Paris.

1. Lario 1898
   56 rue du Four 75006
   45 48 44 65
   Top-quality Italian shoes.

2. Revillon Fourrures
   44 rue du Dragon 75006
   2 rue de Grenelle 75006
   42 22 38 91
   Furs and leather.

3. Laure Bassal
   3 rue de Grenelle 75006
   42 22 44 24
   Avant-garde shoes—deluxe.

4. Marie Martine
   8 rue de Sèvres 75006
   42 22 18 44
   Brigitte Bardot used to buy her clothes here; it is now *bon chic, bon genre.*

5. Sonia Rykiel Enfants
   4 rue de Grenelle 75006
   49 54 61 10
   Madame Rykiel's children's wear.

6. Sonia Rykiel Inscription
   6 rue de Grenelle 75006
   49 54 61 00
   Rykiel's daughter's creations: more youthful, less expensive than her mother's.

7. Guido Pasquali
   8 rue de Grenelle 75006
   42 22 69 00
   Sensible shoes in good taste for teenagers.

8. Sabbia Rosa
   73 rue des Saints-Pères 75006
   45 48 88 37
   Made-to-order cotton and silk nightshirts and underwear.

9. Arche
   21 rue du Dragon 75006
   42 22 98 30
   The most comfortable shoes in Paris.

10 Robert Beaulieu
30 rue du Dragon 75006
45 48 56 80
Fun furs.

11 La Faïence Anglaise
11 rue du Dragon 75006
42 22 42 72
Faïence, selected furniture, and table linens in the Victorian style.

12 Church's
4 rue du Dragon 75006
45 44 50 47
English shoes for men, superb shoe kits, shoehorns.

13 Sonia Rykiel
175 boulevard Saint-Germain 75006
49 54 60 00
The *Maison-Mére* of Sonia Rykiel in a beautiful *hôtel particulier*. Women's wear only.

14 Compagnie Française de l'Orient et de la Chine
163 and 167 boulevard Saint-Germain 75006
45 48 10 31
Chinese and other Asian clothes and household objects.

15 Rykiel Homme
194 boulevard Saint-Germain 75007
45 44 83 19
The smart masculine version of Rykiel.

16 Emerich Meerson
200 boulevard Saint-Germain 75007
42 22 12 89
Sophisticated watches for connoisseurs.

17 Irie
8 rue du Pré-aux-Clercs 75007
42 61 18 28
Young, body-hugging, avant-garde clothes.

18 Klein d'Oeil and Michel Klein
6 rue du Pré-aux-Clercs 75007
47 03 93 76–42 60 37 11
Cutting-edge dressing.

19 Laurence Tavernier
7 rue du Pré-aux-Clercs 75007
49 27 03 95
All-cotton pajamas and other at-home wear for men and women.

A TOUR OF THE SHOPS OF SAINT-GERMAIN-DES-PRÉS

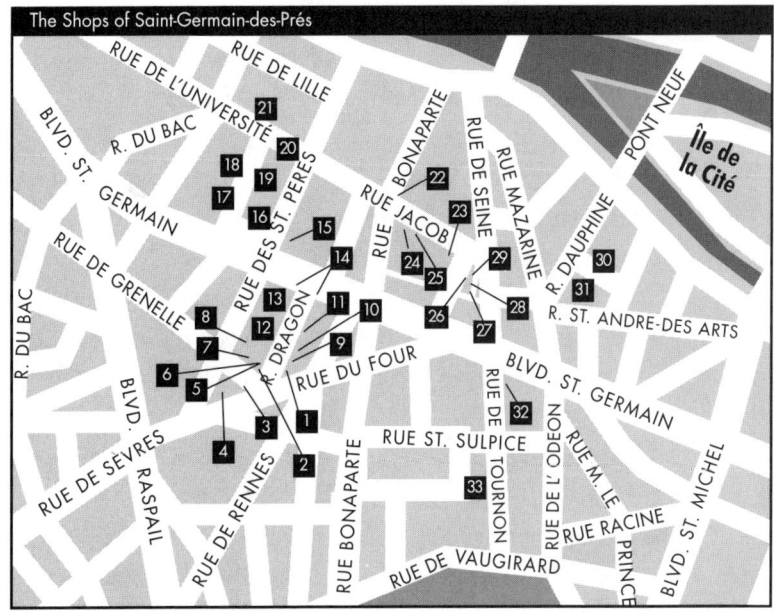

20 Pamina
5 rue de l'Université 75007
42 60 29 49
Tables, carafes, goblets, candelabra, collector's bottles, china.

21 Jean-Charles Brosseau
26 rue de l'Université 75007
40 15 98 72
Panama, cotton, and straw hats.

22 M.C.
21 rue Bonaparte 75006
43 54 91 71
Madeleine Castaing's antiques.
Very trustworthy.

23 Pierre et Patrick Frey
5 rue Jacob 75006 and
2 rue de Furstenberg
46 33 73 00
Luggage, carpetbags, shawls, exceptional fabrics, picnic baskets, beach bags, wallpapers.

24 L'Atelier d'Anaïs
23 rue Jacob 75006
43 26 68 00
Embroideries, tapestry threads, patterns.

25 Michèle Aragon
21 rue Jacob 75006
43 25 87 69
Chandeliers, curtains, plates from the 1930s, embroidered table linens.

26. Manuel Canovas
5 place de Furstenberg 75006
43 26 89 31
Everything for the house, including bed and bath linens, and for picnics and the beach.

27. Métaphore
7 place de Furstenberg 75006
46 33 03 20
Fabrics, beachwear.

28. Etamine
2 rue de Furstenberg 75006
43 25 49 83
Fabrics, parasols.

29. Jacques Dey
1 rue de Furstenberg 75006
43 26 41 55
Modern fabrics for curtains and wall coverings.

30. Hervé Domar
48 rue Dauphine 75006
46 33 88 99
Contemporary eyewear.

31. Frego
61 rue Dauphine 75006
43 54 98 54
Elegant silk clothes for men and women.

32. Optique de Seine
99 rue de Seine 75006
43 29 80 05
Classic eyewear.

33. Emmanuelle Khanh
2 rue de Tournon 75006
46 33 41 03
High-style designs for women.

ALONG THE ROUTE OF FAMOUS AMERICAN AUTHORS: A WALKING TOUR

Paris has been a magnet for American intellectuals since the days of Benjamin Franklin, John Adams, and Thomas Jefferson. In the 19th century, writers such as Washington Irving, Nathaniel Hawthorne, Edgar Allen Poe, and Henry James came to absorb the city's atmosphere.

But it was in the 1920s that Paris attracted more American literati than ever before or since. Spurred by Prohibition, the new American puritanism, faster ships, and a franc at four cents, they all came: Ernest Hemingway, F. Scott Fitzgerald, Gertrude Stein, Sylvia Beach, and many others. Some of their residences and hangouts still stand. Here's a walking tour, and a list of their favorite cafés and restaurants, still dispensing café au lait, gin, and lively conversation.

Residences

1 *58 rue de Vaugirard 75006*
F. Scott and **Zelda Fitzgerald** had an apartment here in 1928–29.

2 *27 rue de Fleurus 75006*
The famous **Stein** headquarters: **Gertrude,** her brother **Leo**, and **Alice B. Toklas** lived here from 1903 to 1938. The place was a veritable pilgrimage for Hemingway, Fitzgerald, Ezra Pound, T. S. Eliot, and so many others.

3 *6 rue Férou 75006*
After his divorce from **Hadley**, **Ernest Hemingway** settled here with **Pauline,** just behind Saint-Sulpice. They lived here when *A Farewell to Arms* was published in September 1929. They left in January 1930—it was Hemingway's last home in Paris.

4 *26 rue Servandoni 75006*
In 1925 **William Faulkner** stayed in a pension here (now the Hôtel des Principautés Unies) with windows overlooking the Luxembourg Gardens.

5 *6 rue Palatine 75006*
F. Scott and **Zelda Fitzgerald** moved here on April 1, 1929. Their apartment was the model for the one in *Babylon Revisited*.

6 *5 rue Christine 75006*
In 1938, when **Gertrude Stein** and **Alice B. Toklas** had to leave the rue de Fleurus, they settled here. After Stein died in 1946, Toklas carried on here for a number of years.

7 *74 rue du Cardinal Lemoine 75005*
Ernest and **Hadley Hemingway**'s first Paris apartment after the hôtel on rue Jacob. It was tiny and not very comfortable, but the Café des Amateurs was across the street on Place de la Contrescarpe.

Cafés and Restaurants

8 Café de Flore
172 boulevard Saint-Germain
75006
45 48 55 26

9 Les Deux Magots
6 place Saint-Germain-des-Prés
75006
45 48 55 25

10 La Closerie des Lilas
171 boulevard du Montparnasse
75006
43 54 21 68

11 Le Dôme
108 boulevard du Montparnasse
75014
43 35 34 82

12 La Coupole
102 boulevard du Montparnasse
75014
43 20 14 20

13 Le Select
99 boulevard du Montparnasse
75006
45 48 38 24

14 La Rotonde
105 boulevard du Montparnasse
75006
43 26 68 84

And a Commemorative Bar

15 Hemingway Bar
Ritz Hôtel
15 place Vendôme 75001
42 60 38 30
In late August of 1944, when **Hemingway** arrived in Paris as a war correspondent with the U.S. Army, he headed for the Ritz Bar and later claimed to have "liberated" it from the German occupation. In appreciation, one of the bars in the hotel bears his name today.

ALONG THE ROUTE OF FAMOUS AMERICAN AUTHORS: A WALKING TOUR

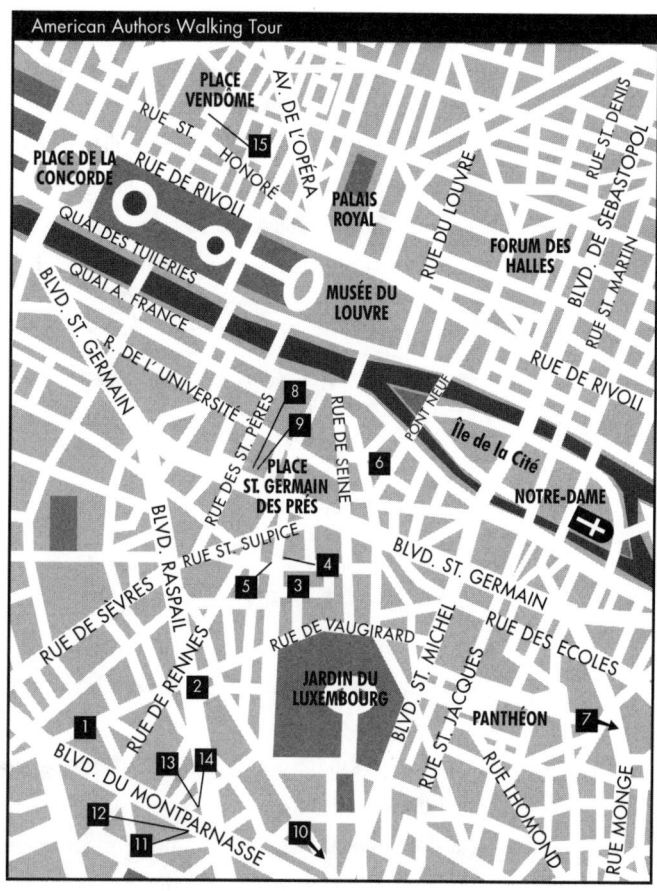

FRANÇOIS REICHENBACH EXPLORES THE 19TH-CENTURY HIDDEN MALLS AND ARCADES

"I love to wander through the streets and byways of Paris where I grew up. I always follow my luck; it takes me to malls and arcades I don't know very well. The old crafts are still practiced in these wonderful covered arcades, built mostly during the 19th century as luxury shops and later taken over by craftspeople. What better way to get to know a city than by getting acquainted with these hidden *passages* and *galeries* and their artisans?"

FRANÇOIS REICHENBACH, *documentary filmmaker* (Les Marines; L'Amérique Insolite; Houston, Texas; *Academy-Award winning* Arthur Rubinstein: L'Amour de la Vie; Sex O'Clock U.S.A.), *contributed this chapter just a few months prior to his death in February 1993.*

1 La Galerie Vero-Dodat
19 rue Jean-Jacques Rousseau 75001
Built in 1826 by two butchers, Mssrs. Vero and Dodat, who lost their fortunes in the undertaking. Robert Capia repairs antique dolls from around the world. There are restaurants, art galleries, a musical instrument shop, a lute maker, and a seller of earthenware ovens.

2 Les Galeries du Palais-Royal
75001
In and around the gardens of the Palais-Royal are three *galeries*—Galerie Montpensier, Galerie Beaujolais, and Pérystile Beaujolais—built at the end of the 18th century. They saw many a prostitute plying her trade during the Revolution and the Empire. Among the shops here are the only ones in Paris that sell medals and decoration ribbons from the world over.

3 La Galerie Colbert
6 rue des Petits-Champs 75002
Built in 1826, entirely destroyed, then rebuilt identical to the original, it belongs to the Bibliothèque Nationale. One of the most beautiful brasseries in Paris, Le Grand Colbert, is here.

4 La Galerie Vivienne
4 rue des Petits-Champs 75002
The queen of the Parisian *galeries*, built in 1778. Here are wine merchants, fashion boutiques (Jean-Paul Gaultier's is here), art galleries, and a tea shop. A bookshop inaugurated in 1825 remains unchanged.

FRANÇOIS REICHENBACH EXPLORES THE 19TH-CENTURY HIDDEN MALLS AND ARCADES

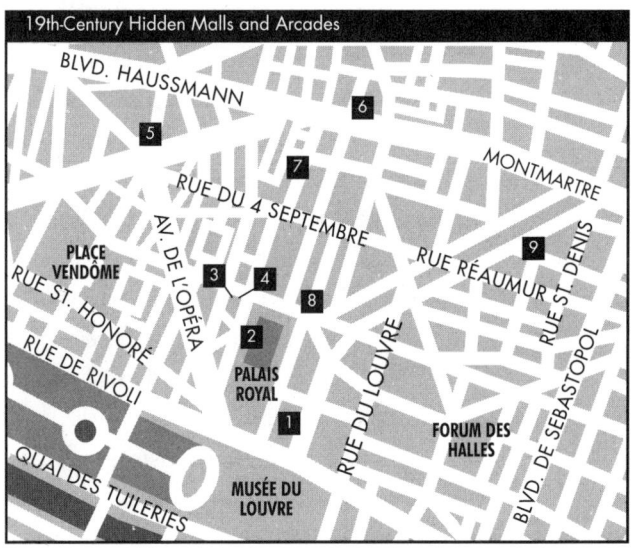

5. **Le Passage des Princes**
5 boulevard des Italiens 75002
The last *passage* built in the 19th century (1860). In the window craftsmen fashion wooden pipes for smoking.

6. **Le Passage Jouffroy**
12 boulevard Montmartre 75009
Built in 1847, its *verrière* (glass roof) is supported by cast-steel columns. There are many restaurants, and the famous Musée Grévin. Built in 1882, it houses Paris' wax museum, showcasing yesterday's and today's celebrities.

7. **Le Passage des Panoramas**
10 rue Saint-Marc 75002
Big panoramas of Paris were installed here in 1799. Today, restaurants, shops for pipe smokers and costume jewelry.

8. **Le Passage Choiseul**
42 rue des Petits-Champs 75002
Built in 1827 between the Palais-Royal and the *grands boulevards*, it has toy shops, fashion boutiques, and a remarkable shop for artists' equipment.

9. **Le Passage du Caire**
2 place du Caire 75002
Built in 1798, it was inspired by the Egyptomania that followed Napoléon's Egyptian campaign. The shops here specialize in mannequins. In the windows you will see heads, busts, feet, arms, hands.

SIR DIRK BOGARDE'S PARK MEANDERS

"Being conceived in Paris (The Crillon, I am assured) does not make me a real Parisian. But I 'feel' that I am. I have known the city since childhood, in gay times and in sad ones. If Paris is not quite as 'green' as, say, London or Munich, Vienna, or even Berlin, it has glorious gardens rather than 'parks.' I have spent many summer (and indeed bitter winter!) days in all of these, which I list and which I love and which, for me, hold infinite memories. The lazy heat of a July day sitting by the pond in the Luxembourg, little white boats skimming the water, the soft whisper of the tiny breeze as silent almost as a sigh, the crunch of wheel and heel on the raked gravel paths, the scarlet of the geraniums, all these and more evoke for me my beloved Paris and its parks and gardens—elegant, calm, lost in the past."

> SIR DIRK BOGARDE, *actor* (The Servant, For King and Country, Accident, The Damned, Death in Venice, Night Porter, Providence), *author* (Voices in the Garden, Jericho), *and frequent contributor to London's* The Daily Telegraph

1 Le Jardin des Tuileries
75001
Entries: Place de la Concorde, rue de Rivoli, avenue du Général Lemoine

The Palais des Tuileries was built in 1564 by Catherine de Medicis and has ever since been the "ballroom," so to speak, of the Elegant People. But the shadows were gathering, the storm was all too near, and in 1792 Louis XVI and his family were forced by the enraged mob to hurry along the path which led to the tragic Pavillon du Manège. This was the start of the fall of the French Royal Family. Here, in this glorious, elegant Royal Park, the last embers of grandeur were extinguished.

But many other, almost capricious, events took place among these paths and lawns. The very first gas balloon soared toward the heavens from this park, and during the period of the Empire a biscuit seller named Madeleine sold biscuits that, years later, were immortalized by Marcel Proust

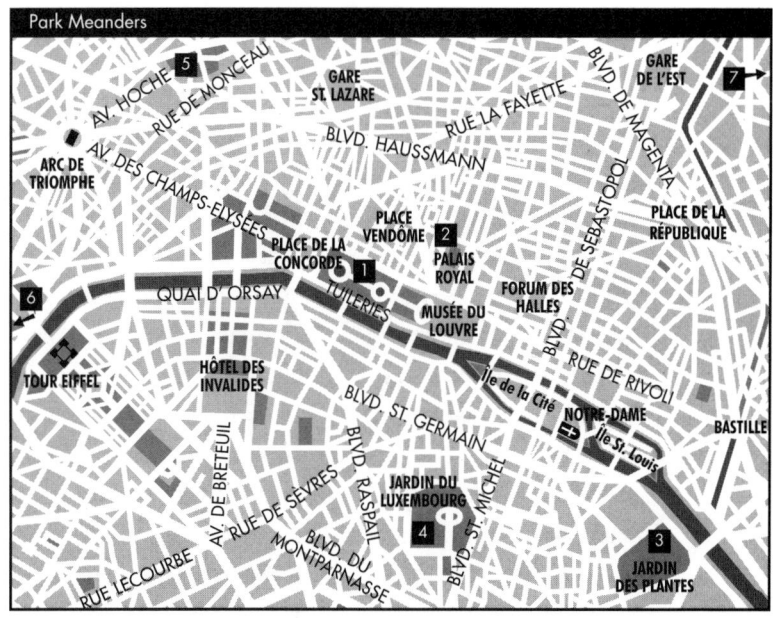

The splendid palace was destroyed by fire during the Commune de Paris in 1871, but the gardens remain almost intact along with some of the original buildings, untouched by the destruction of the palace. This elegant, very French park provides a glorious respite of calm and cool for the almost always exhausted visitors to the Louvre. Here, with the sound of traffic muffled, the chatter of sparrows, the sigh of the summer wind, you can be reminded that Paris, whatever may have happened to her over the many years of her history, is indeed a Royal City.

2 Le Jardin du Palais-Royal
75001
Entries: rue Montpensier, rue de Beaujolais, rue de Valois, Place du Palais-Royal
This secret garden is almost forgotten in the somber elegance of the great buildings that surround it. But it was once a scene of wild debauchery, lust, and greed. It belonged for many years to the Orléans family, and the palace gardens were transformed by them into a rendezvous for the roués and rogues and the Ladies of the Town. The arcades surrounding the park were filled with shops and

bars, and one could walk here, and do a great many more reprehensible things, until the early hours of the morning. It is said that the French Revolution actually started here on the 13th of July, 1789, and in 1787 an unknown lieutenant named Bonaparte made his first feminine conquest here. As the years drifted by, artists and writers and thinkers moved into the apartments above the now empty shops, and the ghosts of Cocteau and beloved Colette draped their shades of elegance and wit over the earlier shades of evil, greed, and lust. You will find one of the most famous *tables* in the world here at Le Grand Véfour (42 96 56 27), a feast for the glutton, but also a feast of beauty for the eye.

3 Le Jardin des Plantes
75005
Entries: Place Valhubert, rue Buffon, rue Linné
I remember being taken here for the first time when I was about five, and being overwhelmed by the heat of the gigantic conservatory filled with thousands of ferns, palms, and tropical splendors. There is also an aquarium and a vivarium (my favorite: toads, frogs, and snakes!). This is a park dedicated to natural history. The museums are here amidst the rare trees and exotic plants. Established as early as 1652, the park still thrives and gives endless pleasure to those who would only stroll under the green canopy of leaves or, as I once did, press their faces as close to an angelfish or a shark—or better yet, a giant salamander or fire-bellied toad—as the glass (and their courage!) will allow.

4 Les Jardins du Luxembourg
75006
Entries: boulevard Saint-Michel, rue Auguste Comte, rue d'Assas, rue de Vaugirard
Perhaps my most favorite park in Paris. Certainly, the one I knew first and best. First built in 1612 by Marie de Medicis (to remind her of her beloved Florence), the gardens took their final form as late as 1790. A completely French garden, with a firm geometric layout,

terraces, and box trees and yew hedges. It is a park, essentially, of the young—I suppose because it is so near the boulevard Saint-Michel and the Université. It is equally a haven for children, as I well remember running in the summer breezes with a gaily colored paper windmill and sailing my glossy tin steamer on the pond. There are statues everywhere, artists, nurses with their perambulators, even a Punch and Judy show. A delectable park indeed.

5 Le Parc Monceau
75008
Entries: boulevard de Courcelles, avenue Velasquez, avenue Ruysdael
When I chose to live in Paris, after having to leave Provence, I decided that a view from the windows must be green and have trees. This is not easy in the city. But I discovered, walking every day on foot, an apartment that overlooked the Parc Monceau. Convenient for the area in which I wished to live and looking out over trees and lawns. But, alas, facing north! So there was never sunlight or even light. I did not stay. But the *parc* had great charm. It was constructed in 1784 as part of a "green belt" round the city, and the very first man in history to jump with a parachute landed in its leafy glades. The Second Empire saw to it that cliffs of imposing buildings surrounded the area—hence no sun and little light. It is always filled with children in prams, on cycles, or simply screaming and yelling. Unrestful; and in my terms Not Worth a Detour! There are, to be sure, trees, dogs, and elderly ladies walking slowly. But it is simply a promenade for the rich *hôtels particuliers* owners and occupiers who surround the overtrodden lawns.

6 Le Parc de Bagatelle
75016
Entry: route de Sèvres 92200 Neuilly-sur-Seine
Across the green boskiness of the Bois de Boulogne. A pond, swans (black ones at that!), and thousands and thousands of roses set in formal beds, this

is the *roseraie*. The grounds were laid out in 1720 and the Marquis d'Estrées built a pretty little pleasure house where, indeed, he enjoyed the company of very elegant, if slightly naughty, ladies. Marie Antoinette's brother-in-law, the future Charles X, had it destroyed and bet that he could rebuild a delicious little *folie* in its place in 64 days. This he did; you can see it still there today.

7 Le Parc des Buttes-Chaumont
75019
Entries: avenue Simon Bolivar, avenue Mathurin Moreau, rue Manin, rue Botzaris
This is the largest green space in Paris. It is also rather a "nonsense." Once on the outskirts of the city, it was a quarry; it then became deserted wasteland, and rather a dangerous area. When Paris annexed two villages, Belleville and La Villette, Napoléon III decided to make the area worthy of the city, a rustic "park for the citizens." To this end, carts and carts of soil were brought to the desolate area and a hilly landscape was instantly constructed! In 1867 a completely faux world was made for the World's Fair. Hills and valleys, waterfalls, lakes, trees, and a kind of Salvator Rosa landscape were born, with rocks and cascades. At its highest point, a reproduction of the Sybil Temple at the Villa in Tivoli emerged. All a complete "nonsense."

CATHERINE DENEUVE'S SECRET GARDENS

"As a child I spent all my summer vacations in the country. My mother had a green thumb. Vegetation in general and especially trees have a real power over me. Nature is a profound part of my life: private gardens, public gardens; all the trees in France 'belong' to me."

CATHERINE DENEUVE, *actress* (The Umbrellas of Cherbourg, Repulsion, Belle de Jour, The Last Metro, The Hunger, *the Academy-Award-winning* Indochine, *and* Ma Saison Preferée)

1 L'Orangerie du Luxembourg
Place Edmond Rostand 75006
From October to May, plants from the Luxembourg Gardens find shelter from the cold here: orange trees (whose flowers are used in the perfume industry), exotic palm trees, pink laurels (which grow over the balustrades of the garden in summer), and pomegranate trees (whose flowers are used to manufacture red ink).

2 Le Verger du Luxembourg
Rue Auguste Comte 75006
This orchard used to be a nursery for Carthusian friars and contained an extraordinary collection of fruit trees. Presently it offers 200 varieties of apple and pear trees, some of which are unknown anywhere else. The trees' growth is guided by metal wires that support the fan-shaped branches. Fruits are protected from birds and insects by small paper bags. You will find here a Caucasian elm, a giant sequoia, a copper beech, and a Judas tree. Also, beehives containing a million bees. Anyone can come for lessons—theoretical and practical—in apiculture.

3 Le Jardin de Babylone
33 rue de Babylone 75007
Hidden behind a huge wall, it used to be the garden of a cloister for the sisters of Saint Vincent de Paul and became a public garden only recently. It has kept its pastoral character and is a joy for the mothers and children of the neighborhood. It includes a real orchard with cherry and apple trees, vines, hazelnut trees, and currant bushes, as well as a playground for tots.

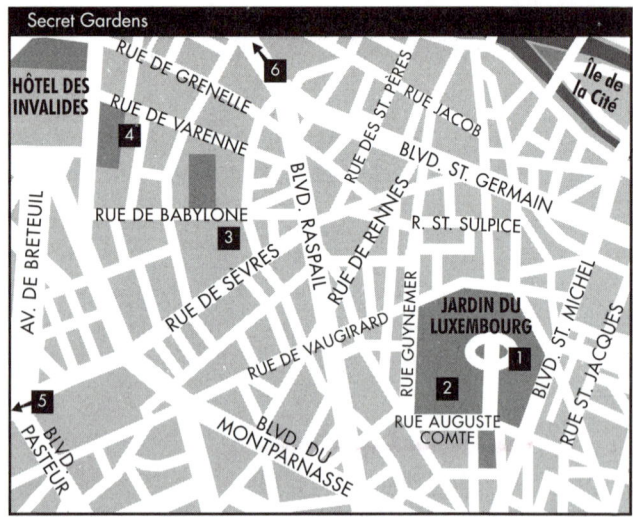

Secret Gardens

4 Le Jardin du Musée Rodin
77 rue de Varenne 75007
Along with *The Thinker, The Burghers of Calais*, and many other Rodin sculptures, this 18th-century garden revels in wonderful roses. A great variety of birds find shelter in its yews, lindens, maples, cherry trees, and vines. And a great variety of lovers find shelter in their shade.

5 Le Jardin des Serres d'Auteuil
3 avenue de la Porte d'Auteuil 75016
This *jardin à la française* is the nursery for all the flowers and plants used to beautify the streets and squares of Paris. Some 64 greenhouses shelter tropical plants and flowers from around the world. Floral exhibitions and concerts are held in the greenhouses.

6 Le Jardin des Epinettes
Rue Maria Deraisme 75017
An oasis of green in a petit-bourgeois neighborhood near Montmartre, it is a typical Parisian square, encircled by chestnut trees. In its center is a bandstand surrounded by silver linden trees. Other unusual trees include the Chinese soapberry, the ginkgo (which has existed for millions of years), the yellow clingstone, the green oak or holm oak with its lasting leaves, and the tulip tree (its roots are the basis for spruce beer).

BROWSING THE FLEA MARKETS WITH PIERRE HEBEY

"Parisians and tourists alike have been flocking to the flea markets—*les puces*—of Paris for over a hundred years, prowling through the crowded stands in search of a treasure, a find, a memento. Here is a personal selection of my favorite sources in Marché Saint-Ouen, the most important of Paris' several flea markets. It is not a guide, but a series of *coups de coeur* stemming from very long personal relationships with the people recommended. They are all trustworthy sellers. Bargaining is always possible, provided it remains courteous."

PIERRE HEBEY, *lawyer, discriminating art collector, and author*

Marché Saint-Ouen is just north of Paris off the Porte de Clignancourt. It is divided into eleven markets, of which Serpette, Paul Bert, and Biron are the most interesting. It is open Saturdays, Sundays, and Mondays. The best time to go is Saturday morning as early as possible (9am).

Marché Serpette and Marché Paul Bert

1 Artémise et Cunégonde
Marché Serpette, Allée 1 Stand 28
40 10 02 21
Antique bed sheets, genuine dresses from Schiaparelli, Dior, Chanel, Jacques Fath. Hats from Paulette. Old laces, embroideries, dolls, table linens, cashmeres.

2 Corinne & Gérard Mahé
Marché Serpette, Allée 1 Stand 31
40 12 81 22
18th- and 19th-century furniture, Minton and Sarreguemines china, charming precious objects. Eclectic and classical.

3 Nicole and Léon Herschtritt
Marché Paul Bert, Allée 1 Stand 2
42 77 53 87
Garden furniture, flower stands, cast iron, painted wooden horses, dolls.

4 Patrick Fortin
Marché Paul Bert Allée 6 Stand 81
40 10 17 87
High-quality Art Déco.

5 Christian Sapet
Marché Paul Bert, Allée 6 Stand 81 bis
40 12 29 12
Sapet could have been a great antiques dealer on one of the chic streets of Paris. He prefers Les Puces and offers high-quality Art Nouveau and Art Déco from 1880 to 1950. Furniture, chandeliers, *coiffeuses* (makeup tables). A favorite of professional decorators.

6 Humeurs
Marché Paul Bert, Stand 280
40 11 27 04
1880s furniture, objects, materials.

7 Roger Besson
Marché Paul Bert, Allée 3 Stand 167, 49 45 02 91
According to Besson, "Everything but 'Louis-Philippe,' which is usually fake." Furniture, objects, fabrics; charming authentic couches.

8 Eric Lombard
Marché Serpette, Allée 6 Stand 2
40 11 73 43 ext.49
1900–1930 objects, decorations.

9 L'Univers du Bronze
M. Richard
Marché Serpette, Allée 6 Stand 1
40 10 04 34
Authentic, rare bronzes.

10 Garaujoud-Balestie
Marché Serpette, Allée 5 Stand 6
40 11 26 69
18th- and 19th-century *haute décoration*, china, tapestries, furniture, armoires, dishes, candelabra, and candlesticks.

11 Lucien Pineau
Marché Serpette, Allée 5 Stand 4
40 11 45 75
M. Pineau is very reliable for everything from 1900–1930.

12 Medianoche—Hubert Badetz
Marché Serpette, Allée 6 Stand 7
40 12 29 69
Lalique glassware, vases, forks and spoons, dishes, carafes.

13 Xavier Cholet
Marché Serpette, Allée 6 Stands 2 & 11
40 12 22 14

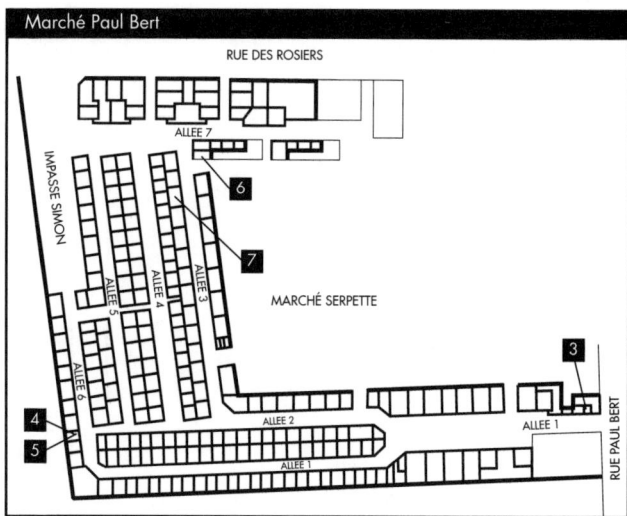

Napoléon III, 1880, end of the 19th century: mantel clocks, furniture.

14 Colette Alnot
Marché Serpette, Allée 5 Stand 19
40 11 54 14
Curiosités, decoration, paintings, objects, pipes, end of the 19th century. First Empire painted velvets.

15 José Sayegh
Marché Serpette, Allée 4 Stand 18
40 10 01 50
18th-century French furniture, English furniture, statues, vases.

16 J. Revellin—Tempesta Marly
Marché Serpette, Allée 4 Stand 6
40 10 13 93
Specializes in *barbotines* (white porcelain vases decorated in violent colors), Baccarat glasses, glass objects, ivory, unglazed porcelain, candelabra.

17 Olwen Forest
Marché Serpette, Allée 3 Stand 7
40 11 96 38
An American lady in Les Puces offers a collection of 1932–1948 jewelry by Eugene Joseff of Hollywood and worn by great stars. Also Schiaparelli, Chanel, and others. Art Nouveau and Art Déco, Christofle tea services, Bohemia crystal glasses.

18 Le Monde des Voyages
Mme. Zisul
Marché Serpette, Allée 3 Stand 15
40 12 64 03
Gorgeous luggage from Hermès, Vuitton, Goyard, Oshkosh: suitcases, wardrobes, cabin trunks. Also old Chanel jewelry and Hermès bags.

19 Edward J. Klejman
Marché Serpette, Allée 1 Stand 21
40 11 54 14
One of the brightest and most competent experts in France on Art Nègre from Africa, Oceania, Borneo. Follow his advice, with your eyes closed.

Marché Biron

20 Sylvie Carpentier
Allée 1 Stand 127
40 12 51 15
Silverware, *orfèvrerie* (wrought precious metals), bronzes.

21 Andrée Vyncke
Allée 1 Stand 14
40 12 92 75
Great specialist for *pâtes de verre,* Art Nouveau: Gallé, Daum, Lalique, Argy-Rousseau, Walter. Everything here is genuine.

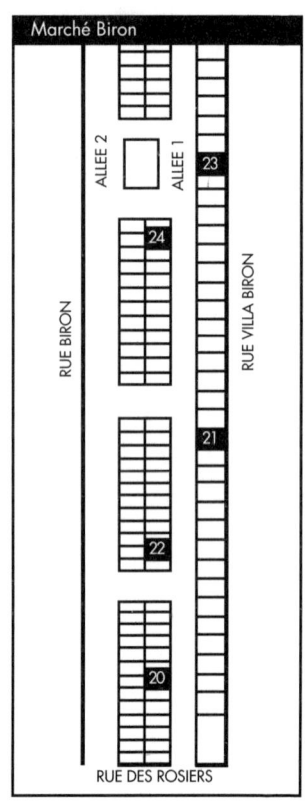

22 Huguette Portefaix
Allée 1 Stand 121
40 10 13 40
Ditto: everything is genuine.

23 Jacqueline Edouard
Allée 1, Stand 29
40 10 23 00
18th-century silverware, Art Déco jewelry, mantel clocks, bronzes, *objets d'art.* Refurbishment of silverware.

BROWSING THE FLEA MARKETS WITH PIERRE HEBEY

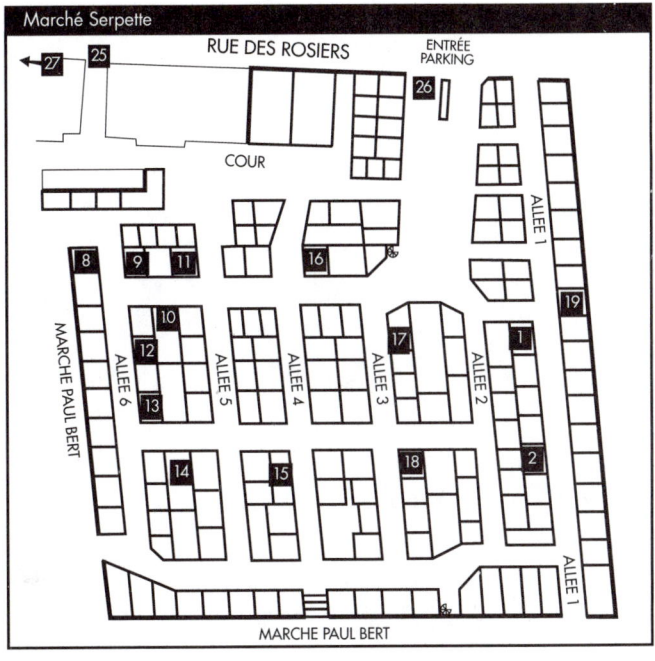

24 Alexia Say
Allée 1 Stand 100
40 12 11 07
Objets d'art, *pâtes de verre*,
Art Nouveau and Art Déco.

Amenities

25 Droguerie Dugay
92 rue des Rosiers
93400 Saint-Ouen
40 11 87 30
The best products for the upkeep of your furniture, restoration of wood, leather, objets d'art, and other items.

26 *110 rue des Rosiers*
93400 Saint-Ouen
A parking lot for your car.

27 Le Coq de la Maison Blanche
37 boulevard Jean Jaurès
93400 Saint-Ouen
40 11 01 23 – 40 11 67 68
A good restaurant to finish your day.

Maps courtesy of Guide Officiel et Pratique des Puces de Paris-Saint Ouen, who periodically publishes up-to-date editions featuring the 2,000 exhibitors under their 85 specialities and locations. Maps include necessary information in French, English, and Japanese.

OUTDOOR MARKETS

Paris has long been a city of open-air markets. Many covered markets were built in the 19th century, in the steel-and-glass architecture of the time. Today, after the destruction of Les Halles, 84 markets remain in Paris. They offer very fresh vegetables, fruits, meat, fish, butter, cheese, and more.

Open-Air Markets
Most are open from 7am to 1:30pm.

1 *Boulevard de Port-Royal 75005*
Open Tuesdays, Thursdays, and Saturdays.

2 Mouffetard
Rue Mouffetard 75005
Open every day.

3 *Place Maubert 75005*
Open Tuesdays, Thursdays, and Saturdays.

4 *Place Monge 75005*
Open Wednesdays, Fridays, and Sundays.

5 Raspail
Boulevard Raspail 75006
Between rue du Cherche-Midi and rue de Rennes
Open Tuesdays and Fridays. Organic foods on Sundays.

6 Saxe Breteuil
Avenue de Saxe 75007
Between avenue de Ségur and Place de Breteuil
Open Thursdays and Saturdays.

7 Aguesseau
Place de la Madeleine 75008
Open Tuesdays and Fridays.

8 Auteuil
Rues d'Auteuil, Donizetti, La Fontaine 75016
Open Wednesdays and Saturdays.

9 Président Wilson
Between rue Debrousse and Place d'Iena 75016
Open Wednesdays and Saturdays.

Covered Markets

10 Saint-Germain
3 ter rue Mabillon 75006
Open every day: 8am–1pm and 4–7:30pm.

OUTDOOR MARKETS

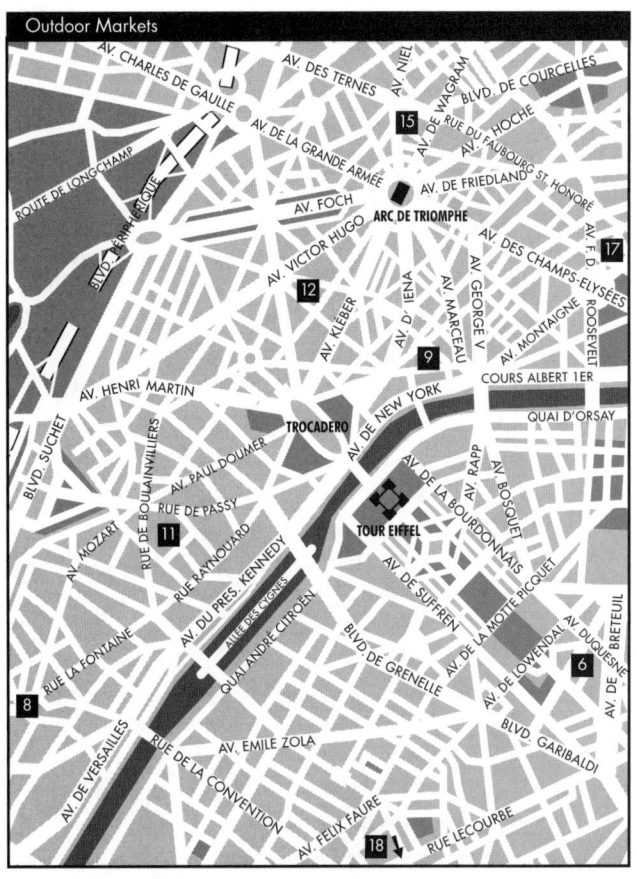

11 Passy
*Rues Bois-le-Vent and Duban
75016*
Open every day: 8am–1pm and 4:30–7:30pm.

12 Saint-Didier
*Rues Mesnil and Saint-Didier
75016*
Open every day: 7am–1pm and 4:30–7:30pm.

Flowers

13 Cité
*Place Louis Lépine
Quai de la Corse 75004*
Open every day except Sunday.

14 Madeleine
Place de la Madeleine 75008
Open every day except Monday.

15 Ternes
Place des Ternes 75017
Open every day except Monday.

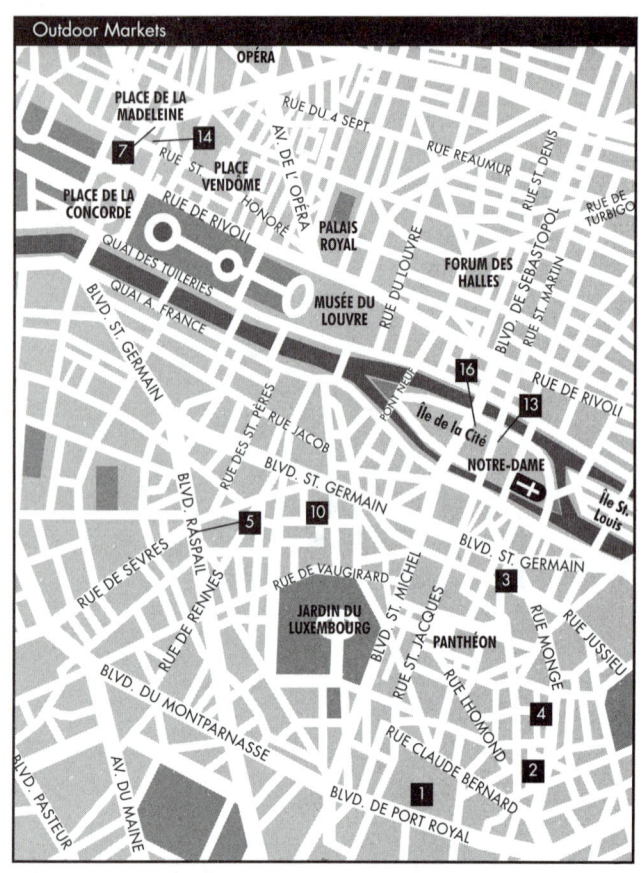

Birds and Pets

16 Marché de la Cité
Quai de la Corse 75004
Open Sundays, 8am–7pm.

Stamps and Pins

17 Carré Marigny
Off the Champs-Elysées at the corner of avenues Marigny and Gabriel 75008
Open all day, Thursdays, Saturdays, Sundays, and holidays.

Flea Markets

18 Puces de Vanves
Avenue de la Porte de Vanves, rue Georges Lafenestre, rue Marc Sangnier 75014
Open Saturdays and Sundays. Secondhand goods are offered from 7am to 7:30pm; new items, from 2pm to 7:30pm.

(Also see *Browsing the Flea Markets with Pierre Hebey*, Chapter 39).

41 FAMOUS GRAVES IN PÈRE-LACHAISE CEMETERY

Inaugurated in 1804 and dedicated to the memory of Louis XIV's confessor, le Père de la Chaise, the Père-Lachaise Cemetery is first and foremost a beautiful garden. The biggest expanse of green in Paris (10,868 acres), it is a *parc à l'anglaise* with over 5,300 trees—maple, ash, chestnut, alder, acacia, linden, and many others. It is also an open-air museum for all sorts of sculptures. One million people are buried here, and a million visitors come every year. There are 14 cemeteries in Paris, but this one is the most famous and has the most illustrious residents.

Cimetière du Père-Lachaise
16 rue du Repos 17020
43 70 70 33

1. *Honoré de Balzac—died 1850.* The prolific giant of French literature *(La Comédie Humaine)* rests in division 48.

2. *Georges Bizet—died 1875.* The famous composer of *Carmen* (and more) rests in division 68.

3. *Frédéric Chopin—died 1849.* Pianist, composer, symbol of the Romantic period. His grave is always covered with flowers. Division 11.

4. *Eugène Delacroix—died 1863.* The great Romantic painter, in division 49.

5. *Théodore Géricault—died 1824.* Another great Romantic painter, in division 12.

6. *Jean de la Fontaine—died 1695.* Famous author of the fables that every French child learns by heart, in division 25.

7. *Georges Méliès—died 1938.* Famous filmmaker who invented cinematographic science fiction, sets, and special effects. Division 64.

8. *Amedeo Modigliani—died 1920.* The doomed painter of the *Années Folles* and of Montparnasse, with his wife, Jeanne Hébuterne, who committed suicide after he died. Division 96.

9. *Molière (Jean-Baptiste Poquelin)—died 1673.* Immortal author of 17th-century comedies, in division 25.

10. *Jim Morrison—died 1971.* The lead singer of The Doors.

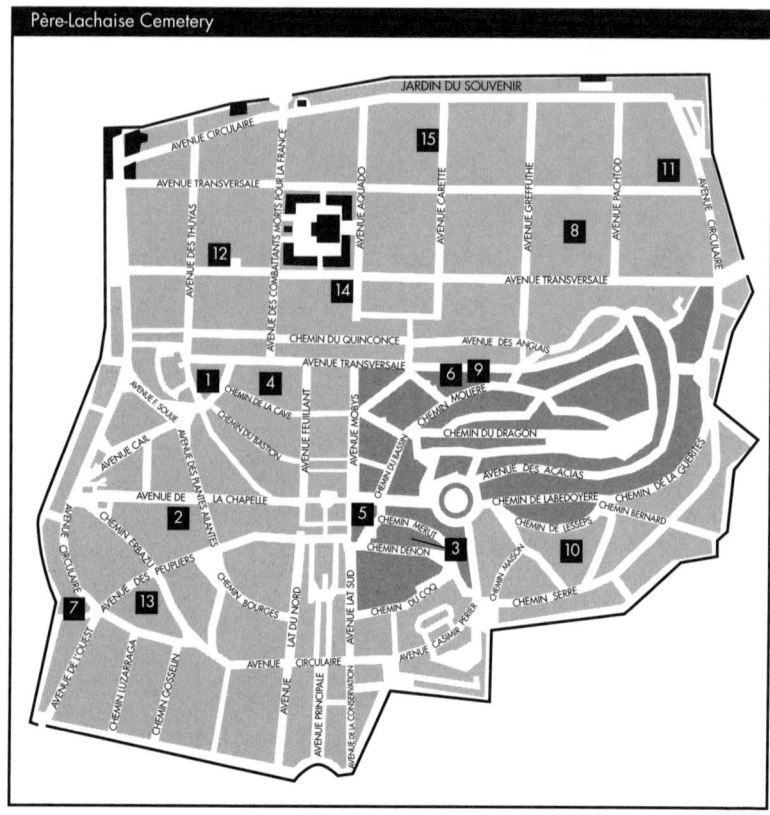

His grave attracts crowds of representatives of the "rock generation." Division 6.

11 *Edith Piaf—died 1963.*
World-famous realist and populist singer, in division 97.

12 *Marcel Proust—died 1922.*
The author of *Remembrance of Things Past,* in division 85.

13 *Georges Seurat—died 1891.*
The master of *pointilliste* painting, in division 66.

14 *Simone Signoret and Yves Montand—died 1985 and 1991, respectively.*
The *couple terrible* of the French cinema at last reunited: a great actress, a famous singer and actor. Division 44.

15 *Oscar Wilde—died 1900.*
The Irish poet, playwright, and satirist, banished from England, lived out his life in Paris. Division 89.

DESIGNER HAUTE COUTURE AND PRÊT-À-PORTER

Their names are known throughout the world. They are so famous, they discourage description—so do their prices. Be sure to check out the big sales, or *soldes*, usually in early June or from mid-December through early January, when you can find the great names and bargains.

1 Chanel
31 rue Cambon 75001
42 86 28 00
Haute couture.

2 Nina Ricci
22 rue Cambon 75001
47 03 35 91
Prêt-à-porter.

3 Ted Lapidus
35 rue Francois 1er 75001
47 20 56 14
Haute couture.

4 Jean-Louis Scherrer
31 rue de Tournon 75006
43 54 49 07
Prêt-à-porter.

5 Paco Rabanne
7 rue du Cherche-Midi 75006
42 22 87 80 – 40 49 08 53
Haute couture.

6 Yves Saint Laurent
6 place Saint-Sulpice 75006
43 29 43 00
Prêt-à-porter.

7 Balmain
44 rue Francois 1er 75008
47 20 35 34
Haute couture.

8 Carven
6 rond-point des Champs-Elysées 75008
42 25 66 50
Haute couture.

9 Chanel
42 avenue Montaigne 75008
47 23 74 12
Haute couture.

10 Christian Dior
30 avenue Montaigne 75008
40 73 54 44
Haute couture.

11 Christian Dior
11 rue Francois 1er 75008
40 73 54 44
Haute couture.

12 Christian Lacroix
*73 rue du Faubourg
Saint-Honoré 75008*
42 65 79 08
Haute couture.

13 Emanuel Ungaro
2 avenue Montaigne 75008
47 23 61 94
Haute couture.

14 Givenchy
3 avenue George V 75008
47 20 81 31
Haute couture.

15 Givenchy
*28 rue du Faubourg Saint-
Honoré 75008*
47 23 81 36
Haute couture.

16 Grès
422 rue Saint-Honoré 75008
42 60 72 00
Prêt-à-porter.

17 Guy Laroche
29 avenue Montaigne 75008
40 69 69 50
Haute couture.

18 Guy Laroche
*30 rue du Faubourg Saint-
Honoré 75008*
42 65 62 74
Prêt-à-porter.

19 Hanae Mori
*17–19 avenue Montaigne
75008*
47 23 52 03
Prêt-à-porter.

20 Hanae Mori
*9 rue du Faubourg
Saint-Honoré 75008*
47 42 78 78
Haute couture.

21 Jean-Louis Scherrer
51 avenue Montaigne 75008
42 65 55 15
Haute couture.

22 Lanvin
*22 rue du Faubourg
Saint-Honoré 75008*
42 65 14 40
Haute couture.

23 Louis Féraud
*88 rue du Faubourg
Saint-Honoré 75008*
42 65 27 29
Haute couture.

DESIGNER HAUTE COUTURE AND PRÊT-À-PORTER

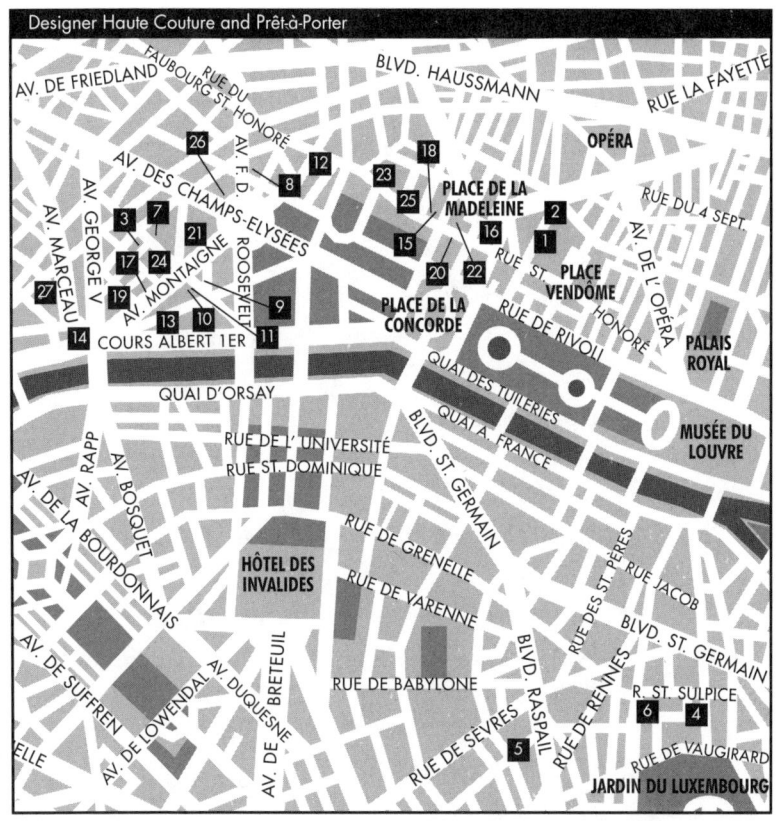

24 Nina Ricci
17 rue François 1er 75008
47 23 78 88
Haute couture and prêt-à-porter.

25 Yves Saint Laurent
32 rue du Faubourg Saint-Honoré 75008
42 65 01 15
Prêt-à-porter.

26 Yves Saint Laurent
12–14 rond-point des Champs-Elysées 75008
45 62 00 23
Prêt-à-porter.

27 Yves Saint Laurent
5 avenue Marceau 75016
47 23 72 71
Haute couture.

HAUTE COUTURE AT DISCOUNT

Quite a few designers maintain stockrooms outside the center of Paris, where you can find last year's collections, seconds, and garments without labels. Here are a few places to shop for great names at reduced prices.

1 Courrèges
7 rue Turbigo 75001
42 33 03 57
Great prices at this Courrèges discount boutique.

2 Pierre Dalby
60 rue de Richelieu 75001
42 96 65 42
A showroom like those in New York for men, women, and children.

3 Boutique Michel Swiss
24 avenue de l'Opéra 75002
47 03 49 11
A 40% discount for great trademarks in fashion accessories (scarves, bags, jewelry).

4 Dépôt des Grandes Marques
15 rue de la Banque 75002
42 96 99 04
Jacques Fath, Cerruti, Louis Féraud, and others.

5 G. D. Expansion
19 rue du Sentier 75002
42 33 38 39
For men: Torrente, Ted Lapidus, Christian Dior, Cerruti. For women: Darel, Beretta, Max Mara, and more.

6 Mendès
65 rue Montmartre 75002
42 36 83 32
Yves Saint Laurent and others.

7 Michel Swiss
16 rue de la Paix, 2nd floor
75002
42 61 61 11
Scarves, bags, and jewelry at a 40% discount.

8 Azzedine Alaïa
18 rue de la Verrerie 75004
40 27 85 58
Styles from the past few years.

9 Biderman
In the courtyard of
114 rue de Turenne 75004
44 54 32 00
Manufactures clothing for Yves Saint Laurent, Kenzo, Hechter. For men only.

HAUTE COUTURE AT DISCOUNT

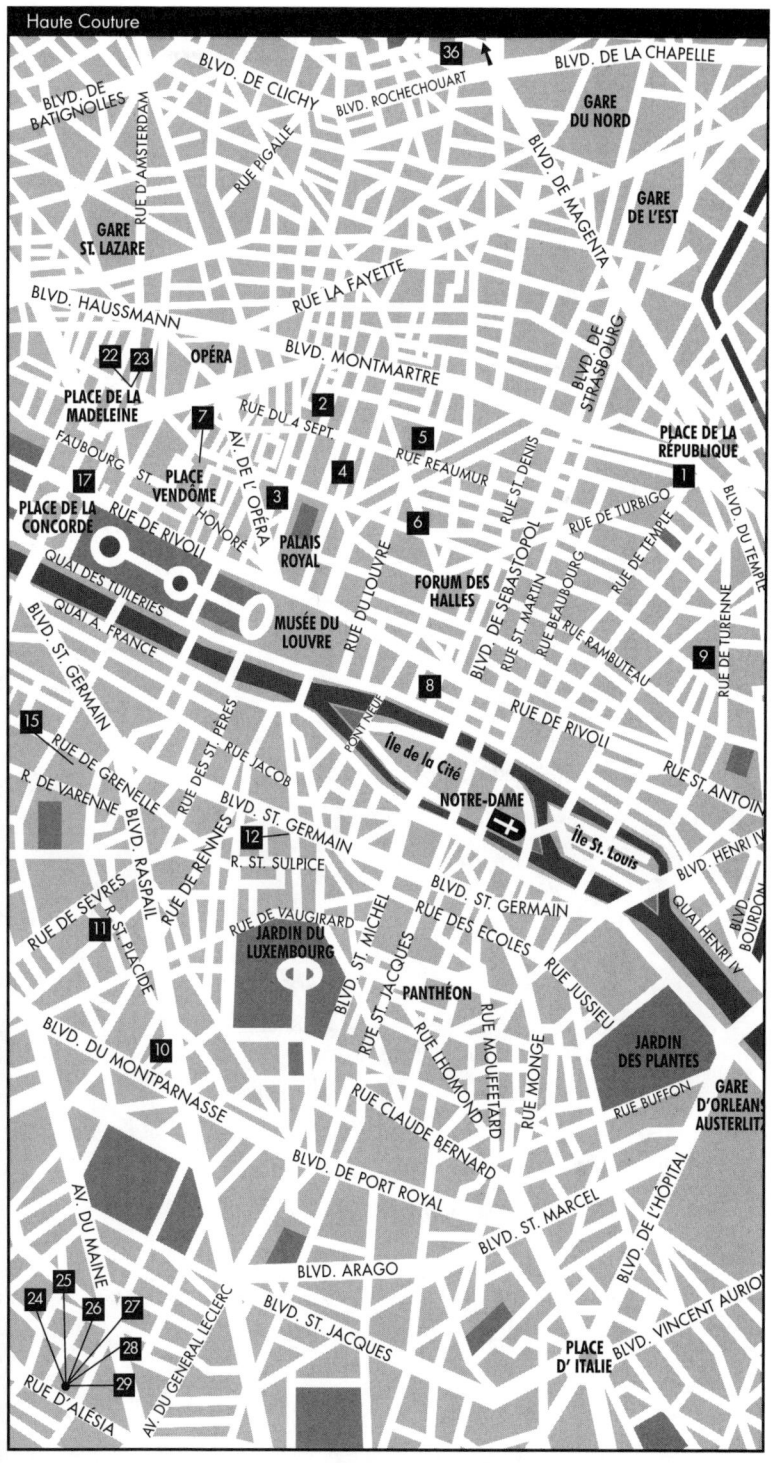

10 La Clef des Soldes
126 boulevard Raspail 75006
45 49 31 00
Suits, shirts, sportswear, shoes, and a children's department.

11 Le Mouton à Cinq Pattes
8, 10, 18 rue Saint-Placide 75006
45 48 82 85
No. 8: women; No. 10: children; No. 18: *soldes des soldes* (ultra inexpensive).

12 Stephane's Men
130 boulevard Saint-Germain 75006
46 33 94 55
Balmain, Lapidus, Dior; also shirts.

13 La Clef des Soldes
99 rue Saint-Dominique 75007
47 05 04 55
Suits, shirts, and a children's department.

14 Dépôt Vente Amélie
15 bis rue Amélie 75007
47 05 90 11
Chanel, Armani, and more at reduced prices.

15 Soldes Bon Point
84 rue de Grenelle 75007
45 48 05 45
The *nec plus ultra* for chic kids. Perennial sales, with labels.

16 Anna Lowe
35 avenue Matignon 75008
43 59 96 61
Haute couture *dégriffés* (with labels removed).

17 Club des Dix/David Shiff
13 rue Royale 75008
42 64 43 21
Chic discount for men and women.

18 Ladysol
221 rue du Faubourg Saint-Honoré 75008
45 63 20 45
Classical ready-made haute couture garments without labels.

19 Modissima
50 boulevard Malesherbes 75008
43 87 93 93
Ready-made by Balenciaga, Torrente, and other great names.

HAUTE COUTURE AT DISCOUNT

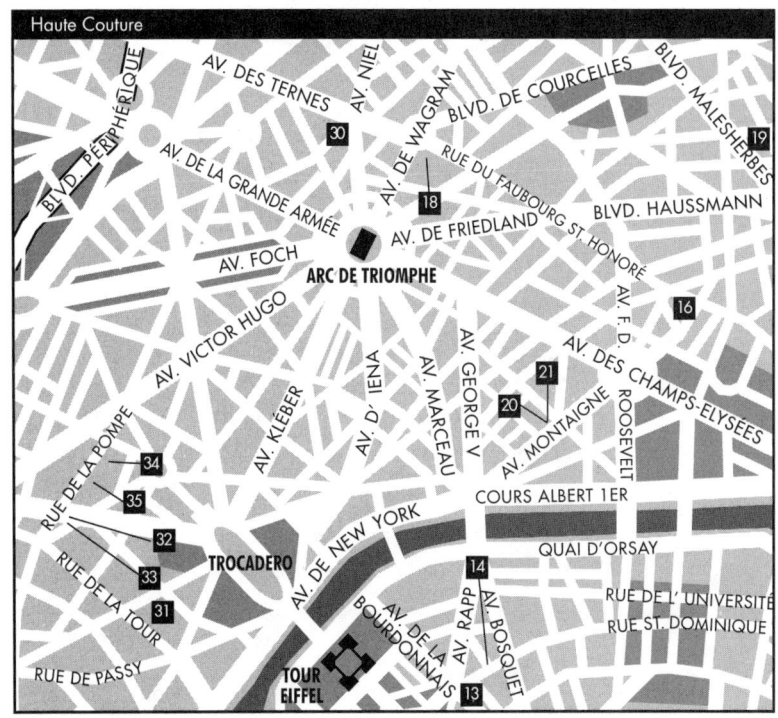

20 Nina Ricci
39 avenue Montaigne 75008
49 52 56 00
In the basement of the main shop, last year's collection at half price.

21 Ricci Club for Men
17 rue François 1er 75008
49 52 56 00
Up to 50% off, with competent and pleasant personnel. Italian selection.

22 Annexe des Créateurs
19 rue Godot-de-Mauroy 75009
42 65 46 40
Mugler, Renata, and others.

23 Rodier
34 rue Godot-de-Mauroy 75009
47 42 62 04
Another source for last year's items, up to 50% off regular prices.

24 Cacharel Stock
114 rue d'Alésia 75014
45 42 53 04
For women and children, the only Cacharel stock in Paris.

25 Chevignon: Majestic by Chevignon
122 rue d'Alésia 75014
45 43 40 25
Sportswear. Last year's collection and seconds.

26 Dorothée Bis Stock
74 rue d'Alésia 75014
45 42 17 11
Dorothy Bis' famous knits and tennis wear at reduced prices.

27 Fabrice Karel
105 rue d'Alésia 75014
45 42 42 61
Women's knits marked down.

28 S. R. Store (Sonia Rykiel)
64 rue d'Alésia 75014
43 95 06 13
Last year's Rykiel at reduced prices.

29 Stock 2—Daniel Hechter
92 rue d'Alésia 75014
45 41 65 57
Large selection for men, women, and children.

30 Bab's
89 bis avenue des Ternes 75016
45 74 02 74
Great labels in ready-to-wear from last year's collections.

31 Catherine Baril
14–16 and 25 rue de la Tour 75016
45 20 95 21
No. 14-16: women; No. 25: men. *Dépot vente*—pricey resale of last year's slightly used collections. All the great labels, including Yves Saint Laurent, Armani, J. L. Scherrer.

32 Réciproque
89 rue de la Pompe 75016
47 27 93 52
Dépôt vente. Gifts.

33 Réciproque
101 rue de la Pompe 75016
47 04 30 28
For men only.

HAUTE COUTURE AT DISCOUNT

- **34** Réciproque
  123 rue de la Pompe 75016
  47 04 30 28
  Raincoats, coats, fake jewelry, leather goods.

- **35** Réciproque
  95 rue de la Pompe 75016
  47 04 30 28
  Dépôt vente.

- **36** Stocks Michel Colin
  15 rue du Ruisseau 75018
  46 06 44 79
  Cashmere blazers and custom-made suits at low prices.

LOUIS MALLE AND CANDICE BERGEN'S PICK OF THE KIDS' SHOPS

"We love to shop for our eight-year-old daughter, Chloe, whenever we're in Paris."

LOUIS MALLE, *film director* (Pretty Baby, Atlantic City, My Dinner with André, Damage), *and* CANDICE BERGEN, *actress* (Carnal Knowledge, Gandhi, "Murphy Brown"), *writer, and photographer*

Toys

1 Jouets et Compagnie
*11 boulevard de Sébastopol
75001
42 33 67 67*
An enormous store with the greatest choice of toys. Reasonable prices, chic address.

2 Le Train Bleu
*55 rue Saint-Placide 75006
45 48 33 78*
Very wide choice for all ages.

3 L'Oiseau de Paradis
*211 boulevard Saint-Germain
75007
45 48 97 90*
A tiny, very pleasant shop with a great number of toys.

4 Le Nain Bleu
*408 rue Saint-Honoré 75008
42 60 39 01*
The most beautiful and most expensive store for toys. Some are handmade.

5 Le Train Bleu
*2, 6, and 11 avenue Mozart
75016
42 88 34 70*
Toys for all ages.

Clothes

6 Agnès B. Enfants
*3 rue du Jour 75001
42 33 04 13*
The loveliest dresses, skirts, sweaters, blouses, and T-shirts for girls up to 12. Elegant yet practical.

7 Pom d'Api
*13 rue du Jour 75001
42 36 08 87*
Shoes of all colors and shapes. Funny and inventive—kids love this place.

8 Jacadi-Diva
*35 rue Saint-Placide 75006
45 49 49 18*
A variety of choices for boys and girls up to 12. Reasonable

LOUIS MALLE AND CANDICE BERGEN'S PICK OF THE KIDS' SHOPS

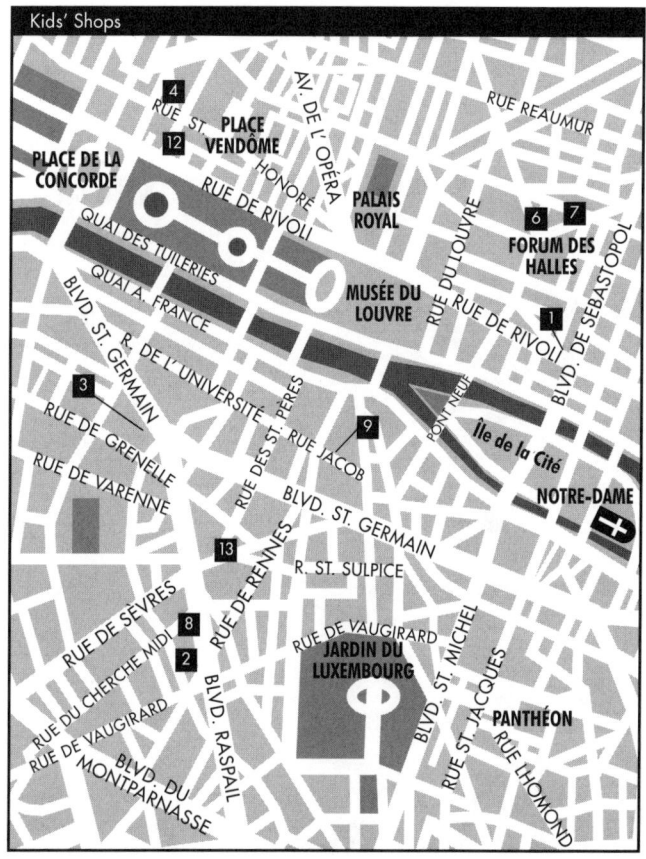

prices. "Solid and chic," as Zazie, the sharp-spoken teen heroine of my film *Zazie dans le Métro,* used to say.

9 Le Petit Faune
33 rue Jacob 75006
42 60 80 72
The best shop for babies. Ravishing clothes, very expensive. Recommended for impressive gifts.

10 Jacadi
51 rue de Passy 75016
45 27 03 01
Durable chic for preteens at reasonable prices.

11 Jacadi
114 rue La Fontaine 75016
42 88 95 95
More affordable dura-chic for preteens.

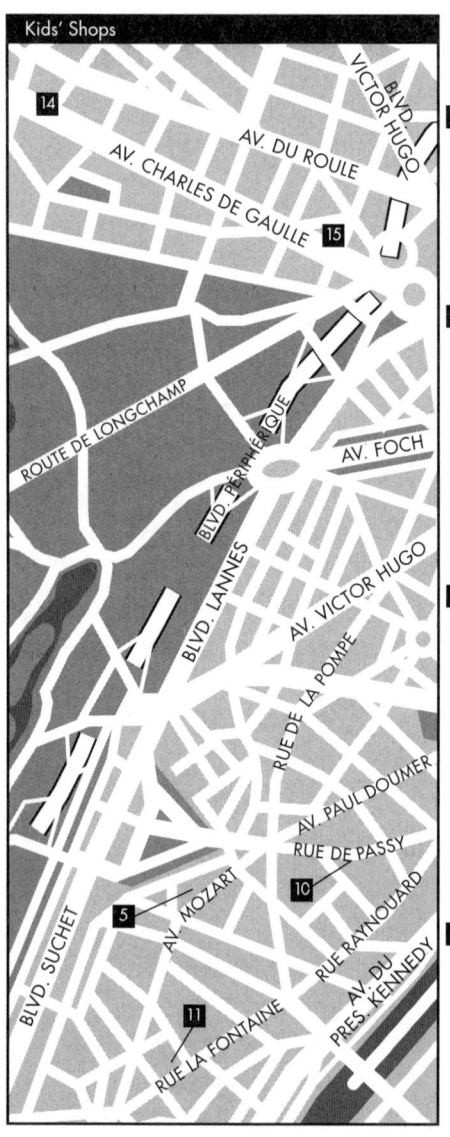

Books

12 W. H. Smith
248 rue de Rivoli 75001
42 60 37 97
Children's books in English.

13 Chantelivre
13 rue de Sèvres 75006
45 48 87 90
A large and beautiful bookshop with a great choice of books, cassettes, and games.

14 La Corde à Sauter
142 avenue Charles de Gaulle
92200 Neuilly-sur-Seine
46 24 82 19
Many, many books and toys in a very pleasant store.

Party Goods

15 Artifices
42 rue de Sablonville
92200 Neuilly-sur-Seine
47 22 62 64
Plenty of ideas for a children's party: balloons, Chinese lanterns, paper hats, costumes, and puppets. Everything to keep children entertained.

DANIÈLE THOMPSON'S TOOLS OF THE TRADE FOR THE SOPHISTICATED HOSTESS

"A home must be a place of refinement. To welcome dinner guests, I like to surprise them with a beautiful setting for the pleasure of the eye. In a modern house with contemporary paintings on white walls, I choose precious table accessories: Queen Anne candlesticks, Venetian glasses, and antique lace tablecloths and napkins."

DANIÈLE THOMPSON, *screenwriter* (Cousin-Cousine, The Mad Adventures of Rabbi Jacob, La Boum, La Neige et le Feu, La Reine Margot) *and one of Paris' most celebrated hostesses*

Kitchenware

1 Dehillerin
18 rue Coquillère 75001
42 36 53 13
Since 1920, the most incredible collection of saucepans of cast iron and copper; cutlery and other instruments. All the chefs of Paris come here to shop.

2 Dîners en Ville
27 rue de Varenne 75007
42 22 78 33
Elegant tablecloths, forks and spoons, glass, table settings.

3 Au Bain Marie
10 rue Boissy d'Anglas 75008
42 66 59 74
For the decoration of your table and home: tea services, elegant trays, place mats, antique knives, English silverware, both antique and modern.

4 La Carpe
14 rue Tronchet 75008
47 42 73 25
Chic hardware store with everything for the table and kitchen, the latest gadgets, pepper and salt mills, pots and pans.

5 Peter
191 rue du Faubourg Saint-Honoré 75008
45 63 88 00
Established in the 19th century as a *coutellerie,* Peter today offers an array of classic and modern items: antique knives, dishes, silverware, glasses, Limoges, German and Italian china, Baccarat. Also beautiful shaving kits.

6 Kitchen Bazaar
6 avenue du Maine 75015
45 48 89 00
Plenty of dishes and gadgets.

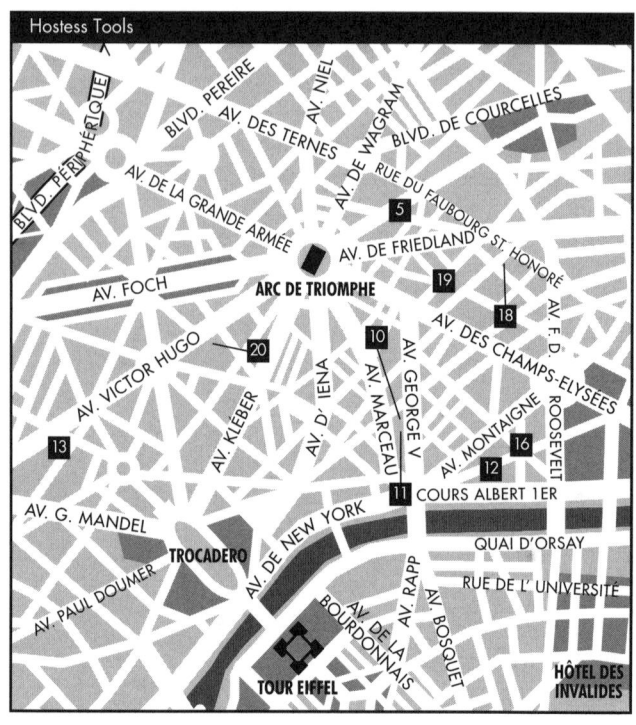

Linens

7 Muriel Grateau
29 rue de Valois 75001
40 20 90 30
In the beautiful setting of the Palais-Royal Arcades, marvelous linen tablecloths and napkins in surprising colors such as baby blue—plus glasses and dishes from Venice.

8 Souleiado/De Mery
78 rue de Seine 75006
43 54 62 25
Original Provence textiles fabricated by the same family for generations, plus tablecloths, bags, toilet kits.

9 Nuit Blanche
41 rue de Bourgogne 75007
45 50 39 29
Lace pillowcases and linens of the romantic 1920s and 1930s.

DANIÈLE THOMPSON'S
TOOLS OF THE TRADE FOR THE SOPHISTICATED HOSTESS

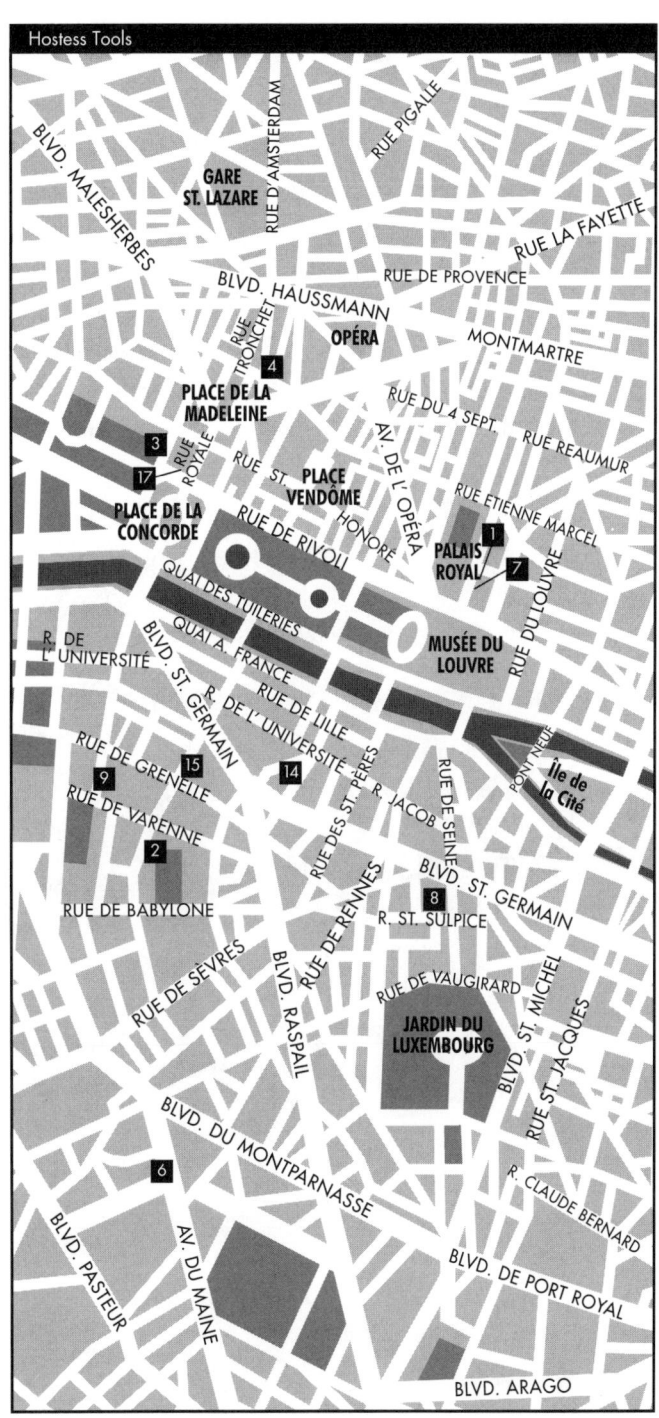

10 Agnès Comar
7 avenue George V 75008
47 23 33 85
Sophisticated designer of tablecloths, napkins, curtains, couches, bedsheets, carpets. Hand-painted fabrics, lamps with leather shades, terrycloth bathrobes.

11 Boutique Manuel Canovas
30 avenue George V 75008
49 52 00 36
Everything for the bathroom, from terrycloth towels to bathrobes. Also tablecloths, place mats, beach bags.

12 Porthault
18 avenue Montaigne 75008
47 20 75 25
The Cadillac of house linens, offering made-to-order linens, china coordinated with your table linen, beautiful tablecloths, towels, terrycloth bathrobes, gorgeous children's wear. Exquisite gifts, and not necessarily expensive.

13 La Châtelaine
170 avenue Victor Hugo 75016
47 27 44 07
In front, a beautiful shop for children's clothes. In back, table linens and bed linens not found anywhere else. Also, embroidered and ladder-hemstitched linens, lacquered trays. A classical and beautiful selection.

Miscellany

14 Debauve et Gallais Chocolates
30 rue des Saints-Pères 75007
45 48 54 67
The best of the chocolates. Specialty: chocolate-covered coffee beans, to be served after dinner.

15 Liliane François
119 rue de Grenelle 75007
45 51 74 65
The best florist in Paris creates beautiful bouquets for the house. Beauty, simplicity, originality.

16 Christian Dior Boutique
30 avenue Montaigne 75008
40 73 54 44
For signed gifts, plates, vases, wooden Thermos bottles. Large turnover of stock, always something new.

17 Lalique
11 rue Royale 75008
42 66 52 40
Vases, glasses from 1920 to today. Also glass rings, carafes, decanters, beautiful perfume bottles, powder boxes, finger bowls, and salad bowls. Extremely refined.

18 Parfumerie Caillau
124 rue du Faubourg Saint-Honoré 75008
43 59 06 86
Brushes, clips, and everything else for the hair.

19 Patricia Delorme
26 rue Washington (3 cité Odiot) 75008
42 56 33 86
Patricia creates modern jewelry to order—brooches, earrings. She also repairs broken jewelry, replaces lost pearls. Many other personalized services. By appointment only.

20 Au Gant d'Or
118 avenue Victor Hugo 75016
47 27 06 46
Vast and chic haberdashery with everything for sewing. Pantyhose and patches. Also uniforms for household help, striped vests, *maître d'hôtel* jackets, aprons, headbands, serving gloves.

DIANE VON FURSTENBERG'S MOST PRECIOUS PAPER SHOPS

"I love *papeteries*, stationery, fountain pens, notebooks. A blank page and colored pencils have always inspired me to make things, create concepts, design fabrics, invent. In Paris, I lose my head and accumulate all sorts of accessories that look useless but can eventually be an inspiration and become useful tools in my work. Here are some addresses in my own neighborhood, the Quartier des Beaux-Arts on the Left Bank, where so many artists lived and still live; on the Right Bank, where the 'chic' stationery shops are; and on rue du Pont Louis-Philippe, which, if you love paper, you must not miss."

DIANE VON FURSTENBERG, *designer of clothing, bed linen, accessories, and author of* Beds

The Left Bank

1 Esquisse
3 rue des Beaux-Arts 75006
43 26 06 86
I buy my fountain pens, stationery, and all sorts of copy books here. Esquisse makes the most beautiful color Xeroxes in the world.

2 Sennelier
3 Quai Voltaire 75007
42 60 29 38
This shop, which has made paints for artists since 1887, reminds me of Picasso and Matisse. Here I buy my paints, drawing books, and wonderful pastels.

3 Cassegrain
81 rue des Saints-Pères 75006
42 22 04 76
An extraordinary variety of fountain pens; British stationery.

The Right Bank

4 Armorial
98 rue du Faubourg Saint-Honoré 75008
42 65 08 18
The most chic shop for calling cards and engraving. I ordered my wedding invitations here.

5 Cassegrain
422 rue Saint-Honoré 75008
42 60 20 08
Exceptional fountain pens and British stationery.

DIANE VON FURSTENBERG'S MOST PRECIOUS PAPER SHOPS

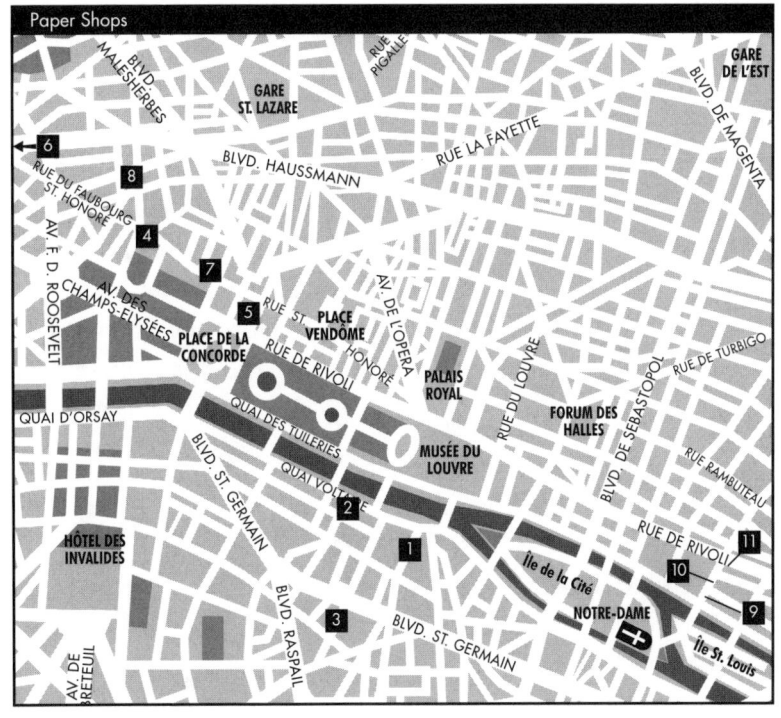

6 Dupre Octante
*141 rue du Faubourg
Saint-Honoré 75008*
45 63 10 11
Everything connected with paperwork, writing, drawing, office work.

7 Hermès
*24 rue du Faubourg
Saint-Honoré 75008*
40 17 47 17
Heaven for little notebooks, telephone books, datebooks, diaries, deluxe desk organizers.

8 Papeterie Saint-Philippe du Roule
71 rue La Boétie 75008
43 59 02 51
Elegant *papeterie*, fountain pens, engraving.

Rue du Pont Louis-Philippe

9 Calligrane
4 rue du Pont Louis-Philippe
75004
48 04 31 89
An original shop where you can find Fabriano paper, an ancient deluxe paper made in Italy. Also photograph albums, colored stationery, and the wonderful Charisma colored pencils from England.

10 Calligrane
6 rue du Pont Louis-Philippe
75004
48 04 09 00
Sister shop of the above offers deluxe Japanese, Chinese, Indian, and French papers in all colors and textures. Specializes in vegetable-fiber paper made from oats, melons, pineapple, tea leaves, and more. My favorite: banana leaf paper.

11 Papier Plus
9 rue du Pont Louis-Philippe
75004
42 77 70 49
An incredible selection of notebooks covered in canvas of different colors, maple-wood pots for pencils, recycled paper sold by weight, large-size stationery in all colors, superb filing boxes in kraft paper, archive boxes, very chic portfolios.

EMMANUELLE KHANH'S FLOWER BASKET

"I design dresses for women in the prime of life, active women, women who are an inspiration. But as much as my work is important to me, my home is also very important. And I cannot live without flowers. There are flowers in every corner of my boulevard Saint-Germain apartment. White, pale colors, mauve—they are mostly in high vases holding only one flower. Here are the florists I like in Paris."

EMMANUELLE KHANH, *fashion designer*

1 Au Nom de la Rose
4 rue de Tournon 75006
46 34 10 64
"Et rose elle a vécu ce que vivent les roses/L'espace d'un matin." ("She was like a rose and she lived the life span of a rose: one morning"—François de Malherbe.) Roses everywhere, garden roses, wild roses. Gertrude Stein ("A rose is a rose is a rose") lived nearby.

2 Marchand des Quatre Saisons
In Marché de Buci
Rue de Buci 75006
Old-style cart, selling flowers in the streets, a century-old tradition. Marcel has been selling flowers in the rue de Buci for 25 years. He prepares delicate bouquets.

3 Tortu
6 carrefour de l'Odéon 75006
43 26 02 56
Tree branches, field flowers, gigantic leaves. Tortu set the fashion for bouquets made of vegetables.

4 Liliane François
119 rue de Grenelle 75007
45 51 74 65 – 45 51 73 18
Parisian bouquets composed with the colors that suit you.

5 Les Fleuristes
Place de la Madeleine 75008
A flower market along the Madeleine Church. Casablanca lilies, beautiful flowers that last a long time. Be sure to inspect everything before making up your mind.

6 Lachaume
10 rue Royale 75008
42 60 57 26 – 42 60 59 74
Flowers in baskets.

7 Monceau-Fleurs
92 boulevard Malesherbes 75008
45 63 88 23
Wise Parisians come here for the cheapest flowers in town.

8 Monceau-Fleurs
60 avenue Paul Doumer 75016
40 72 79 27
Another site for the cheapest flowers in town.

9 Elyfleurs
82 avenue de Wagram 75017
47 66 87 19
Sells flowers and champagne 24 hours a day, 7 days a week.

10 Monceau-Fleurs
2 place Général Koenig 75017
45 74 61 39
Some of the best prices in Paris.

11 La Cueillette de Gally
Jardin de Gally
Ferme de Vauluceau
78870 Bailly
39 63 20 20
Just outside Paris, fields of flowers. Wear wooden clogs: you can roam through the fields and pick your own. Different flowers every season.

12 *Rungis 94150*
The wholesale market just outside Paris for fruits, vegetables, meats, fish . . . and flowers. (It replaces the old Halles.) Pretend you are a florist: this is the paradise of flowers. If you are feeling depressed, the best place to go is Rungis, where among miles of flowers you will find a new *joie de vivre*.

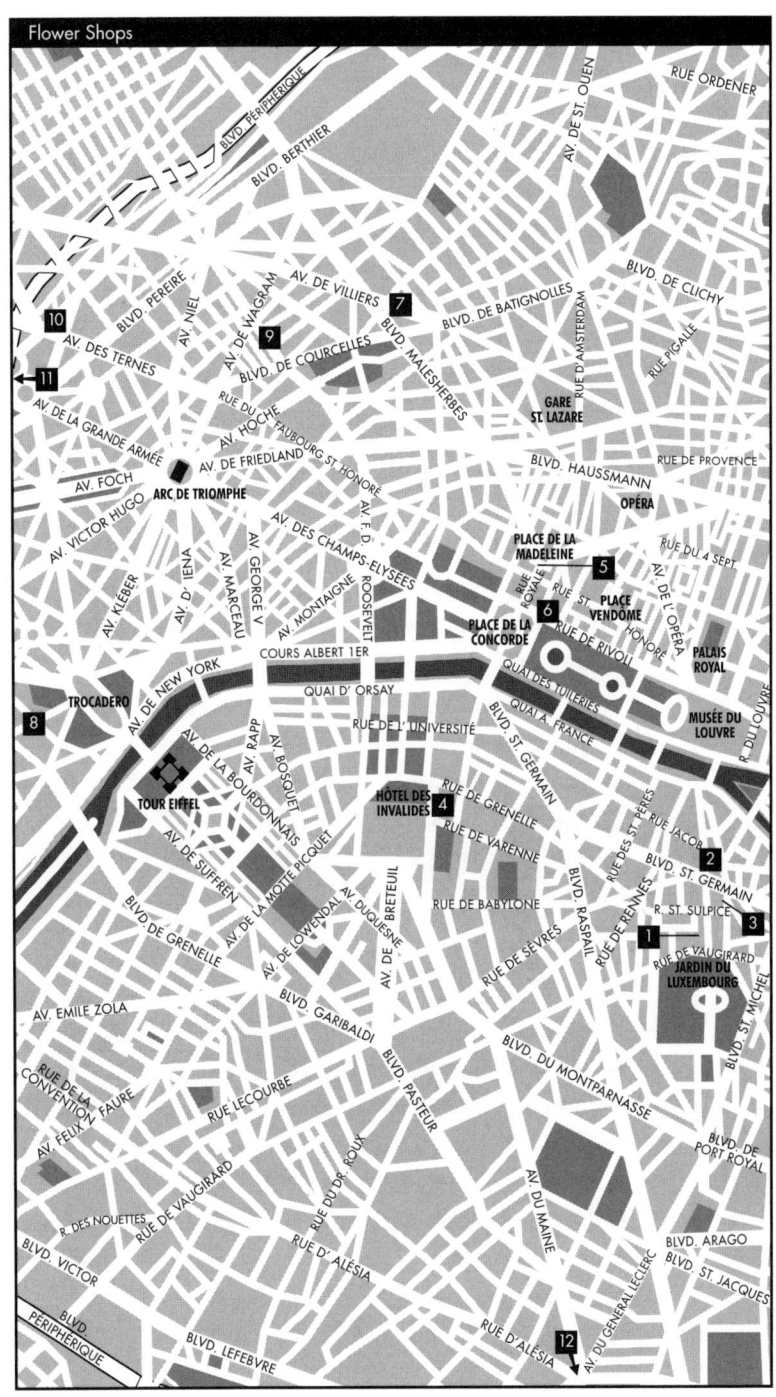

"Jim has been my constant companion for over eight years. He means everything to me. Beatrice and Armelle, who work for me, are just as much in love with him as I am. They consider him a son and are always happy to baby-sit him when I have to go away. His breed? Jim is a 'Royal Trottoir,' meaning he is a mongrel."

INÈS DE LA FRESSANGE, *model and fashion boutique manager*

Animal Clinic

1 Dr. Michel Klein
4 rue Linois 75015
45 75 07 00
The best clinic for animals in Paris. Michel Klein has such love for animals that the girl at the reception desk has a monkey on her shoulder. With Dr. Klein anything is possible to save your pet. Perhaps his real name is Dr. Doolittle.

Canine Fashion

2 Les Etats-Unis
229 rue Saint-Honoré 75001
42 60 73 95
A Parisian dog must be elegant. This shop has the most chic leashes and collars, which can be made to order. For my wedding (Jim was my best man) he wore a "dinner jacket" collar of black leather with a white bow tie.

Dog Walking

3 Tuileries Gardens 75008
For his outings I always take Jim to the Tuileries along the rue de Rivoli, which is the only part of the garden open to dogs and where he meets his regular pals.

Hairdresser

Sorry, but my dog does not go to a hairdresser.

Hotel

4 Hôtel Vernet
25 rue Vernet 75008
47 23 43 10
Some Parisian hotels are not too kind about pets. But the Vernet welcomes them graciously. They have wonderful room service for dogs, and the concierge takes very good care of them.

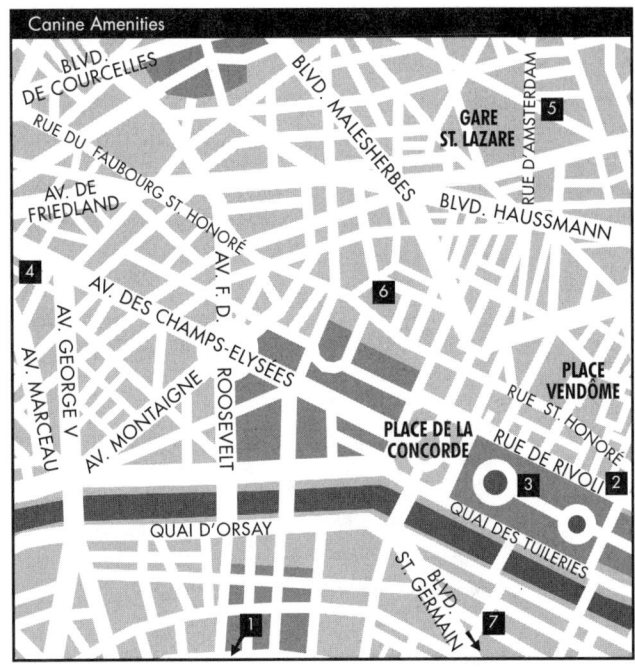

Insurance

5 Assurance Concorde
5 rue de Londres 75009
42 80 66 00
An insurance company that specializes in coverage for animals, including reimbursement for health care and damages.

Meat

6 La Boucherie de la Présidence
15 rue Montalivet 75008
42 65 62 08
I always buy Jim's meat here.

Taxicabs

French taxi drivers are often awful with people. Imagine how they are with dogs. One special company is an exception, Les Taxis Bleus (phone 49 36 10 10). Mention that you have a dog when you call to order a cab.

7 Taxi Canine
62 rue Regnault 75013
45 85 12 74–46 38 74 01
Taxis and ambulances for animals, alone or accompanied.

49 JAPAN IN PARIS: FASHION, FOOD, BOOKS, ART

"Japan's cultural invasion of Paris began in the 1980s with Japanese fashion, followed by décor, art, dance (Butoo), Zen, literature, and very organic Japanese food. The significant though silent presence of Japanese businessmen and the mass arrival of Japanese tourists (no less silently) contributed to the rise of a 'Little Tokyo' in Paris, whether or not to the liking of the French."

KUNIKO TSUTSUMI, *in charge of European activities of the Seibu-Saison Group*

Designer Boutiques
Don't look for kimonos in these boutiques, as the work of these famous Japanese designers is definitely contemporary.

1 Kenzo
3 place des Victoires 75001
40 39 72 02
The most Parisian of Japanese designers, totally integrated into the circle of Paris fashion.

2 Yohji Yamamoto
47 rue Etienne Marcel 75001
45 08 82 45
Another top-flight designer.

3 Yohji Yamamoto
25 rue du Louvre 75001
42 21 42 93
More top-flight design.

4 Comme des Garçons–Rei Kawakubo
42 rue Etienne Marcel 75002
42 33 05 21
The stylist for Comme des Garçons. Women's fashions.

5 Comme des Garçons–Rei Kawakubo
40 rue Etienne Marcel 75002
42 36 91 54
Men's fashions.

6 Issey Miyake
3 place des Vosges 75004
48 87 01 86
Contemporary collection; new designs presented every 6 months.

7 Issey Miyake
201 boulevard Saint-Germain 75007
45 48 10 44
Permanent collection (classics).

High-Fashion Designer Shops
Less avant-garde, more classic couture.

8 Hanae Mori
9 rue du Faubourg Saint-Honoré 75008
47 42 76 68
Headquarters for the only Japanese designer registered as a haute couture member in Paris.

9 Hanae Mori
17 avenue Montaigne 75008
47 23 52 03
The studio of Paris' only registered Japanese haute couture designer.

10 Ichiro Kimijima
48 rue François 1er 75008
42 25 11 00
His dresses have a distinct personality.

11 Jun Ashida
34 rue du Faubourg Saint-Honoré 75008
42 65 09 30
Very elegant—Ashida was designer to the Empress of Japan.

Kimonos

12 Kimono-Ya
11 rue du Pont Louis-Philippe 75004
48 87 30 24
Traditional robes beautifully made.

Restaurants

13 Kinugawa
9 rue du Mont-Thabor 75001
42 60 65 07
Kyoto cuisine and traditional Kaiseki meals.

14 Takara
14 rue Molière 75001
42 96 08 38
The oldest Japanese restaurant in Paris. Family atmosphere.

15 Tsukiji
2 bis rue des Ciseaux 75006
43 54 65 19
Very good sashimi and sushi. Alas, this place is very small.

16 Suntory
13 rue Lincoln 75008
42 25 40 27
One of the best Japanese restaurants in Paris. A widely varied menu, including *teppanyaki* meals cooked in front of you.

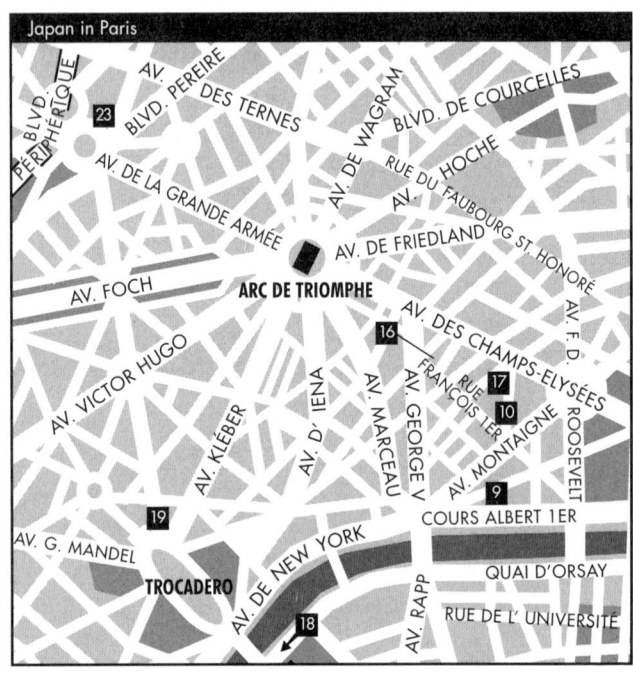

Japan in Paris

17 Yakitori
24 rue Marbeuf 75008
42 25 77 77
One of a chain of Yakitori grill rooms. Also at Place du Marché Saint-Honoré, Opéra, Montparnasse, Saint-Germain, and Saint-Michel.

18 Ben Kay
61 quai de Grenelle 75015
40 58 20 00
At Hôtel Nikko, for sushi, *teppanyaki, sukiyaki,* and more. View of the Seine.

19 Shiki
47 avenue Raymond Poincaré 75016
47 27 10 47
A small restaurant with a very talented chef-owner.

Tea Room—Patisserie

20 Toraya
10 rue Saint-Florentin 75001
42 60 13 00
Very artistic traditional cakes.

Food & Things Japanese

21 Genji
6 rue d'Amboise 75002
42 96 01 19
Japanese caterer.

JAPAN IN PARIS: FASHION, FOOD, BOOKS, ART

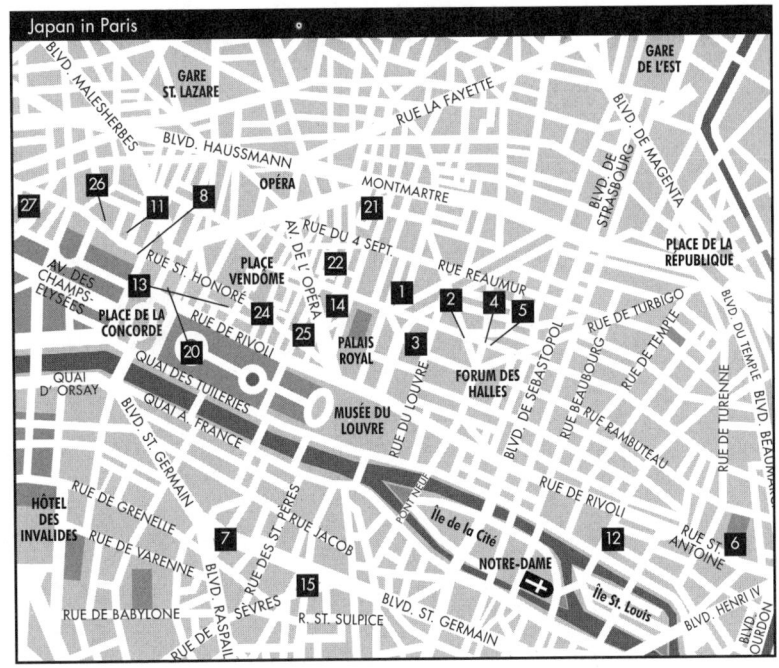

22 Kyoko
46 rue des Petits-Champs 75002
42 61 33 65 – 42 61 33 66
Japanese foods.

23 Daimaru
Palais des Congrès
2 place de la Porte Maillot
75017
40 68 21 05
Japanese handicrafts, groceries.

Bookshops

24 Junku
262 rue Saint-Honoré 75001
42 60 89 12
Contemporary art is sometimes displayed in this bookshop.

25 Tokyo-Do
4 rue Sainte-Anne 75001
42 61 08 71
Japanese books.

Art Galleries

26 Nichido
61 rue du Faubourg
Saint-Honoré 75008
42 66 62 86
Originals and prints.

27 Yoshii
8 avenue Matignon 75008
43 59 52 37
Contemporary Japanese art.

THE MÉTRO: SUBWAY AND CULTURE

The Métro is the easiest, fastest, and cheapest way to get around in Paris. Trains run from 5:45am to 12:45am and cover all corners of the city. But the Métro is not just transportation—it's art. Sculptor Hector Guimard's original station entrances were some of the treasures of Art Nouveau (one is on display in the garden of the Museum of Modern Art in New York City). The sinuous met portals still welcome riders at the Porte Dauphine, Abbesses, and Monceau stations. Some Métro station interiors are beautifully decorated; others offer exhibits from nearby museums.

Here are some of the most interesting stations:

1 Châtelet–Les Halles 75001
RER Ligne A
Salle des Echanges
Discoveries from recent archeological digs are exhibited here.

2 Louvre 75001
Ligne 1 Vincennes—Défense
Copies in stone, brass, and glass of Egyptian, Greek, Roman, Medieval, and Oriental sculptural masterpieces in the museum.

3 Bourse 75002
Ligne 3 Pont de Levallois—Galliéni
Coins and currencies from around the world.

4 Hôtel de Ville 75004
Ligne 1 Vincennes—Défense
Murals recall the history of the ancient Place de Grève (now Place de l'Hôtel de Ville). The City Hall of Paris built in the 16th century, burned to ashes during the 1870 Commune uprising and was later reconstructed.

KEY TO MÉTRO MAP LINES
LINE 1: GRANDE ARCHE DE LA DÉFENSE CHÂTEAU DE VINCENNES
LINE 2: NATION/PORTE DAUPHINE
LINE 3: PONT DE LEVAILLOIS-BÉCON/ GALLIENI
LINE 4: PORTE DE CLIGNANCOURT/ PORTE D'ORLEANS
LINE 5: BOBIGNY-PABLO PICASSO/ PLACE D'ITALIE
LINE 6: NATION/CH. DE GAULLE-ETOILE (PAR DENFERT ROCHEREAU)
LINE 7: LA COURNEVUE-8 MAI 1945/ VILLE JUIF-LOUIS ARAGON OR MAIRIE D'IVRY
LINE 8: CRÉTEIL-PRÉFECTURE/BALARD
LINE 9: PONT DE SÈVRES/MAIRIE DE MONTREUIL
LINE 10: GARE D'AUSTERLITZ/BOULOGNE PONT DE ST CLOUD
LINE 11: MAIRIE DES LILAS/CHÂTELET
LINE 12: PORTE DE LA CHAPELLE/MAIRIE D'ISSEY
LINE 13: CHÂTILLON-MONTROGUE/ GABRIEL PÉRI-ASNIÈRES-GENNEVILL OR ST DENIS BASILIQUE

THE MÉTRO: SUBWAY AND CULTURE

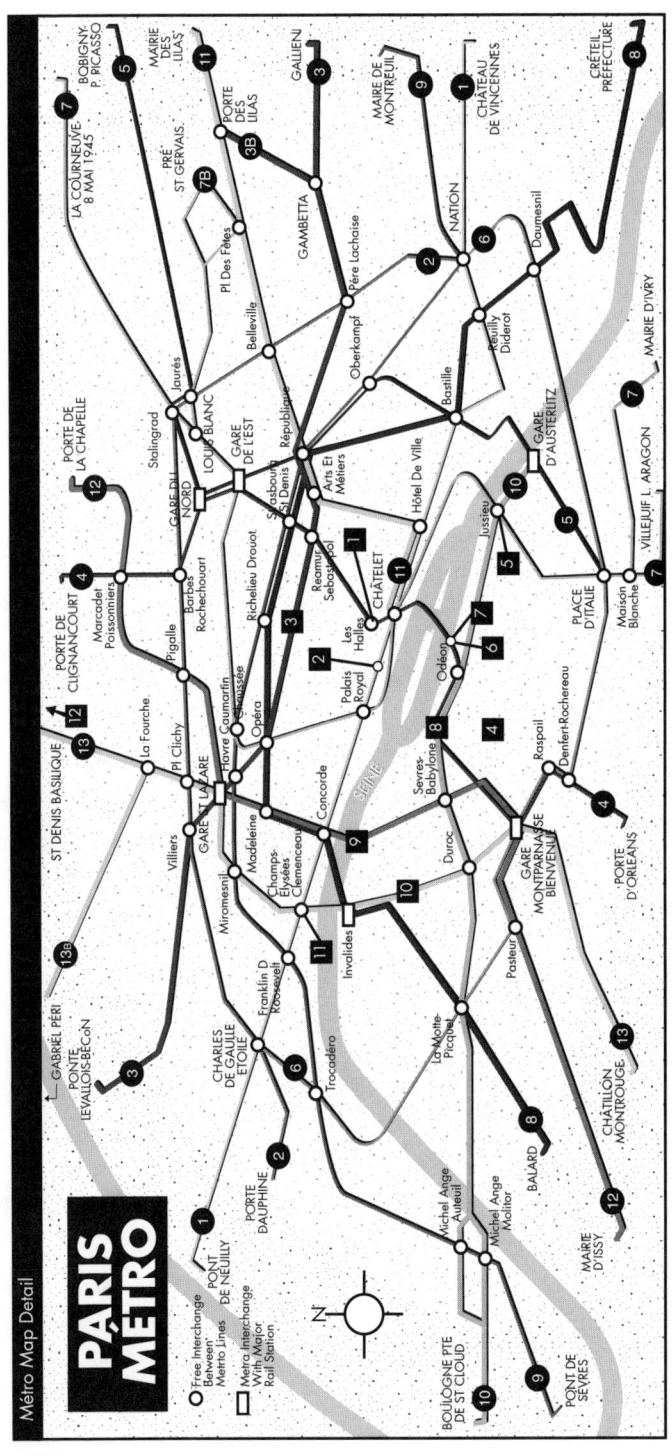

5 Jussieu 75005
Ligne 10 Gare d'Austerlitz—Boulogne/Pont de Saint-Cloud
Items from the Musée National d'Histoire Naturelle are displayed here.

6 Saint-Michel/Notre-Dame 75005
RER Lignes B and C
Decorated by Claude Maréchal.

7 Cluny–La Sorbonne 75005
Ligne 10 Gare d'Austerlitz–Boulogne/Pont de Saint-Cloud
Decorated by Jean Bazaine.

8 Saint-Germain-des-Prés 75006
Ligne 4 Porte d'Orléans—Porte de Clignancourt
Works of art evoke the history of the Abbey, the Church, and the Quartier Saint-Germain-des-Prés.

9 Assemblée Nationale 75007
Ligne 12 Mairie d'Issy—Porte de la Chapelle
Alternating décor by Jean-Charles Blais: rows of human silhouettes evoke the members of the nearby National Assembly.

10 Varenne 75007
Ligne 13 Châtillon/Montrouge—Saint-Denis/Basilique
Copies of statues, the originals of which can be found in the Musée Rodin just above the station.

11 Champs-Elysées–Clemenceau 75008
Ligne 1 Vincennes—Défense
Here you'll find information about the Palais de la Découverte science museum next door.

12 Saint-Denis Basilique 93200
Ligne 13 Châtillon/Montrouge—Saint-Denis/Basilique
Great bay windows overlook antique stones in a garden and the Royal Basilique. Portraits of several kings of France.

The Paris Métro Map on the preceding page illustrates the thirteen Métro lines "in the city." RER lines, which reach the suburbs but also cross Paris, are not included on this map. Please refer to the RATP Métro map for more detailed information on the Paris Métro.

ACKNOWLEDGMENTS

We are deeply grateful to the following people, whose contributions have made this book possible.

Hervé Aaron
Isabelle Adjani
Candice Bergen
Paul Bocuse
Sir Dirk Bogarde
André Courrèges
Hubert de Givenchy
Inès de la Fressange
Catherine Deneuve
Patrice de Nussac
Alain Dutournier
Costa-Gavras
Pierre Hebey
Emmanuelle Khanh
Michel Legrand
Claude Lelouch
Louis Malle
Sophie Marceau
Jeanne Moreau
Michèle Morgan
Gérard Oury
Charlotte Rampling
Jean-Paul Rappeneau
Régine
François Reichenbach
Bridget Restivo
Mstislav Rostropovitch
Jean-Louis Scherrer
Danièle Thompson
Kuniko Tsutsumi
Diane Von Furstenberg
Andrzej Zulawski

... and to ...

André Asséo
Tanya Blumstein
Basha and Christian Ferry
Anne Germain
Arlette Gordon
Edith Grant
Christiane Graziani-Traube
Martine Guerrand-Hermès
Genevieve Hebey
Olga Horstig
Marie-José Nat
Maureen O'Donnell
Philippe Payelle—
  Service de la Communication, Musée du Louvre
Beverly and Julia Pimsleur
Marie-Laure Reyre
Pierre and Gille Schneider
Jane Vilardebo

... and to the following organizations ...

La Délégation à l'Action Artistique de la Ville de Paris
La Direction des Parcs, Jardins, et Espaces Verts de la Ville de Paris
La Direction de la RATP
Guide Officiel et Pratique des Puces de Paris-Saint Ouen
La Syndicat d'Initiative du Vieux Montmartre

INDEX

A

Aaron, Hervé
  Louvre favorites, 72, 74-75
Abbaye Saint-Germain, 61
Acabo, Denise, 54
Accatone, 110
Action Christine, 110
Adjani, Isabelle
  favorite health spots, 55-56
Agnès B. Enfants, 164
Aguesseau market, 150
Ajani, 41
Alain Demachy, 70
Alexia Say, 149
Alexandros, 38
Allard, 18
Al Mouna, 41
Al Rosenberg, 40
Alsatian cuisine, 10, 31
Amazigh, 41
Ambassade d'Auvergne, 7
Ambassadeurs, 58
Ambroisie, 7
American authors' landmarks, 133-135
American Museum, 98
Ami Louis, 33
Amphiclès, 8
amusement park, 91
An 2000, 66
Anahï, 33
Andrée Vyncke, 148
Angelina, 42
Annexe des Créateurs, 161
antique shops, 70-71, 122, 131
Apicius, 16
aquariums, 90, 140
Arabian, Ghislaine, 16
Arc de Triomphe, 124
Arc de Triomphe du Carrousel, 125, 128
arcades, 19th century, 136-137
Arche, 129
Argentine cuisine, 33
Arlequin, 110
Armani, 160, 163
Armorial, 172
Artcurial, 49, 89
Artémise et Cunégonde, 145
Artifices, 166
Arvers, Félix, 121
Ashida, Jun, 181
Assiette, 14
Atelier d'Anaïs, 131
Atelier, Théâtre de l', 116
Au Bain Marie, 167
Auberge du Bonheur, 23
Auberge du Relais Breton, 25
Auberge Pyrénées-Cévennes, chez Philippe, 11
Au Coin des Gourmets, 36
Au Délices de Szechuen, 36
Auditorium du Musée du Louvre, 101
Au Gant d'Or, 171
Au Jardin d'Espagne, 46
Au Nom de la Rose, 175
Au Petit Montmorency, 15
Au Petit Riche, 14

Au Sauvignon, 28
Au Senteurs de Provence, 11
Auteuil market, 150
Auvergne cuisine, 7
Auvers-sur-Oise, 93
Aux Lyonnais, 30
Azzedine Alaïa, 158

B

Bab's, 162
Bac à Glaces, 44
Badetz, Hubert, 146
Badier, Gilles, 46
Badier, Simone, 46
Baie d'Ha Long, 38
Bains, 64
Baiser Salé, 106
Balenciaga, 161
Balmain, Pierre, 155, 160, 162
Balzac, Honoré de, 85-86, 153
Balzar, 31, 66
Bardau, Philippe, 15
Bas-Bréau, 25
Basquaise, Lulu la, 14
Bateau Lavoir, 115
Baudelaire, 120
Baumann, 10
Bauta, 38-39
Bazaine, Jean, 186
Beaubourg, 76
Beauharnais, 97
Beauvilliers, 113
Bellecour, 10
Bellini, 39
Ben Kay, 182
Benoit, Chez, 31, 34
Beretta, 158
Bergen, Candice, 164
Berro, Martial, 49
Berthillon, 44, 120
Besson, Roger, 146
Biderman, 158
Bistrot d'à Côté, 11
Bistrot de Breteuil, 30
Bistrot de l'Etoile, 30
Blérancourt, 93
Bocuse, Paul, 7
Boeuf sur le Toit, 66
Bofinger, 31, 66
Bogarde, Sir Dirk, 138
Bois de Boulogne, restaurants in, 21, 23, 24, 33
Boissier
  avenue Marceau, 54
  avenue Victor Hugo, 54
book shops, 56, 120, 166
Bouché, Daniel, 15
Boucherie Renaissance-Marbeuf, 46
Bouchons, 66
Boulevard de Port-Royal market, 150
Bourdelle, Antoine, 77, 125
Bourdonnais, 15
Boutique de Layrac, 64
Boutique Manuel Canovas, 170

INDEX 189

Boutique Michel Swiss, 158
Brasserie Flo, 10
brasseries, 31, 33, 35, 136
Brialy, Jean-Claude, 120
Bricard, Eugène, 78
Bristol, 58

C

cabarets, 64
Cacharel Stock, 162
Café de Flore, 134
Calligrane, 174
Cambodian cuisine, 36
Camondo, Count Moïse de, 80
Capia, Robert, 136
Cardin, Pierre, 20, 22
Carpaccio, 39, 60
Carpe, 167
Carré des Feuillants, 10, 15
Carré Marigny market, 152
Carrette, 43
Carven, 155
Cassegrain, 49, 172
catering, 48
Catherine Baril, 162
Cave Vignon, 46
Caviar Kaspia, 32
Cazaudehore, 25, 99
cemetery *See* Cimetière
Centre de la Mer et des Eaux, 90
Centre de Traitement de Cheveux Leonore Greyl, 55
Centre Georges Pompidou, 76, 110
Cernuschi, Henri, 79
Cerruti, 158
Chalet des Iles, 23
Champs-Elysées, restaurants on, 15, 20, 22, 23
Champs-sur-Marne, 94
Chanel, 155, 160
Chanel, Coco, 57, 79
Chantelivre, 166
Chantilly, 94
Chartres, 96
Château de Blérancourt, 93
Château de Chine, 38
Château de Ferrières, 96
Château de Monte Cristo, restaurant near, 25
Château des Brouillards, 114
Chateaubriand, François René, home of, 99
Châtelaine, 170
Châtelet Théâtre Musical de Paris, 101
Chevignon: Majestic by Chevignon, 162
Chez Benoît, 31
Chez Jenny, 31, 34
Chez Lipp, 66
Chez Moissonnier, 7
Chez Pauline, 7
Chieng-Mai, 36
children
    activities for, 90-92
    shops, 164-166
china shop, 131
Chinese cuisine, 36, 38
chiropractor, 55
chocolate shops, 42-45, 50-51, 54, 170

Chocolatière, 44
Christian Constant, 54
Christian Dior Boutique, 171
Christian Lacroix, 156
Christian Sapet, 146
Church's, 130
Cimetière de Montmartre, 115
Cimetière du Père-Lachaise, 153
Cinémathèque Française, 111
Cité des Sciences et de l'Industrie, 91
Cité market, 151
Cité Universitaire, restaurant near, 23
Clef des Soldes, 160
Clemenceau, Georges, home of, 80
Clodenis, 11, 114-115
Closerie des Lilas, 66, 134
clothing shops, 129-130, 132, 155-163
Club des Dix/David Shiff, 160
Club Lionel Hampton, 105
Coat, Micheline, 15
Coco Passion, 44
Cognacq, Ernest, 78
Colette Alnot, 147
Colonne Vendôme, 128
Comme des Garçons-Rei Kawakubo, 180
Comoglio, 69
Compagnie Française de l'Orient et de la Chine, 130
Comptoir des Thés et Cafés, 51
concert halls, 101-104
Conciergerie, 118
Constant, 44
Conti, 39
Copenhague-Flora Danica, 22
Coq de la Maison Blanche, 149
Coq Hardi, 25
Corde à Sauter, 166
Cordonnerie Vaneau, 48
Corinne & Gérard Mahé, 145
Costa-Gavras
    favorite movie houses, 107, 110-111
Coupole, 31, 35, 134
Courcel, Nicole, 11, 116
Courrèges, 158
Courrèges, André
    favorite museums, 76-77
Crazy Horse Saloon, 64
Crillon, 58
Cueillette de Gally, 176
cuisine *See by region or type*

D

Daimaru, 183
Dali, Salvador, 21
Dalloyau
    place Edmond Rostand, 42, 44, 51
    rue du Faubourg Saint-Honoré, 43, 54
Dauphiné cuisine, 8
day trips outside of Paris, 93-100
Debauve et Gallais Chocolates, 170
Dehillerin, 167
Délices d'Aphrodite-Mavrommatis, 38
Deneuve, Catherine
    secret gardens, 143-144
Dépôt des Grandes Marques, 158

Dépôt Vente Amélie, 160
Deux Magots, 134
Didier Aaron, 71
Dîners en Ville, 167
Dior, Christian, 155, 158, 160, 162, 171
Dôme, 134
Dorothée Bis Stock, 162
Doyen, 16
Droguerie Dugay, 149
Drouant, 18
Duc, 33
Duc des Lombards, 105
Dullin, Charles, 116
Dupre Octante, 173
Dutournier, Alain, 10, 15
Dynastie Thai, 38

E

Ecu de France, 25, 94
Edward J. Klejman, 148
Eglise de la Madeleine, 102
Eglise Saint-Eustache, 101
Eglise Saint-Louis-en-l'Ile, 120
Eglise Saint-Pierre-de-Montmartre, 112
Eiffel Tower, 124
  restaurant in, 32
Elyfleurs, 176
Elysée Lenôtre, 20
Emanuel Ungaro, 156
embroidery supplies, 131
Emerich Meerson, 130
Entrepôt, 110
Epi d'Or, 28
Escurial, 110
Espace Bleu, 56
Espace Cardin, 22
Espadon, 57
Esquisse, 172
Etamine, 132
Etangs, 96
Etats-Unis, 178
Etoile d'Or, 54
eyewear shops, 132

F

Fabre, Denise, 11, 16
fabric shops, 48, 69, 131
Fabrice Karel, 162
Faïence Anglaise, 130
Fakhr El Dine
  rue de Longchamp, 41
  rue Quentin Bauchart, 41
farm, 90
Fath, Jacques, 158, 160
Fauchon, 50
Faugeron, Henri, 16
Fauvette-Gaumont, 110
Féraud, Louis, 156, 158
Ferme Georges Ville, 90
films *See* movie houses
flea markets, 145-149, 152
  See also outdoor markets
Flemish cuisine, 15, 16
Fleuristes, 175
Flore en l'Ile, 44

florists, 68, 71
flower markets, 117, 151, 175-176
Folies Bergères, 64
Fontaine aux Chocolats, 51
Fontaine Médicis, 128
Fontaine Molière, 128
Fontainebleau, 97
food shops, open late, 64, 66
Forum Horizon, 107
Fouquet, 48
Fournier, Bernard, 7
Foux, 10
Frego, 132
Fressange, Inès de la, 178
furniture shop, 130

G

Galerie Adrien Maeght, 88
Galerie Beaubourg, 88
Galerie Beaujolais, 136
Galerie Colbert, 136
Galerie Daniel Templon, 88
Galerie d'Apollon, 75
Galerie de France, 88
Galerie Denise René, 89
Galerie Froment-Putnam, 88
Galerie J.G.M., 88
Galerie Karsten Greve, 88
Galerie Lahumière, 89
Galerie Lelong, 89
Galerie Montpensier, 136
Galerie Prazan-Fitoussi, 88
Galerie Vero-Dodat, 136
Galerie Vivienne, 136
Galerie Yvon Lambert, 88
Galeries du Palais-Royal, 136
Garage Lamartine, 68
Garaujoud-Balestie, 146
garden restaurants, 22-27
gardens, 138-144
  See also parks
Gare de Lyon, restaurant at, 21
gas stations, all-night, 68
Gascogne cuisine, 10, 15
Gaudriole, 22
Gaumont Grand Ecran, 107
Gaumont Opéra, 107
Gaumont Rama Ambassade, 107
Gautier, Théophile, 120
G.D. Expansion, 158
Génin, André, 7
Genji, 182
Géode, 91, 110
Gilles Vilfeu, 45
Givenchy, 156
Givenchy, Hubert de
  Paris preferences, 69-71
Giverny, 97-98
Goyard, 48
Grand Action, 110
Grand Chinois, 38
Grand Colbert, 136
Grand Hôtel de Sully, 122
grand hotels, 57-60
Grand Monarque, 96

Grand Palais, 125
Grand Pavois, 107
Grand Véfour, 18, 32, 140
Grande Cascade, 21, 24
Graziano's, 115
Greek cuisine, 38
Grès, 156
Groult, Philippe, 8
Guenmaï, 55
Guido Pasquali, 129
Guimard, Hector, 21
Guini, Alex, 10
Guy Laroche, 156, 160
Guy Savoy, 8, 30

H

hair care salon, natural, 55
hairdressers, 49, 130
Hanae Mori, 156, 181
Harel, 49
hat shops, 132
haute couture, 155-163
 at discount, 158, 160-163
health food restaurants, 55
Hebey, Pierre
 flea market tour, 145-149
Hechter, Daniel, 158, 162
Hédiard
 avenue Paul Doumer, 50
 boulevard de Courcelles, 51
 place de la Madeleine, 48, 50
 rue Donizetti, 51
 rue du Bac, 50
Hemingway Bar, 134
Henri Maupiou, 48
Hermès, 173
Hervé Domar, 132
Holocaust memorials, 120, 122
homeopathic pharmacies, 56
Hostellerie de l'Aigle d'Or, 97
Hostellerie du Country Club Samois, 100
hotel, pet-friendly, 178
Hôtel, 62
Hôtel Aubert de Fontenay (Musée Picasso), 123
Hôtel Chatignon, 123
Hôtel d'Angleterre, 61
Hôtel de Lauzun, 120
Hôtel de l'Université, 63
Hôtel des Deux Continents, 62
Hôtel des Deux Iles, 62
Hôtel des Grands Hommes, 62
Hôtel des Monnaies, 84
Hôtel des Principautés Unies, 133
Hôtel des Saints-Pères, 63
Hôtel du Conseiller au Parlement Pierre
 Vuole, 121
Hôtel du Danube, 62
Hôtel du Duc de Saint-Simon, 63
Hôtel Esmeralda, 61
Hôtel George V, 58-59
Hôtel Guénégaud, 82-83
Hôtel Intercontinental, 57
Hôtel Lambert, 120
Hôtel Lancaster, 59
 restaurant in, 23, 59
Hôtel Le Colbert, 61
Hôtel Lenox Saint-Germain, 62
Hôtel Lutetia, 57-58
Hôtel Marle, 123
Hôtel Meurice, 57
Hôtel Montalembert, 62
Hôtel Raphaël, 60
 restaurant in, 60
Hôtel Saint-Grégoire, 63
Hôtel Sainte-Beuve, 62
Hôtel Salé, 83, 123
Hôtel Vernet, 178
houseware shops, 131, 167-168, 170-171
Hubert Badetz, 146
Huguette Portefaix, 148
Hun, Patrick, 7

I

ice cream, 44-45
Ichiro Kimijima, 181
Ile de la Cité, tour of, 117-119
Ile Saint-Louis, tour of, 120-121
Indian cuisine, 36
Institut du Monde Arabe, 41
Institut Lancôme, 55
Irie, 130
Issey Miyake, 180
Italian cuisine, 33, 38-40

J

Jacadi, 165
Jacadi-Diva, 164-165
Jacqueline Edouard, 148
Jacques Dey, 132
Japan in Paris, 180-183
Japanese cuisine, 181-183
Jardin, 60
Jardin d'Acclimatation, 91
Jardin de Babylone, 143
Jardin des Epinettes, 144
Jardin des Plantes, 140
Jardin des Tuileries, 138-139
Jardin du Carré d'Or, 22
Jardin du Luxembourg, 140-141
Jardin du Musée Rodin, 144
Jardin du Palais-Royal, 139-140
Jardins de Bagatelle, 24, 33
Jardins de Giverny, 98
Jardins des Serres d'Auteuil, 144
Jardins du Belvèdère, 40
jazz clubs, 105-106
Jean-Charles Brosseau, 131
Jean Charles et ses Amis, 14
Jean-Michel Eté, 55
Jewish cuisine, 40
Jo Goldenberg, 40, 64
Joël Robuchon, 16
José Sayegh, 147
Jouets et Compagnie, 164
J. Revellin—Tempesta Marly, 147
Jules Verne, 32
Jun Ashida, 181
Junku, 183
Junot, Avenue, 114
Jura/Franche-Comté cuisine, 10

K

Kenzo, 158, 180
Khanh, Emmanuelle, 132, 175
Kimono-Ya, 181
Kinugawa, 181
Kitchen Bazaar, 167
Klein d'Oeil and Michel Klein, 130
Kyoko, 183

L

Lachaume, 71, 176
Lacroix, Christian, 156
Ladurée, 43
Ladysol, 160
Lalanne, Mme. Claude, 49
Lalique, 171
Lamaison, 7
Landowski, Marcel, 121
Lanvin, 156
Lapérouse, 18
Lapidus, Ted, 155, 158, 160, 162
Lapin Agile, 112-113
Lario 1898, 129
Laroche, Guy, 156, 160
Lasserre, 20
Laure Bassal, 129
Laurence Tavernier, 130
Laurent, 32
Lebanese cuisine, 41
Left Bank hotels, 61-63
Legrand, Michel
    favorite jazz spots, 105-106
Lelouch, Claude
    activities for children, 90-92
Lemaison, Alain, 8
Lenôtre
    avenue Victor Hugo, 54
    rue d'Auteuil, 48, 54
    rue du Bac, 54
Lenôtre, André, 94
Lenôtre, Gaston, 24
Lepic, rue, 115
Lescure, 28
Lido, 64
Liliane Françoise, 170, 175
Linxe, Robert, 50
Lipp, 31, 34, 66
Louis Féraud, 158
Louis G., 49
Louis XIV, 21
Louis XIV, 26, 98, 99, 100
Louvre See Musée du Louvre
Lowe, Anna, 160
Lucas-Carton, 16
Lucien Pineau, 146
Lyons cuisine, 7, 10-11

M

Ma Bourgogne, 28
Mac-Mahon, 110
Madeleine market, 151
Maison de Balzac, 85-86
Maison de l'Amérique Latine, 22
Maison de Victor Hugo, 78

Maison du Chocolat
    rue du Faubourg Saint-Honoré, 50
    rue François 1er, 43
    rue Pierre Charron, 50
Malle, Louis
Malle and Bergen's children's shops, 164-166
malls, 19th century, 136-137
Malraux, André, 20
Manoir de Paris, 16
Mansart, François, 82
Manuel Canovas, 132
Manufacture des Gobelins, 85
Mara, Max, 158
Marais, tour of, 122-123
Marceau, Sophie
    tour of the Marais, 122-123
Marchand des Quatre Saisons, 175
Marché aux Fleurs, 117-118
Marché Biron, 148-149
Marché de la Cité market, 152
Marché Minute, 66
Marché Paul Bert shops, 145-146
Marché Saint-Pierre, 116
Marché Serpette shops, 145-148
Maréchal, Claude, 186
Mariage Frères
    rue des Grands-Augustins, 43, 46
    rue du Bourg Tibourg, 42
Marie Martine, 129
Marionnettes des Champs-Elysées, 92
Marionnettes du Champ de Mars, 92
Marionnettes du Luxembourg, 92
Marly, Pierre, 79
Marriott, 60
massage salon, 55
Max Linder, 110
Maxim's, 20, 33
M.C., 131
Mediterranean cuisine, 16, 24
Mendès, 158
Mer de Sable, 91
Mère Catherine, 114
Mery, Gilles, 16
Métaphore, 132
Métro stations decorated, 184-186
Michel Rostang, 8, 11
Michel Swiss, 158
Michèle Aragon, 131
Mickiewicz, Adam, 121, 125
Midi—Pyrénées cuisine, 11
Miyake, Issey, 180
Mme. Lagautrière (Moreaux), 71
Modigliani, Amedeo, 153
Modissima, 160
Moissonnier, Chez, 7
Moissonnier, Louis, 7
Molay, Jacques de, 119
Mollard, 21
Monceau-Fleurs, 176
Monde des Voyages, 148
Montespan, Mme. de, 98
Montmartre, walking tour of, 112-116
monuments, Zulawski's favorites, 124-125, 128
Moreau, Gustave (museum), 80
Moreau, Jeanne
    favorite shops, 46, 48-49

INDEX

Morgan, Michèle
   favorite art galleries, 88-89
Moroccan cuisine, 41
Mosquée de Paris, 42
Mouffetard market, 150
Moulin de la Galette, 115
Moulin d'Orgemont, 26
Moulin d'Orgeval, 26
Moulin Rouge, 64, 115
Moulié-Savart, 49
Mouton à Cinq Pattes, 160
movie houses, 91, 107, 110-111
Mugler, 158
Muriel Grateau, 168
Muscade, 22
Musée
   Adam Mickiewicz, 121
   Bourdelle, 77
   Bricard, 78
   Carnavalet, 76, 122-123
   Cernuschi, 79
   Cognacq-Jay, 78
   Condé, 94
   d'Art Moderne de la Ville de Paris, 86
   de Balzac, 85-86
   de la Chasse et de la Nature, 70, 82-83
   de la Contrefaçon, 86
   de la Marine, 80-81
   de la Mode et du Costume, 81
   de la Monnaie, 84
   de la Parfumerie Fragonard, 85
   de la Police, 83
   de la Poste, 80
   de la Serrure, 78
   de la Serrure: Musée Fontaine, 82
   de l'Homme, 87
   de l'Orangerie, 85
   de Neuilly, 87
   de Radio-France, 86-87
   Delacroix, 84
   Départemental du Prieuré, 98
   des Antiquités Nationales, 98
   des Arts Africains et d'Océanie, 77
   des Arts Décoratifs, 82
   des Equipages, 100
   des Lunettes et Lorgnettes, 79-80
   d'Orsay, 76
   du Louvre, 72
   du Vieux Montmartre, 112
   du Vin, 87
   Georges Clemenceau, 80
   Grévin, 90, 137
   Guimet, 77
   Gustave Moreau, 80
   Henri Langlois, 110
   Marmottan, 77
   National de la Céramique, 81
   National de la Légion d'Honneur et des Ordres de Chevalerie, 78-79
   National des Arts et Traditions Populaires, 81
   National du Moyen Age, 84
   Nissim-de-Camondo, 80
   Picasso, 83, 123
   Rodin, 84-85
Muséum d'Histoire Naturelle, Le, 90
museums in Paris
   18th-century art/antiques, 80
   anthropology, 87
   Art Déco, 82
   Art Nouveau, 82
   Art of Africa and Oceania, 77
   Asian art, 77, 79
   Balzac, Honoré de, 85-86
   binoculars, 79-80
   Bourdelle, Antoine, 77
   Clemenceau, Georges, 80
   Cognacq collection, 78
   counterfeiting, 86
   Courreges' favorites, 76-77
   Delacroix, Eugène, home of, 84
   eyeglasses, 79-80
   figurines, antique wind-up, 87
   French art, 19th-20th century, 85
   French art, 19th century, 76, 85
   French arts and crafts, preindustrial, 81
   French clothes, 81
   French history, 76
   French life, Middle Ages to 1920s, 82
   French naval history, 80-81
   French police archives, 83
   Givenchy's favorites, 70
   Hugo, Victor, home of, 78
   hunting, 70; 82-83
   locks and keys, 78, 82
   mail-handling technology, 80
   middle ages, 84
   military uniforms and regalia, 78-79
   modern art, 76, 86
   Monet, 77
   Moreau, Gustave, 80
   natural history, 90
   Neuilly, 87
   numismatics, 84
   Parisian history, 76, 122
   perfume, 85
   Picasso, 83, 123
   Polish, 121
   porcelain, 81
   radio, 86-87
   Rodin, Auguste, 84-85
   science, 90
   stamps, 80
   telescopes, 79-80
   wax, 90, 137
   wine-making, 87
   Zadkine sculpture, 76
museums outside of Paris
   American-French relations, 93
   archeology, 98
   art, American, 98
   art, Postimpressionist, 98-99
   Chateaubriand's home, 99
   coach-making and horse-drawn carriages, 100
   horse and pony, 94
   military art and history, Napoleonic, 97
   Monet, Claude, home of, 97-98

N

Naïla de Montbrison, 49
Nain Bleu, 164
Napoléon, 79, 140

Natori, 48
Nerval, Gérard de, 114
New Morning, 105
Nezard-Lubré, 51
Nice—Provence cuisine, 11
Nichido, 183
Niçoise, 11
Nicole and Léon Herschtritt, 145
nightclubs, 64
Nina Ricci, 155, 157, 161
Nini, 40
Normandy cuisine, 8
North African cuisine, 41
Norvins, rue, 114
Notre-Dame de Paris, 117
Nouveau Musée de la Toile de Jouy, 69
Nuit Blanche, 168
Nussac, Patrice de
    favorite chefs, 15-16

O

Obelisque, 58
Oeillade, 30
Oiseau de Paradis, 164
Olwen Forest, 147
Opéra Bastille, 104
Opéra Comique, 102
Opéra Garnier, 103
opticians, 132
Optique de Seine, 132
Orangerie, 32, 69
Orangerie du Luxembourg, 143
Oury, Gérard
    walking tour of Montmartre, 112-116
outdoor markets, 150-152
    See also flea markets

P

Pacaud, Bernard, 7
Paco Rabanne, 155
Pagode, 110
Palais de Chaillot, 80
Palais de la Découverte, 90
Palais d'Orsay, 20
Palais Galliera, 81
Palais Royal gardens, restaurants in, 22
Pamina, 131
Panoramic, 99
Papeterie Saint-Philippe du Roule, 173
Papier Plus, 70, 174
Paradis Latin, 64
Parc de Bagatelle, 141-142
Parc des Buttes-Chaumont, 142
Parc Monceau, 141
Parc Zoologique de Paris, 91
Parc Zoologique de Thoiry, 92
Parfumerie Caillau, 171
Paris history on video, 90
Paris, 58
Parking George V (gas), 68
parking lot, 149
parks, 138-142
    See also gardens
Parvis, 117
Passage Choiseul, 137

Passage des Panoramas, 137
Passage des Princes, 137
Passage du Caire, 137
Passage Jouffroy, 137
Passard, Alain, 15
Passy market, 151
Patricia Delorme, 171
Patrick Fortin, 146
Paul Bocuse, 7
Pavillon du Manège, 138
Pavillon Henri IV, 26
Pavillon Montsouris, 23
Pavillon Puebla, 24
Peltier, 52
Père-Lachaise Cemetery, 153
Pérystile Beaujolais, 136
pet services and supplies, 178-179
Peter, 167
Petit Faune, 165
Petit Journal Montparnasse, 105
Petit Opportun, 105
Petit Palais, 125
Petit Sully, 122
Petit Train de Montmartre, 116
Petite Bretonnière, 8
Peyrot, Claude, 7
Pharmacie Azoulay: La Grande Pharmacie
    de la Place, 67
Pharmacie Basire, 56
Pharmacie de Wagram, 56
Pharmacie des Champs-Elysées, 67
Pharmacie Matignon, 56
pharmacies, 56, 67
phytotherapy salon, 55
Pierre Dalby, 158
Pierre et Patrick Frey, 131
Pineau, Lucien, 146
Piousseau, 52
Pitchi Poï, 40
Place Charles Dullin, 116
Place Dauphine, 118
Place de la Concorde, restaurant at, 22
Place des Abbesses, 116
Place des Pyramides, 128
Place des Vosges, 122
Place du Tertre, 113-114
Place Emile Goudeau, 115
Place Maubert market, 150
Place Monge market, 150
planetarium, 90-91
Plaza-Athénée, 60
Poissonnerie du Champ de Mars, 46
Pom d'Api, 164
Pom'Cannelle, 44
Pompidou, Georges, 121
Pompidou, Mme., 121
Pomponnette, 114
Pont Alexandre III, 124
Pont de Bir Hakeim, 124
Pont de la Tournelle, 121
Pont de l'Alma, 125
Pont Neuf, 118, 125
Port Marly, restaurant in, 25
Porthault, 170
postal codes, 1
Poularde Saint-Honoré, 46

Pré Catelan, 24
Président Wilson market, 150
prêt-à-porter, 155-157
Prince de Galles (Marriott), 60
Princes, 59
Prix Goncourt, 18
Procope, 66
Provence cuisine, 11
provincial cuisine, 7-8; 10-11; 14
Publicis Champs-Elysées, 67
Publicis Matignon, 67
Publicis Saint-Germain, 67
Puces de Vanves, 152
puppet shows, 92

Q

Quai de Bethune, 121
Quai d'Orléans, 121
Quatorze Juillet Parnasse, 110

R

Rampling, Charlotte
  tour, Ile de la Cité, 117-119
  tour, Ile Saint-Louis, 120-121
Rappeneau, Jean-Paul
  favorite Left Bank hotels, 61-63
Raspail market, 150
Récamier, 11
Réciproque, 162-163
Régence-Plaza, 60
Régine
  favorite chocolate shops, 50-51, 54
Reich, Georges, 160
Reichenbach, François
  malls and arcades, 136-137
Relais Chablis, 28
Relais Christine, 61
Relais Plaza, 33, 60
Renata, 158
Renoma, 158
Restaurant A, 36
Restaurant de la Fondation Cartier, 26
Restaurant du Musée d'Orsay, 20
restaurants
  See by name, region, & type of cuisine
Restivo, Bridget, 78
Revillon Fourrures, 129
Rex, 107
Ricci Club for Men, 161
Ricci, Nina, 155, 157, 161
Richart, 45
Ritz, 57
Robert Beaulieu, 130
Robuchon, Jamin-Joël, 16
Rodier, 161
Rodin, Auguste, home of, 84-85
Roger Besson, 146
Rostang, Michel, 8, 11
Rostropovich, Mstislav
  concert hall survey, 101-104
    Rotisserie du Chat qui Tourne, 94
Rotonde, 134
Royal Monceau, 60
  restaurants in, 60
Rubenstein, Helena, 121

Rue des Deux Ponts, 120
Rue des Francs-Bourgeois, 122
Rue des Hospices Saint-Gervais, 122
Rue des Rosiers, 122
Rue des Saules, 112-113
Rue Payenne, 123
Rue Quincampoix, 123
Rue Saint-Louis-en-l'Ile, 120
Rue Saint-Paul, 122
Rue Saint-Vincent, 113
Rungis, 176
Russian Church, 103
Rykiel Homme, 130
Rykiel, Sonia, 129, 162

S

Sabbia Rosa, 129
Sacré-Cœur, 112, 124
Saint-Didier market, 151
Saint-Germain-des-Prés shops, 129-132
Saint-Germain-en-Laye, 98
Saint-Germain market, 150
Saint Laurent, Yves, 155, 157-158, 162-163
Saint-Moritz, 10
Sainte Chapelle, 118
Salle à Manger, 60
Salle du Palais de Chaillot, 111
Salle Gaveau, 102
Salle Pleyel, 102-103
Samaritaine, 78
Sapet, Christian, 146
Savoie cuisine, 8
Savoy, Guy, 8, 30
Saxe Breteuil market, 150
Scherrer, Jean-Louis
  favorite places to eat, 32-35
seafood, 26, 33
Segoura, 71
Select, 134
Senderens, Alain, 16
Sennelier, 172
Serbource, Philippe, 11
Sévigné, Mme. de, 76, 123
Shakespeare & Company, 134
Shiki, 182
shops
  antique doll repair, 136
  antiques, 70-71, 122, 131
  bathroom supplies, 170
  beach gear, 131, 132
  birds, 152
  bronzes, 146
  children's books, 166
  children's clothing, 164-165
  children's party supplies, 166
  china, 130
  clothing and shoes, 129-130
  embroidery supplies, 131
  eyewear, 132
  fabric, 48, 69, 131
  flowers, 49, 68, 71, 117, 151, 170, 175-176
  food, 46, 48
  furniture, 130
  hair care supplies, 171

hats, 132
housewares, 131, 167, 171
jewelry
   artists', 49
   repair, 171
   to order, 171
leather goods/repair, 48
linens, 167, 168, 170
luggage, 48, 131, 148
mannequins, 137
medals and ribbons, 136
pipes for smoking, 137
shoes, 129-130
stationery, 49, 70, 172-174
tea, 46
toy, 137, 164, 166
uniforms for household help, 171
watches, 130
Soldes Bon Point, 160
Sonia Rykiel, 130
Sonia Rykiel Enfants, 129
Sonia Rykiel Inscription, 129
Sormani, 40
Souleiado/De Mery, 168
Southwest cuisine, 14
Square du Vert Galant, 119
S.R. Store, 162
Station Ciel Murat, 68
Station Elf, 68
Stephane's Men, 160, 162
Stock 2—Daniel Hechter, 162
Stocks Michel Colin, 163
Stresa, 33, 39, 69
Studio 106, 104
Sunset, 106
Suntory, 181
Sylvie Carpentier, 148
Szechuan cuisine, 36

T

Table de Pierre, 14
Taghit, 55
Takara, 181
Tan Dinh, 36
tapestry production, tour of works, 85
Tastevin, 26
Tea and Tattered Pages, 43
tea salons, 42-43, 136, 182
Ternes market, 151
Terrasse de l'Etang, 26
Thai cuisine, 36, 38
Théâtre de la Petite Ourse, 92
Thoumieux, 31
Tokyo-Do, 183
Toraya, 182
Torrente, 161
Tortu, 175
Touchagues, 20
Tour Eiffel, 124
   restaurant in, 32
Touraine cuisine, 14
Tournier, Nicole, 14
Train Bleu—Gare de Lyon, 21
Train Bleu (toys), 164
train trip, sightseeing, 116
Trois Marches, 100

Trou Gascon, 14
Tsukiji, 181
Tsutsumi, Kuniko, 180
Twinings of London, 48

U

U.G.C. Normandie, 107

V

Vagenende, 66
Valadon, Suzanne, 112
Vallée aux Loups, 99
Vandenhende, Francis, 16
Le Vau: Galerie d'Apollon, 75
Vaux-le-Vicomte, 99-100
Veggie, 55
Verger du Luxembourg, 143
Versailles, 100
veterinarian, 178
Vidéothèque de Paris, 90, 111
Vieille Fontaine, 27
Vietnamese cuisine, 36, 38
Vigato, Jean-Pierre, 16
Villa, 105
Villa Vinci, 40
vivarium, 140
Vivarois, 7
Voltaire, 35
Von Furstenberg, Diane
   favorite stationers, 172-174

W

walking tours, 112-123, 129-137, 145-149
watch shop, 130
W. H. Smith, 166
Willie's Wine Bar, 28
wine bars, 28
wine, Parisian, 113

X

Xavier Cholet, 146

Y

Yakitori, 182
Yohji Yamamoto, 180
Yoshii, 183
Yugaraj, 36
Yves Saint Laurent, 155, 157-158, 162-163

Z

Zadkine, Ossip, 76
zoos, 90-92
Zulawski, Andrzej
   favorite monuments, 124-125, 128